*Family and Divorce in California, 1850-1890*

SUNY Series In American Social History
Elizabeth Pleck and Charles Stephenson, Editors

# Family and Divorce in California, 1850-1890

VICTORIAN ILLUSIONS AND EVERYDAY REALITIES

*Robert L. Griswold*
University of Oklahoma

*State University of New York Press* ALBANY

Published by
State University of New York Press, Albany



Printed in the United States of America



For information, address State University of New York Press, State University Plaza, Albany, N.Y., 12246

Library of Congress Cataloging in Publication Data

Griswold, Robert L., 1950-
Family and divorce in California, 1850-1890.

(SUNY series in American social history)
Bibliography: p.
Includes index.
1. Family—California—History—19th century. 2.Divorce—California—History—19th century. 3. Rural families—California—History—19th century. 4. Sex role. 5. Social change. I. Title.
II. Series.
HQ555.C2G74 1982 306.8′09784 82-16759
ISBN 0-87395-633-8
ISBN 0-87395-634-6 (pbk.)

*To Ellen*

# *Contents*

# *Tables*

# *Illustrations*

# *Acknowledgments*

This study began as a seminar paper, mushroomed into a doctoral thesis, and has ended as a book. Along the way, my intellectual debts have grown apace. I have drawn most heavily on the account of Professor Carl Degler who, as my dissertation adviser, guided an earlier version of this study. Ever helpful and encouraging, Professor Degler tirelessly critiqued the argument, edited the prose, and sustained my commitment: his suggestions were always given with a perfect blend of critical sense and good cheer. To Professor Barton Bernstein I am indebted for helping me develop a critical perspective on all major issues in American history and for insisting that I develop more carefully many of the issues raised in this book. I also wish to thank Professors Carolyn Lougee and Paul Gilje for their suggestions and critical comments on earlier versions of the manuscript. A special word of thanks to Professor Terrence McDonald who read and critiqued every chapter of the manuscript and assisted me in the computer work. My editors, Elizabeth Pleck and Charles Stephenson, provided many thoughtful comments and criticisms. All of these scholars helped me formulate and reformulate the issues addressed in the following chapters. To them many thanks and much credit are due. I, of course, am responsible for any errors of fact or interpretation.

My debts do not end here. The staffs at the San Mateo County Hall of Justice and Records and the Santa Clara County Superior Court House helped in many ways; so, too, did the librarians at Stanford University. My thanks to Valerie Matsumoto for helping with the selection of the photographs and Martha Penisten for typing and retyping, with remarkable speed and accuracy, the manuscript. *Pacific Historical Review* kindly permitted me to use parts of my article, "Apart But Not Adrift: Wives, Divorce, and Independence in California, 1850–1890," 49 (1980), in Chapter Four. The staffs of the San Jose Historical Museum and the San Mateo County Historical Association generously allowed reproduction of photographs selected from their extensive collections. To the Whiting Fellowship Program, the Center for Research on Women at Stanford University, and the

University of Oklahoma Research Council, I am thankful for the financial assistance they provided at different stages of the researching and writing of this book.

Finally, my wife, Ellen Wisdom, deserves special mention. She offered advice, made suggestions, registered her questions and doubts, and helped shape the argument as it progressed through various stages of development. Her own professional knowledge of family relations helped immeasurably. Equally important, she supplied the kind of sustained emotional support that would have warmed the heart of any nineteenth-century moralist. Thanks, too, to my daughter, Sarah, for making family life a personal as well as a historical phenomenon.

# 1

# *Introduction: From Patriarchy to Companionship*

A personal drama came to an end in San Mateo County in early 1878. Emily Chandler had suffered enough. She had tolerated her husband's epithets, and she had even stayed with him after he tried to break her arm across his knee. But Samuel went too far in January 1878. In the presence of her neighbors, he humiliated her by "discharging his water" on the front door of her house. When she protested, he pulled a knife and threatened to kill her. Fortunately, Emily lived to file for divorce, and in March 1878 she and Samuel legally parted company.[1]

Between 1850 and 1890, hundreds of disenchanted Californians like the Chandlers appeared in San Mateo and Santa Clara County divorce court to sever one of the nineteenth century's most sacred bonds. Their decision was neither easy nor common, given the cultural importance of the nineteenth-century family: on it depended social order, public morality, civic virtue, and individual happiness.[2] To break a marriage, therefore, represented a direct challenge to nineteenth-century morality, but more and more Americans were willing to take this risk. For reasons that will become clear later, Californians along with other Americans would not tolerate behavior that their parents and grandparents accepted as a normal part of marriage. In the United States from 1870 to 1880, the population rose 30.1 percent but the divorce rate jumped by 79.4 percent; in the next decade the population increased 25.5 percent and the divorce rate 70.2 percent; and in the last decade of the century, the population went up 20.7 percent and the divorce rate 66.6 percent. Though the increase in the divorce rate did slow down, the difference in the relative size of the two rates was in fact greater in the last decade than in the first.[3] In California, the figures were even more dramatic: the state's population grew by 54.3 percent from 1870 to 1880, but the divorce rate jumped by 129 percent.[4]

Why this increase occurred, an increase that gave rise to the "divorce crisis" of the late nineteenth and early twentieth centuries, is central to this book. This dramatic surge in the divorce rate produced, as William O'Neill demonstrated, great social concern, starting with the formation of the New England Divorce Reform League in 1881. For the next several decades, clergymen, women's groups, and other concerned citizens sought for a way to stem the tide of divorce.[5] Similar concern is echoed today, when a divorce rate approaching 50 percent has produced consternation—most of it historically uninformed—about the future of the family. Although speculation abounds as to why the divorce rate has risen steadily since the mid-nineteenth century—the decline of the extended family, women's selfishness, the erosion of patriarchy, the lifting of legal restrictions, increased employment opportunities for women, urbanization, women's search for autonomy, consumerism, the emergence of the companionate family—these speculations are seldom based on the evidence most likely to illuminate the issue: the divorce documents themselves.[6] By analyzing California divorce documents during the early years of this upward trend and by sifting through not only formal legal documents but the far richer witness testimony, we will find that the "divorce crisis" was a logical consequence of the emergence of the modern family and that the high rates of today merely reflect, albeit more dramatically, the same kinds of tensions and shattered expectations found in the previous century.

The four hundred San Mateo and Santa Clara County, California divorce cases from 1850 to 1890 that form the core of this study reveal more than the source of the divorce crisis. They also permit the reconstruction of the family life of farmers and laborers, housewives, and domestics. Few of the men and women who came to California after the discovery of gold had the opportunity—or even, perhaps, the inclination—to record their thoughts about family life. Their experience is obscured by time and an absence of sources; the rare letters and diaries that have survived generally reflect the values of literate middle- and upper-class Americans. In fact, most studies of the nineteenth-century family have relied upon the letters, diaries, and memoirs of the literate or upon the caveats and exhortations of well-meaning family moralists, but neither approach touches the lives of Americans who neither wrote memoirs nor published or read moralistic tracts. Even the inferences made about family values in demographic studies—evidence that certainly gets closer to the lives of common Americans—seldom provide direct access to the actual opinions and values of people. Divorce records circumvent this problem because men and women from all walks of life brought their cases into court; and, as they testified about their marriage, we, in a sense, eavesdrop on their private lives. What were the expected roles for husbands and wives? How was power in the family distributed? Did wives' domestic contributions warrant recognition? What did being a parent, or a child, mean in the nineteenth century? Divorce records, despite some limitations, offer a way to answer these questions.[7]

The records also clarify the relationship between prescriptive norms and the values and behavior of everyday people. Many scholars have noted the dangers of using prescriptive literature—the tendency to confuse prescription and description, its class bias, the question of whether such material was even read much less accepted by everyday folk—but if, as John Faragher has argued, one important "object of historical scholarship is to show how prescribed norms and values reflected, conflicted with, or were translated into behavior," then the divorce cases offer a means to explore this connection.[8] Did farm women, for example, describe their own behavior in terms consonant with the "cult of true womanhood," and did husbands highlight their allegiance to the companionate ideal or to an older patriarchal ethos?

A related point concerns the function of ideology in the divorce setting. Whether people's behavior corresponded to the ideals professed in court is difficult to answer, but uncontestable is the fact that prescribed ideals provided couples with a powerful source of appeal when marriage soured. That is, as the expectations and importance of marriage went up in the nineteenth century and as companionship, love, affection, and mutuality became the accepted norm, husbands and wives who fell short of such high standards found themselves vulnerable in divorce trials. For what defense did the cruel, abusive husband have when local newspapers urged him to be affectionate, loving, considerate, and kind? How could an intemperate, cursing wife defend herself in light of literature that insisted that her sex was the foundation of morality?[9] If such allegations were proven true, the defendant's case was hopeless, but if the defendant could prove that his or her behavior was actually in line with prescribed morality, he or she would likely win the case in a countersuit, or at least have the case dismissed.

The families in this study are from a non-urban, predominately agricultural area, a selection based on the fact that throughout the nineteenth century, most Americans lived on farms and in small communities of less than twenty-five hundred people (the census definition of a city). By studying the family life of individuals in rural areas, we examine the residential experience of most American men and women in the nineteenth-century, and though generalizations must be cautious, the family values found in California likely infused the lives of thousands of other Americans as well. This case study of rural families, then, allows us to examine if and how prescriptive ideals affected the lives of Americans from a variety of class backgrounds, how men and women conceived of proper sex roles, and how parents viewed their children.

Like other cultural values, attitudes about the family are a product of history. These Californians inherited certain ideas and assumptions about the family that would have been foreign to people a century earlier, and although nineteenth-century writers tried continuously—just as moralists do today—to mold, shape, and redefine family relations, the direction of change, the overall vision of proper family relations was clear by the middle to late nineteenth century. By 1850 the modern family had emerged: men and women who came into divorce court alleging that their spouse failed to meet certain standards were, in essence, complaining that their mates failed to meet the demands of modernity. In order to understand the significance of the divorce data, an overview of the broad contours of change is in order: by seeing how family values changed from the seventeenth century to the nineteenth century, the meaning of these nineteenth-century Americans' discontent becomes clear.

### *The Companionate Family*

The popular image of Victorian family life consists of a patriarchal tableau in which women fussed in the front parlor or fluttered about the nursery, while men, for their part, commanded obedience from wives and gave severe looks to whispering children. Women were sentimental, nurturing, and intuitive; men, by contrast, were unemotional, austere, and rational. In all matters, the husband was the master of the house, and his stern requests demanded obedience from wife and children alike. And a specter haunted the upstanding family, the specter of sex; women fainted at the very thought, and men, too, found the subject unsettling—the piano legs wrapped in pantaloons have become, to modern minds, the symbol for this allegedly repressed, inhibited age.

While this view buoys confidence in today's social–sexual mores, it is condescending and ahistorical, as well as inaccurate. The nineteenth-century family must be judged on its own terms, not in light of today's sexual and familial attitudes. Fortunately, recent historical scholarship has already begun the reinterpretation of women's and men's roles in the last century. For women, the nineteenth century has emerged, not as the century of oppression, but as the period when women's sphere began "the process of shattering the hierarchy of sex and, more directly, in softening the hierarchical relationship of marriage";[10] for men, these years witnessed the emergence of a corollary phenomenon in the full flowering of the companionate ideal, an ideal predicated on the notion of domestic equality between husbands and wives. The nineteenth century, in this interpretation, is the decisive century in the development and realization of the companionate family. Signs of change were evident in the eighteenth century, to be sure, but people in the nineteenth century witnessed the arrival of family relations grounded in a partnership between husbands and wives who, although working in different spheres, owed each other mutual deference, respect, kindness, and love.[11]

This interpretation, based largely on analyses of guidance books and tracts directed at middle- and upper-class urbanites and on letters and memoirs from among the educated, erodes the patriarchal stereotype but scarcely touches the lives of most nineteenth-century Americans who lived not in cities but in rural areas. Fortunately, the use of the California divorce documents fills part of this gap. These records reveal that the companionate ideal did, indeed, affect the lives of rural men and women from all social classes. The legal documents and witness testimony make it clear that men and women from all social classes conceived of family relations in affective terms, placed a premium on emotional fulfillment in the family, considered women's opinions and contributions worthy of respect and consideration, emphasized male kindness and accommodation, and assumed that children were special members of the household in need of love and affection. Day laborers and clerks, blacksmiths as well as storekeepers, housewives and laundry-women all shared these basic perceptions of family values. It is this companionate ideal that resonated so strongly in the divorce testimony; this ideal that offered powerful ammunition for unhappy husbands and wives and provided the standards by which people judged their own marriages; this ideal that gave rise to the steady and rapid rise in the divorce rate. Such bold claims for the companionate ideal require elaboration, so let us examine in some detail the shift from patriarchy to companionship between the seventeenth and nineteenth centuries.

Although historians dispute why the companionate family emerged in America, they agree that the years of the late eighteenth and early nineteenth centuries were decisive. This is not to say that seventeenth-century marriages were devoid of any hint of companionship; the Puritans, for example, believed that marriage was a union of partners, entailed mutual respect and shared responsibility, and required love and devotion between the two partners.[12] But the Puritans' emphasis on wifely submission cautions against our making too great a claim on their behalf. Their marriages were partnerships between unequals, partnerships in which the husband exercised a patriarchal role and the wife a submissive one. As Edmund Morgan noted of the Puritan wife, "Even in her proper sphere of housewifery she could not rightly have anything 'of any great moment disposed of, without his Knowledge and Approbation'; in other matters she was expected to depend entirely upon his judgement."[13] Puritans compared this submission of wives to husbands with the covenant between God and the visible saints; just as the covenant with God was an agreement between unequals, so, too, was the covenant between husband and wife.[14] Moreover, because God created order and not chaos, Puritan social theory defended hierarchy and rank and held that authority in society should mirror authority in the family, authority built on patriarchal assumptions.[15]

In his study of Plymouth Colony, John Demos described the workings of seventeenth-century patriarchy and noted the presence in the colony of a "deep and primitive kind of suspicion of women, solely on account of their sex."[16] This suspicion, whose roots went back to Eve's treachery, helped justify women's duty to obey men in a spirit, as the minister John Robinson put it, of "reverend subjection."[17] Women in Plymouth were the "weaker vessel," less intelligent than men and less capable of rational discourse; moreover, their first sin in the Garden of Eden forever condemned them to a secondary status. Although women's position in Plymouth was better than that of their counterparts in England—they had better control over widows' rights, land transfers, the making of contracts, and the "putting out" of their children—subjection remained the basic duty of a wife to her mate.[18] Even seventeenth-century and early-eighteenth-century Quakers, justifiably famous for their elevation of women's religious status, insisted on the necessity of women's domestic subordination, again partly due to Eve's temptation of Adam. Despite evidence of affection between husbands and wives, wives were to yield to husbands, and when disputes arose, to take care, as Thomas Gwin advised in the early eighteenth century, "never to upbraid or provoke him; to be careful of his Concerns, prudent in your Carriage to his Relations; to love him with an entire Affection."[19]

Men exercised control over other members of the family as well. In seventeenth-century Andover, Massachusetts, Philip Greven found first- and second-generation fathers unwilling to grant adult sons full title to family lands, thereby maintaining patriarchal control by keeping their sons in a state of semidependence even after marriage. It was this control, argued Greven, that "was of the utmost importance in creating, and in maintaining, the extended, patriarchal families characteristic of the first and second generations in Andover. In this seventeenth-century American community, at least, patriarchalism was a reality, based firmly upon the possession and control of the land."[20] Greven's evidence is especially important because it reveals how ideology translated into actual behavior, how a social theory predicated on hierarchy and patriarchal control became manifest in land policies that enabled fathers to maintain power over their adult sons.

Nor does evidence from the Chesapeake contradict this image of patriarchy. Despite demographic features that made extended paternal control difficult—extremely high mortality rates left few fathers surviving to old age—those that did survive, especially those with wealth, tried to control their offspring's marriages in much the same way as their New England counterparts. Seventeenth-century Chesapeake fathers did not, however, match New England fathers' prolonged power over their children's lives. Recognizing the high probability of early death, Southern fathers granted surviving sons early control of the family estate, thereby protecting heirs from the machinations of stepfathers and guardians. This unwillingness to exercise protracted paternal control came not from more modern, less patriarchal attitudes but from the simple demographic reality of high mortality. Even so, a minority of fathers did, in their wills, exercise control from the grave, stipulating that sons, for example, provide for mothers and younger siblings in return for their inheritance.[21]

Chesapeake data on the emotional level of seventeenth-century marriages are quite sketchy. The evidence gleaned by Lorena Walsh suggests that sexual fidelity, peaceful cohabitation, and economic support were the "minimal duties that spouses must perform," but aside from some weak evidence implying that wives were due a measure of affection and respect from husbands, little is known about the affective bonds of early Southern marriages. Perhaps high mortality rates were the key variable: with marriages broken early by death—in one Maryland county from 1650 to 1700, mortality ended the majority of marriages within seven years—spouses had good reason to avoid deep emotional ties.[22] For seventeenth-century colonists, then, little evidence of the companionate family exists. Aside from an emphasis on sexual fidelity and a rational love growing out of a Godly union, these marriages were too patriarchal to deserve the term companionate. Invested with many social responsibilities and characterized by a lack of social boundaries between household and society, colonial families reflected the hierarchical principles on which all of society was organized. Husbands ruled, wives obeyed, and when family governance appeared to break down, social authorities intervened to reestablish proper order and lines of authority.

Evidence from the pre-Revolutionary period suggests the persistence of patriarchal relations. Eighteenth-century divorce records, in dealing with family economic matters, "clearly differentiated the two spouses' economic roles: the husband's, to supply or provide; the wife's, to use goods frugally and to obey." Nancy Cott added that in its economic aspects, "The traditional marriage contract resembled an indenture between master and servant."[23] Even upper-class homes in the first half of the eighteenth century revealed, as studied by Daniel Blake Smith, a noticeable absence of true companionship. Wealthy planter families in the Chesapeake prior to 1750 exhibited "a strong sense of order, authority, and self-restraint," and marriage choices were dominated by "matters of paternal preference, economic class, and social status, rather than companionship or romantic love." Smith described the precompanionate nature of these early-eighteenth-century families: "In these rather authoritarian, patriarchal families, moderation and restraint governed family relationships. Strong emotional attachments between family members were muted in the overriding concern for order and clear lines of authority and obedience within the household."[24]

The clear lines of authority and hierarchy that characterized early-eighteenth-century families presupposed a disparity of power and esteem between husbands and wives. Studies of women in the eighteenth century document their inferior position and reveal that women's self-conceptions had to change before a marriage based on equality, mutual respect, and companionship could emerge. Mary Beth Norton found that forms of address between husbands and wives prior to the Revolution suggested a hierarchy; wives often used the formal "Mr." when corresponding with their husbands, but husbands used first names or expressions like "dear child" when writing to their wives. Such evidence suggested to Norton that American white men in the eighteenth century "clearly expected their wives to be submissive, and many wives consciously and deliberately met that expectation."[25] Norton also found that women's letters and diaries exhibited a lack of self-confidence. Women often apologized for their sex, complained of their sex-based inability to reason properly, critized their poor writing style (again on the basis of sex), and were sometimes self-deprecating in the extreme. Loyalist women who made claims of compensation before the British government after the Revolution, likewise perceived themselves as "helpless," dependent, and inferior; moreover, they knew little of their family's finances, precise property holdings, and debt and mortgage obligations.[26] Certainly this female sense of inferiority precluded the existence of true companionship.

Eighteenth-century law institutionalized this sense of inferiority. Under the concept of coverture, the law submerged a wife's legal identity in that of her husband's; therefore, women could not sue or be sued, draft wills, make contracts, buy or sell property, manage their own wages, or supervise their own real estate. Although prenuptual agreements might protect the property a bride brought to her marriage, the law of coverture expressed women's secondary position in society and their subordinate place within marriage.[27] Even a wife's traditional veto power over the sale of land she brought to her marriage began to erode in the eighteenth century as courts, husbands, lawyers, and purchasers all assumed that a husband represented the best interests of his wife.[28]

Coverture also functioned in the realm of politics by assuming that the husband alone expressed the family's political interests. Although conflicting Revolutionary loyalties of husbands and wives strained the concept of coverture, American courts in the postwar years stood behind it. Linda Kerber concluded her analysis of coverture and revolutionary loyalties with words that go to the heart of female subordination in eighteenth-century America: "Faced with a choice between encouraging a woman's support for the Revolution and her loyalty to a tory husband, even some Revolutionaries insisted that she choose loyalty to her husband. Faced with a choice between coverture and independence, the Revolutionary chose coverture."[29]

All of this evidence suggests that eighteenth-century women occupied a subordinate position in the family and in society. Additional evidence could be presented—women's limited educational opportunities, for example, insured their dependence—but the point should be clear: a marriage of equals, a true partnership, could not develop as long as both sexes perceived women as inferior and subordinate to men.[30] So complete, in fact, was women's secondary position that commentators made little analysis of the female role. Women's destiny involved marriage, children, and household work, but eighteenth-century moralists left the proper fulfillment of these duties (especially when compared to what followed in the next century) largely unexamined.[31] A woman's identity was ascribed rather than achieved; it grew "naturally" out of her role as childbearer and rearer.[32]

This ascribed status, growing out of biology, is reflected in demographic evidence. Women in the eighteenth century spent a good portion of their lives moving from one pregnancy to the next, a constant cycle that not only took its toll on women but hampered the development of companionate marriages. It is not coincidental that the companionate family and a drastic decline in fertility emerged simultaneously: the two are part of the same process.[33] For women in the eighteenth century, large families were the norm. As late as 1800, the average number of births for white women who reached menopause (and hence the completion of their fertility) was 7.04, a figure that plummetted to 3.56 by 1900.[34] Such large families meant that women spent years bearing children: in the case of eighteenth-century Quaker women, over seventeen years elapsed between the birth of the first and last child, a figure that fell to 11.3 years for wives born between 1880 and 1889. Of course the longer span of childbearing meant that eighteenth-century women (and men) spent more of their lives rearing children. Whereas almost forty years passed in the eighteenth century between marriage and the departure of the last child, that figure had been cut to thirty-five years by the late nineteenth century. Moreover, eighteenth-century parents could expect that almost all of their years of marriage would also be years of child rearing. Among eighteenth-century Quakers, one spouse would generally die before the last child left home, and the surviving spouse could expect to die within five years after the last child married.[35] These statistics translated into a life of never-ending child care and domestic work for women. The cycle of pregnancy and birth for over fifteen years meant that mothers were sixty before the last child departed from home. No wonder there was so little discussion of women's responsibilities—they stood all around her.

Beginning in the middle to late eighteenth century, the family began to shift from a patriarchal to a companionate form. Although the roots of the change may be earlier—perhaps extending back to the Reformation—the years after 1750 decisively reshaped the family, changed the relative status of men and women in the home, made new demands on both husbands and wives, and significantly altered the importance of children in the family. This new family ideal is apparent in prescriptive literature, where the trend is clearly evident, and in the actual behavior and attitudes of men and women, data that is more elusive but no less convincing.

Demography provides some of the most provocative evidence on the transformation of the family. Studies of mid- to late-eighteenth-century America reveal a relaxation of parental authority over children, certainly a precondition for the establishment of a truly companionate family based on mutuality and a willingness to consult and cooperate with each other. This evidence does not mean that all fatherly authority evaporated, but it does suggest that the more rigid patriarchy of colonial times began to ease in the second half of the eighteenth century. Philip Greven's study of four generations in Andover, Massachusetts, documented the relative independence of fourth-generation sons because of their fathers' inability or unwillingness to exercise traditional paternal control over the family estate. Indeed, these sons, coming to maturity in the mid-eighteenth century, increasingly established control over their estates and inheritances before their fathers died, thereby avoiding the semidependent status of earlier generations, whose fathers maintained paternal control through their resolute hold on family land.[36] Daniel Scott Smith found evidence of a similar decline in paternal authority in late-eighteenth-century Hingham, Massachusetts. By using a series of imaginative tests on data involving mate selection, he discovered that fathers' control over their childrens' marriage partners declined after 1780. Smith concluded that beginning in the 1780s, marriage shifted from a stable, parent-run system to a stable, participant-run system.[37]

The reduction of paternal control over children is supported by other evidence showing how the increasing independence of children translated into a new emphasis on emotion and affection in the family. By the middle of the eighteenth century, the children of Chesapeake planters chose their own mates on the basis of personal attraction, romance, and love.[38] As marriage became less a union of families and more a bond of companionship between two people, the role of parents in forging economic connections through their children's marriages declined. Parents could only hope that their children's upbringing in an environment of self-government and rational discipline would enable them to make a wise mate selection.[39]

Left to make their own marriage choices, people in the late eighteenth and nineteenth centuries emphasized the importance of romantic love and companionship to their marraiges. Courting and married couples filled letters and diaries with sentimental and romantic expressions of love, devotion, and mutual admiration. By the late eighteenth century, Daniel Blake Smith found Chesapeake couples, who earlier emphasized the rationality of their love, giving vent to expressions of unrestrained romance. In the 1780s, St. George Tucker courted Frances Randolph and hoped that his affection for her would be reciprocated: "If the Ardor of my Affections and the sincerity of a heart wholly devoted to you can inspire you with a Tender Sentiment towards me suppress not the Emotion." In another letter he told her that "Satisfaction of beholding you is a pleasure which my heart now pants-after."[40] Even late-eighteenth-century couples seeking divorces reflected this trend. In her analysis of eighteenth-century Connecticut divorce records, Linda Kerber discovered that petitions during and after the Revolution more frequently mentioned the absence of love and affection than had prewar petitions.[41]

Carl Degler's analysis of private letters, journals, and diaries of nineteenth-century couples uncovered many examples of heartfelt expressions of devotion. In a letter to her husband, Henry, Mary Poor wrote that "the love I feel for you is different from any other love, that to be with you is my life." On another occasion, she informed him that "such a feeling of longing for you, dearest, comes over me that I feel as if I must fly to you." Husbands, too, expressed their emotional dependence on their wives. Reverend Robert Mallard wrote his wife that her absence "is an affliction to me and I long for it to end."[42] Women on the nineteenth-century frontier also expressed feelings of love and affection. Julie Jeffrey's study of such women concluded that despite the rigors of their life, they believed in the romantic ideal. Susannah Willeford, for one, described her husband as "my first and only choice. The man to whom I first gave my heart and confidence." Roselle Putnam, another pioneer, referred to her husband as "the idol of my heart."[43]

The emphasis on love and romance also appeared in popular prescriptive literature of the period. A content analysis of New England magazines from 1750 to 1800 revealed that writers considered romantic love the core of the ideal marriage. A similar analysis of magazines in the mid-nineteenth century found that "ego happiness" was at the heart of marriage. Given the absence of such expressions in the early eighteenth century, this evidence strongly suggests that after the mid-eighteenth century, marriage began to take on a new meaning for people and that people's emotional expectations for marriage began to rise. Ultimately, this development would have dramatic repercussions in divorce court.[44]

Love, affection, and companionship comprised the essence of the companionate family after the mid-eighteenth century, but these romantic sentiments were not the only new developments in family life: as affective expectations changed, so too did the position of men and women in the family. With love and mutuality now dominating the ideal marriage, it followed that sex roles would change and male power would diminish. Although the growth of emotion did not necessarily imply a democratization of authority within the household—planter husbands, for their part, sought loving, intimate bonds but still instructed their wives and expected them to obey—evidence from the early nineteenth century points to a rising status for women in the family and a softening of male authority.[45]

Advice literature to husbands in the early nineteenth century revealed this trend most clearly. In an effort to restore conjugal unity threatened by urban life and the separation of home and work, moralists enunciated what one scholar has called "the doctrine of companionship and collaboration." Writers advised men, now gone from home for hours on end, to develop closer psychological ties with their wives, to treat their wives as coequals in the home, to ask their opinions on domestic matters, to spend their leisure time with their wives, to place themselves under their wives' moral guidance, and even to consult with their wives in business matters.[46] An article from *Godey's Lady's Book* captured the essence of the new view with this advice: "A good husband always regards his wife as his equal; treats her with kindness, respect, and attention; and never addresses her with an air of authority, as if she were, as some husbands appear to regard their wives, a mere housekeeper."[47] Such literature, appearing in profusion beginning in the 1830s, increased women's authority in the home, enlarged the significance of their work there, and presupposed a real sharing of domestic authority. Some commentators even urged that wives be given control of the domestic sphere. The first annual report of the U.S. Department of Agriculture in 1862 directed farm husbands to recognize their wive's emotional needs and to treat them with tenderness, affection, and sympathy. The report added that rather than contradicting their wives' domestic authority, farmers should "make the wife's authority in her domain as imperative as their own."[48]

This increase in women's power in the home was central both to the emergence of the companionate family—for how could a true partnership exist where one party was manifestly inferior to another?—and to the ideology of domesticity. Linked to women's rising domestic status was the infusion of women's household duties and the home itself with high moral and even political purpose. Although husbands might still make most important decisions (whether to move, buy or sell property, or start a business), moralists ascribed to wives and mothers an even more important source of influence: they were responsible for the moral well-being of the family and, through that influence, the destiny of the country as well. To that end, prescriptive literature expected women to make the home a refuge from the immoral outside world, to guide their husbands' moral development, and perhaps most important, to see to it that the children received a proper upbringing. These crucial responsibilities increased women's influence in the family, reduced male authority, and accelerated the trend toward companionship; as we shall see, they also provided a powerful appeal when wayward husbands violated wives' finer moral sensibilities.[49]

The transformation of women's work in the home from unexamined duty to high moral calling began in the wake of the American Revolution, when writers politicized women's traditional work and gave it new meaning. If their sphere had not changed, the significance of women's domestic duties certainly expanded: the future of the Republic, argued many postwar commentators, depended upon the virtue of its citizens, a virtue shaped and molded by republican mothers who were themselves to exhibit qualities of confidence, self-reliance, rationality, and benevolence.[50] Helped by a new style of education that would prepare future mothers for this task, women were expected to play a crucial role in forging the destiny of the new nation.[51] A free, republican government could survive only if mothers properly guided their sons' moral training. Thus, after the Revolution, women's status rose, not by repudiation of their traditional tasks but by politicization of their sphere and expansion of female responsibilities. Their sphere, although different than men's, would be equal to and complement the male sphere. But beyond this point, women would not go. Mary Beth Norton's study concluded that although many female writers recognized women's intellectual abilities, highlighted women's key role as republican mothers, and argued that male and female spheres were equally important, they were unwilling to challenge the assumption that woman's destiny was to marry, bear children, and manage a household.[52] Still, the heightened significance of women's domestic role redounded to the benefit of women, by increasing their social status and legitimating demands for companionate relations based on mutual respect and affection.

As revolutionary fervor and republicanism waned, so too did the emphasis on republican motherhood. But while motherhood lost its explicitly republican purpose, domesticity took on a new dimension as women became the moral guardians of a society beset by bewildering social change. Many commentators in the first half of the nineteenth century lamented the apparent erosion of stability and community brought on by a decline in religious authority, industrialization and class antagonisms, increased mobility, urban problems, and the erosion of political hierarchy and stability. Establishing morality and order amidst this hubbub became, for many commentators, the central task facing society, and just as republican theorists had turned to women, nineteenth-century moralists also looked to them to establish a moral harbor safe from the "storms of democratic liberty."[53]

Proponents of the new ideology of domesticity started with the assumption that women were by nature more moral than men. This assumption derived from a century-long transformation in Anglo-American social attitudes about women. Between the seventeenth and the nineteenth centuries, but especially after 1780, and under the impact of early-eighteenth-century opposition to aristocratic libertinism, upper-class desires to protect men's property in women, and, most important, evangelical fears of disorder, women were transformed from the more lustful and carnal gender to the "passionless" sex. This belief in women's passionlessness served as the foundation for women's imputed moral superiority and functioned, as Nancy Cott observed, "to enhance women's status and widen their opportunities in the nineteenth century." Passionlessness translated into moral superiority, and moral superiority translated into both enhanced self-respect and the obligation to exercise moral power in reforming society.[54]

Catherine Beecher, the foremost exponent of domesticity, revealed just why and how women could perform this reforming role. In her view, only women could bring stability to the nation, only they, acting as moral guardians and uniquely qualified for the task, could heal the divisions so threatening to society. Women, and the moral home they created, would create a new national unity free from class and regional antagonisms. Gender, a biological phenomenon, would be the only recognized division in society. Although Beecher praised women's voluntary submission and self-sacrifice as an example of how to achieve order in a democratic society, the weight of her writings elevated women's importance in the home and society. Her biographer, Kathryn Sklar, is correct in asserting that Beecher was a feminist "insofar as she was trying to shape American society to respond to the needs and talents of women."[55]

Beecher's assumption that domesticity should play a social and political role is reflected in women's involvement in reform efforts. Although domesticity contained negative implications—some scholars insist that it functioned to keep women powerless, submissive, and confined—more compelling is the view that the infusion of women's sphere with high moral purpose not only increased women's status in the home but expanded the acceptable limits of women's activity in society. As early as the 1830s, women in New York sought to end prostitution and the sexual double standard. Organizing the New York Female Moral Reform Society in 1834, these pious, evangelical women hoped to extend women's natural, domestic morality into society: in the process, they fought male licentiousness, tried to help prostitutes by establishing a refuge, and insisted that mothers' influence on sons held the key to ending predatory male sexuality. To accomplish their goals, these women organized a network of church-related reform societies, formed a statewide and then a national organization, published a widely circulated newspaper, and called for a national crusade to ostracize men guilty of sexual immorality. In building a reform organization that explicitly emphasized women's vital moral role in society, the women of the society also affirmed the sororal nature of their effort. Members' letters to their newspaper and even official correspondence invariably began with "Sisters," "Dear Sisters," or "Beloved Sisters," evidence that led Carroll Smith Rosenberg to conclude that such reform organizations helped women overcome the isolation of life in rural America.[56]

Despite the obvious political role of the Reform Society, the membership rejected the challenge to traditional domesticity posed by radical feminists. When Sarah Grimke, writing in the society's newspaper, urged women to reject the domestic role, the membership responded with letters defending women's role in the family. What the members wanted was not a repudiation of domesticity but the extension of domestic morality into the public domain. Throughout the nineteenth century, other women made similar claims. Frontier women, as guardians of civilization, struggled against prostitution, built schools, enforced the Sabbath, fought for temperance, and generally tried to build a new civilization in the West, all under the auspices of the domestic ideal.[57] The moral basis of women's sphere also led them to work in the Sunday-school movement, orphan asylums, charity organizations—where they were more sympathetic than their male counterparts—abolitionism, education reform, temperance crusades, and the settlement-house movement.[58]

By no means, then, did domesticity exclude women from a social role. Although women were denied direct access to the political world, the moral assumptions of domesticity meant that women had a crucial role to play both within and beyond the family. The ideology of domesticity transformed and ennobled traditional tasks and in the process elevated the status of women in society, a development that fit perfectly with the assumptions of the companionate ideal. While writers underscored the moral importance of women, they simultaneously urged husbands to respect, admire, and consult with their wives. Women's new influence in the home and society required a revision of traditional authority, if not to total equality, then at least toward mutual respect and cooperation and the recognition that women's sphere was different than but equal to that of men's.

That family values changed from the seventeenth to the nineteenth century is clear. Our task now is to see how this century-long transformation in the family affected Californians in the second half of the nineteenth century, how men and women struggled with the implications of the companionate ideal, and how marriages dissolved as one party or the other fell short of the ideal. The divorce records, in short, offer a window on the private side of family life, on aspirations, expectations, attitudes, and values.

# 2

# *Divorce Documents and Divorce Seekers*

The breakup of a marriage is only in part played out in private. When one party decides that his or her unhappiness outweighs the desire to continue the bond and files for divorce, the marital split assumes a public dimension. Rules and procedures now take over; lawyers are contacted, witnesses called. From this public side of the breakup we can reconstruct the family values of nineteenth-century Californians, but to do this it is necessary to understand not only the incidence of divorce in California but how divorces were obtained. For unless that is done, it may be thought that evidence from divorce records was not representative or significant in delineating the nature of family life.

## *Divorce Law and Procedure*

From the start, California law provided wide-ranging grounds for divorce, and this latitude—if it did not invite divorce suits—certainly did not discourage them either. Rare would be the man or woman who could not subsume his or her complaint under one of the several grounds provided by the law as a legitimate basis of marital dissolution. Moreover, securing a divorce was relatively easy once the allegations were filed; throughout the period of this study, roughly 90 percent of the plaintiffs either received a divorce or dismissed their own charges. By an act of 1851, a man or woman who had established residence for six months could bring a divorce suit on the following grounds: natural impotency, adultery, extreme cruelty, willful desertion or neglect, habitual intemperance, fraud, and conviction of a felony.[1] In 1870, the law became even more liberal when an act reduced the required period of intemperance, desertion, or neglect from three years to two, and more liberal still in 1872 when the same period was cut to one year.[2] These changes all made divorces more easily obtainable. After 1872, the divorce statutes remained relatively unchanged, and the six grounds available to the plaintiff—adultery, cruelty, desertion, neglect, intemperance, and conviction of a felony—provided ample legal opportunity for unhappy California husbands and wives to escape from their bonds.[3]

Several important appellate court decisions provided further legal latitude and revealed how the companionate ideal became embodied in law. The demand that husbands consult with and respect their wives, the belief that affection, love, and mutual admiration was at the core of the family, the hope that marriage would become a true partnership—all of these developments ultimately reshaped divorce law, nowhere more clearly than in the expansion of unacceptable marital behavior. In the appellate cases that follow, the California Supreme Court expanded the legitimate basis of allegations of cruelty and—because women brought most of the cruelty complaints—thereby reduced the power of the husband over the wife.[4] In particular, early appellate decisions offered important definitions of mental cruelty. An 1857 decision affirmed that women's finer sensibilities deserved respect and that imprecations as to her sexual conduct constituted cruelty. The judge noted that under the "old common law," cruelty could be proved only if there "be personal assault and battery, and even this be permissible provided the stick was not larger than the fore-finger." He then rejected the adequacy of this viewpoint and in so doing revealed his allegiance to the belief, central to domesticity, that women were naturally more moral than men: "But the present condition of refined society will not admit of this severity of construction. To a lady of delicacy of feeling, purity of thought and refined sensibilities, I can conceive of no greater cruelty than by falsely charging her with prostituting her person." To the judge, false accusations of adultery were even more cruel than physical assault: "She would readily forgive a blow, when her pride and virtue could never permit her to overlook or forebear the aspersion and defamation of character."[5] Echoing this theme, another decision in the same year maintained that the law must recognize that a false accusation of adultery is "the grossest act of cruelty which can be perpetrated against an innocent female." In a revealing statement about nineteenth-century legal attitudes toward women, the judge added that courts have a duty "to society to see that woman is respected, and that all good citizens should aid in her elevation, and that every legal means should be brought to the advancement of that object."[6] Just as important, the court in yet a third 1857 case contended that cruelty could result from repeated inconsideration and not just one clear act of brutality: "But an accumulation of acts, all of an unkind, harsh or cruel character, but none of which would, by itself, authorise [*sic*] a divorce, may, when considered together, constitute extreme cruelty."[7]

Five years later the Supreme Court again interpreted the nature of mental cruelty and again increased protection for wives. This time the Supreme Court overturned a lower court's opinion that conflicts, sometimes even violence, naturally arose between husbands and wives and that cruelty "must be so extreme in its nature that in itself it furnished an apprehension that the continuancy of the cohabitation would be attended with bodily harm to the wife." The Supreme Court emphatically denied the lower court's ruling and thereby implied that women need not prove themselves fearful of future acts of violence in order to secure a divorce: "This charge, we think, also was too strong. Acts of cruelty such as are specified need not be persistent, need not become a fixed habit, before relief and safety can be had by a divorce."[8] The last important Supreme Court interpretation on curelty between 1850 and 1890 came in 1863, when the court specifically recognized the reality of mental cruelty and explicitly rejected the idea that only physical assault constituted cruelty: "The better opinion, however, is opposed to this view, and we think that any conduct sufficiently aggravated to produce ill-health or bodily pain, though operating primarily upon the mind only, should be regarded as legal cruelty." In 1870 the state legislature redefined cruelty to explicitly include "mental suffering."[9]

In these decisions, the law is being reshaped to reflect the companionate ideal, and although both sexes might profit from the liberal interpretation of cruelty, women clearly had the most to gain by these changes. This, too, was in keeping with a desire to establish more equal marriages, for it was husbands' arbitrary power that needed reduction. As later evidence will make clear, women effectively used these expanded notions of cruelty to end unhappy marriages. The changes in divorce law were also in keeping with women's rising status in other areas of the law. In the course of the nineteenth century, coverture broke down, and women gained the power to make contracts, lend and borrow money, transfer and control property, and manage their own wages. As one nineteenth-century commentator concluded, "in domestic control the irresistible movement is in the direction of the most perfect *legal equality of the married partners, consistent with family unity.*"[10]

Though the laws changed and legal definitions broadened, the procedures themselves remained essentially the same. Once a marriage became sufficiently intolerable to warrant a divorce, a man or woman who had resided in California for at least six months filed a complaint in Superior Court based on one of the six grounds already described.[11] The court then served notice of the suit, and the defendant either responded to the accusations or, as was more common, defaulted. In either case, the court then gathered evidence—the state statutes in 1851 stipulated that no divorce could be granted simply by default—and after assessing the evidence ruled either for or against the plaintiff's suit.[12]

The divorce records used here contain two basic types of evidence. All cases include a collection of legal documents drafted by lawyers, such as complaints, motions, answers, and demurrers. Many cases, in addition, especially until the mid-1880s, contain testimony taken by a court-appointed referee (or court commissioner) about the family life of the couple involved in the proceedings. Buried in these questions and answers is a rich vein of information about family life, because the referee asked witnesses direct questions and then recorded their answers—so far as one can tell—*verbatim.* How did the defendant treat his wife? Were they happy? Was the woman chaste? Was the man a good worker? Altogether, 120 cases (30 percent of the total) included witness testimony, and in these cases, 451 people testified under oath before the commissioner; of that number 82 were husbands and wives involved as litigants and 369 were people called as witnesses on behalf of a plaintiff or a defendant.[13]

But is evidence from divorce records reliable information about family experience? After all, although my intention is to examine the family life of Americans, the average American in the nineteenth century did not get divorced.[14] Can such evidence shed much light on the attitudes and behavior of Americans in general, especially those who did not seek to dissolve their marriages? When we understand the assumptions behind the divorce procedures, I think it can. Because nineteenth-century divorce was an adversarial procedure, and because community mores frowned on marital dissolution, people spent considerable time explaining why they wanted to get divorced, what they had expected from their spouse, how they felt about their children, and what they perceived their own behavior to have been. In short, the attitudes of the society in general are exposed as we read how couples justified the need for a divorce; moreover, the great variety of witnesses also brought to the surface submerged, private aspects of family life, and in many cases the historian sees a community emerge from the record as one neighbor or relative after another answered questions about a given couple. It should be emphasized that the focus of this study is on attitudes and values; we cannot possibly know whether a man was actually "honest, frugal, and loving," but the fact that a neighbor described him as such suggests what values comprised the proper role for men, not only in the eyes of the neighbors, but of the court and therefore of society as well.

In addition, although these men and women were perhaps more courageous than most, although they were willing to break what most agreed was a sacred bond, the kinds of arguments they made in court were consonant with the values held by society at large; most of the testimony, in fact, shows one partner or another explaining how his or her marriage failed to meet expected standards, standards presumably shared by most members of the community. Their appeals to the court—whose judgment they needed to win—revealed their sad disappointment that marriage did not meet socially recognized standards, rather than any fierce desire for a unique marital arrangement.[15]

Nor should it be thought that the records represent no more than a simple pandering to the prejudices of middle-class judges who heard the cases. Here a note on the distinction between formal legal documents and witness testimony is in order. The information, it is true, drawn up by lawyers for the court in the form of complaints, motions, and answers outlined—insofar as it was written by middle-class men for middle-class men—the contours of "polite" thought on acceptable marital behavior. But the fact that the same lawyer in appearing before the same judge in two different cases alleging the same grounds offered different amounts of detail suggests that the pleas were not simply conventional but reflective of the facts of the marital experiences of the couple. Why, if the records do not give an accurate sense of family relations, would the same lawyer describe cruelty allegations in one case in horrifying detail and in the next (to the same judge) give only the briefest description of an isolated incident? Why would the same lawyer describe one woman's poverty in pitiful terms and the next woman's deprivations so matter-of-factly?

Although these formal documents are certainly useful, the actual testimony of witnesses provides the real opportunity to hear what Californians thought about family relations. Yet, how do we know that the witnesses who offered such fascinating testimony were not simply repeating the instructions of lawyers? First, although witnesses might have been coached or might have known what was expected of them, this is unlikely, and, in any event, no evidence suggests that coaching took place. Moreover, witnesses would be unlikely simply to parrot the instructions of a lawyer if they did not in some basic sense share the same values. Second, there is at least one example that suggests that witnesses could be quite independent of even a judge's views. Judge David Belden of San Jose tried a large percentage of the cases in Santa Clara County from the early 1870s through most of the 1880s. In his decision on a case in 1886 he proffered his conception of proper power relations in the home: "The husband," he wrote, "is the head of and THE MASTER OF THE HOUSE. He is accountable for its management and responsible for what transpires within it. He can say who shall and who shall not be received there and can command anyone to who *[sic]* he may object to remove from his house."[16] If coaching were common, we would expect witnesses in Belden's court to concentrate on the presence or absence of a woman's Pauline virtues, but the fact that so few witnesses singled out obedience as a female virtue (despite Belden's views on the subject) strongly suggests that witnesses gave their own honest opinions and not simply words supplied by lawyers aware of a judge's views. Certainly we must not forget that people sometimes perjure themselves and that judges are sometimes cajoled, but my sense of the testimony is that of men and women trying their best to discuss frankly the family experience of themselves or of their neighbors. Before we explore this testimony in depth, it is necessary to examine who exactly comprised the divorce seekers.

## *The Divorce Seekers*

The divorce cases start with a Santa Clara case in December 1850—San Mateo's first case came fourteen years later in 1864—and end with cases tried in December 1889. In both counties, the first date is that of the earliest case on record, the second marks that point where the written testimony appeared infrequently and the cases, therefore, provide less valuable evidence for historical analysis. The San Mateo evidence is actually more than a sample—it includes every case: 197 suits. In Santa Clara County, however, the larger population necessitated a systematic sample of every fifth case, a procedure that yielded 204 cases. Thus the total number in the study is 401 cases involving 276 female plaintiffs (68.8 percent) and 125 male plaintiffs (31.2 percent).[17]

Though the cases span the years 1850 to 1890, the period of time covered by the study is actually longer and encompasses much of the nineteenth century. This projection back to the antebellum period occurs because testimony or complaints about family relations in 1865, for example, most probably represent the expression of at least two decades of prior experience. That is, a woman married in 1865 was almost certainly born before 1845, and the twenty-odd years between birth and marriage decisively shaped her attitudes about family life. Furthermore, to extend the linkage still further back, her parents, relatives, and friends transmitted their ideas about sex roles and family patterns to her, and their experience dates from the first quarter of the century. Though aware of the absurdity of extending this generational linkage to Plymouth Colony, my point is that attitudes about family life do not miraculously appear the day a divorce suit is filed. Table 1 shows, by decades, the year of marriage of the litigants.

*Table 1.* Decade of Marriage

| Decade Married | Percent | (N) | Cumulative Percent |
|---|---|---|---|
| 1830s | 1.0 | (4) | 1.0 |
| 1840s | 6.0 | (24) | 7.0 |
| 1850s | 14.3 | (57) | 21.3 |
| 1860s | 28.1 | (112) | 49.4 |
| 1870s | 33.6 | (134) | 83.0 |
| 1880s | 17.0 | (68) | 100.0 |
| Missing | | (2) | |
| (N) | | (401) | |

As the table makes clear, one-fifth (21.3 percent) married in the 1850s or earlier, meaning—given an average age of at least twenty at marriage—that some eighty couples spent their premarital years in the first half of the century. Since by 1869, one-half of the couples (49.4 percent) had married, about two hundred couples in the sample had absorbed their values about marriage and family life in the antebellum years. Thus, although the divorce complaints span the years 1850–1890, a good portion of the cases reflect values and attitudes formed in antebellum America.

Who were these Californians who found themselves in divorce court? One might reasonably guess that most came from the middle and upper classes. They would be the people with the economic wherewithal to afford a divorce. They would also be the people with high enough expectations about marriage to suffer disappointments sufficient to warrant filing for divorce. After all, moralists wrote for middle-class audiences, and if middle-class people accepted this advice, if they infused their marriages with so much emotion, mutual regard, and personal commitment, then they might also suffer the tensions and disappointments that led to divorce. Meanwhile, to continue this line of argument, the small-town laborer and his wife would continue to muddle through, not very happy but not expecting very much either.

Actually, though, this plausible expectation and the actual divorce evidence do not square; a surprisingly high percentage of people were from among the farming and the working classes.[18] Farmers, rural laborers, teamsters, saddle makers, carpenters, and bakers all appeared in the records, suggesting—as later evidence will demonstrate—that heightened marital demands and expectations affected the family life of people from all social classes. The non-industrial nature of San Mateo and Santa Clara County precluded the class cleavages characteristic of a mill town, but even rural and small town society had discernible divisions. By various methods, the occupations of more than one-half the sample were found, and these occupations were then grouped into six classes.[19] The Appendix includes a complete list of the occupations comprising the six divisions and the number of men in each, but before proceeding to Table 2—which provides a class breakdown of the sample—a few examples might serve to make the divisions more concrete: (1) the upper class included businessmen, merchants, lawyers, and all those who identified themselves as ranchers; (2) bookkeepers, dentists, druggists, and storekeepers were combined to form the middle class; (3) farmers are self-explanatory, but any landowner clearly identified as wealthy was counted as being in the upper class; (4) skilled trades included bakers, carpenters, cooks, and tailors; (5) miners, teamsters, and mill workers were grouped in the unskilled trades; and (6) laborers were those men who identified themselves as such or were so identified by others; their ranks included both town and rural laborers as well as men described as "unemployed" who were clearly not tradesmen.

*Table 2*. Social Classes in the Sample

| Social Classes | Number of Husbands in Each Class | % of Total |
|---|---|---|
| Upper Class | 35 | 17 |
| Middle Class | 34 | 17 |
| Farmers | 28 | 14 |
| Skilled Trades | 38 | 19 |
| Unskilled Trades | 19 | 9 |
| Laborers | 49 | 24 |
| Total | 203 | 100 |

The striking point of this table is the concentration at the lower end of the economic scale. The bottom three classes are taken to comprise the working class, and they represent 52 percent of the known occupations; if we admit farmers to the ranks of workingmen, the percentage of blue-collar litigants rises to 66 percent. In short, divorce courts were not the exclusive province of the middle and upper classes but offered relief from marital problems to workingmen as well. Though comparisons with national statistics are difficult because the census grouped the occupations differently, the figures in Table 2 are in line with the nation at large. Nationally, from 1887 to

1906, farmers made up 25.2 percent of the divorced, laborers 17.9 percent, and workers in manufacturing 22.7 percent, for a total of 65.8 percent.[20] Therefore, if divorce signifies the lack of congruity between marital expectations and reality, this disjunction was not confined to one class or to one part of the class structure.

If the middle and upper classes did not dominate the divorce docket, neither were the illiterate excluded from the remedy of divorce. Altogether, 9.6 percent of the female plaintiffs and 3.8 percent of the male plaintiffs were illiterate, but note in Table 3 that in the first two decades, 21.2 percent of the female plaintiffs could not sign their names but instead marked the documents with an "X".[21]

*Table 3*. Male and Female Illiteracy by Decade of Complaint

| Decade of Complaint | Illiterate Male Plaintiffs | | Illiterate Female Plaintiffs | |
|---|---|---|---|---|
| | % | (N) | % | (N) |
| 1850s and 1860s | 10.0 | (1) | 21.2 | (7) |
| 1870s | 0.0 | (0) | 12.0 | (10) |
| 1880s | 4.5 | (3) | 5.2 | (7) |

Not surprisingly, most of the illiterates came from the bottom rungs of society. Dividing the sample into blue collar and white collar reveals that among women, 85.7 percent came from the working class and that among men, all came from the blue-collar group.[22]

The fact that in the first two decades of this study over 20 percent of the female plaintiffs were illiterate and that in the 1870s over 10 percent could not sign their name suggests that "modern" attitudes about marriage can exist even in the absence of basic literacy. These twenty-four illiterate women—although lacking a basic component of modern consciousness—acted to end marriages that their great-grandmothers would surely have continued to tolerate.[23] The transformation of the family that started in the mid-eighteenth century affected the lives of all Americans, but especially women, who gained the most from the softening of male power. That even illiterate women took the difficult step of deciding to divorce, securing a lawyer, and pursuing their case through the courts suggests the far-reaching scope and consequences of the emergence of the companionate family.

Although the records yielded the class background and literacy of the litigants, they provided neither racial nor ethnic information. But a safe assumption is that almost all of the divorce seekers were white. In Santa Clara County in 1860, whites made up 98 percent of the population; in 1870, 93 percent; and in 1880, 92 percent. The percentage decline stemmed from the influx of Chinese laborers who in 1860 were insignificant in numbers but by 1870 comprised 6 percent of the total population and by 1880, 8 percent. San Mateo County's racial composition was similar. In 1860 the population was 96 percent white, but by 1870 the same figure fell to 92 percent and in 1880 stood at 93 percent. Again, Chinese accounted for the failing percentage of whites; in 1870 Chinese represented 8 percent of the total population and ten years later, 7 percent. The only figures for 1890 show that the town of San Jose in that year was 93 percent white, 6 percent Chinese, and the remaining 1 percent Black, Japanese, and Indian.[24] The fact that Chinese made up the largest percentage of the nonwhite population suggests, for two reasons, that these California couples consisted almost exclusively of whites; first, the Chinese population was almost wholly comprised of single men; second, any Chinese that might have appeared in the divorce records would be easily identifiable by surname, but no such names appeared in the sample.

The question of race is not complicated, but the issue of ethnicity is more difficult. Unfortunately, the divorce documents provide no direct information on the ethnic background of the litigants. Census data offer a portrait of the ethnic makeup of the two counties, but it is no substitute for knowing the actual ethnic background of the litigants. Neither county, however, had a high percentage of foreign-born from any one country. In 1890, five countries dominated Santa Clara County's foreign-born population; Ireland, 5 percent; Germany, 4 percent; England, 3 percent; and Canada, 2 percent. The same figures in San Mateo County reveal different countries of birth but the same low percentage of the total population: Ireland, 9 percent; Italy, 6 percent; and China, Portugal, and Germany, 4 percent each.[25] Thus, although the sample surely contains foreign-born, it is unlikely that couples from any one country far outnumbered couples from other nations.

How many of the divorce seekers were foreigh-born is impossible to say, but we do know that most were married in the United States. Among the 401 cases, 93 percent (373) involved couples who married in the United States; only 7 percent (28) married outside the country. Table 4 provides the country of marriage among the twenty-eight couples wed abroad.

*Table 4.* Country of Marriage

| | Total Foreign Married | | | |
|---|---|---|---|---|
| Country of Marriage | San Mateo County % | (N) | Santa Clara County % | (N) |
| England | 43 | (6) | 21 | (3) |
| Italy | 14 | (2) | 7 | (1) |
| Canada | 14 | (2) | 14 | (2) |
| Australia | 7 | (1) | 7 | (1) |
| Belgium | 7 | (1) | 7 | (1) |
| France | 7 | (1) | 36 | (5) |
| Germany | 7 | (1) | 0 | (0) |
| Mexico | 0 | (0) | 7 | (1) |
| Total | 99 | (14) | 99 | (14) |

Note in Table 4 that among the foreign-married, 54 percent (15 of 28) came from England, Canada, and Australia, countries that shared a cultural heritage with that of the United States. Though the evidence on the place of marriage is no substitute for actual knowledge of ethnic background, the above figures help to minimize the importance of ethnic variations in this sample as a factor in determining family values and attitudes.

These rural Californians who came into divorce court—whether wealthy or poor, educated or illiterate—all had one thing in common: the desire to improve their own personal life by sundering a bond that the society of nineteenth-century America both cherished and advocated. Why one person did so and another in similar circumstances did not is a question we cannot answer, but the central point is that increasing numbers of people took that dramatic step as the century advanced. No statistic better reveals the existence of rising marital expectations than does the increase in the divorce rate.[26] In the United States from 1860 to 1900, the divorce rate went up fourfold, jumping almost 80 percent in the 1870s alone. In California, divorce grew even more rapidly as the number skyrocketed by almost 130 percent in the 1870s, far outdistancing the 54 percent growth in the population. The ratio of married couples to one divorce, given in Table 5, also shows the increase and provides a useful comparison between California and the country as a whole.[27]

*Table 5.* Married Couples to One Divorce

| | 1870 | 1880 |
|---|---|---|
| California | 355:1 | 239:1 |
| Nationally | 644:1 | 481:1 |

The divorce cases from the two countries reflect this pattern of growth. Before comparing the population growth rate with the divorce growth rate, Table 6 provides the number of complaints by decade, showing their concentration in the latter decades.

*Table 6.* Divorce Complaints by Decade

| Decade of Complaint | Number | % of Total |
|---|---|---|
| 1850s | 10 | 2.5 |
| 1860s | 37 | 9.2 |
| 1870s | 118 | 29.4 |
| 1880s | 236 | 58.9 |
| Total | 401 | 100.0 |

The rise in population accounted for a percentage of the shift—more people meant more divorce suits—but divorce complaints rose considerably faster than the population. Table 7 compares the percentage in population change with the percentage of change in divorce complaints and grants by decade.[28]

*Table 7.* Increase of Population and Divorce Complaints in San Mateo and Santa Clara Counties by Decade

| Decade of Complaint | Percent Population Increase | Percent Divorce Complaint Increase | Percent Divorce Grant Increase |
|---|---|---|---|
| 1860-1870 | 117 | 266 | |
| 1870-1880 | 33 | 211 | 233 |
| 1880-1890 | 33 | 114 | 101 |

Throughout these years of growth, the comparative percentage of men and women filing complaints changed only slightly, despite the large increase in the number of complaints being filed. Whether the percentage of male and female suits are compared by decade of marriage, as presented in Table 8, or by decade of complaint, as presented in Table 9, the figures show that women brought roughly two-thirds of all suits.

*Table 8.* Male and Female Suits by Decade of Marriage

| Decade of Marriage | Suits by Men | | Suits by Women | |
|---|---|---|---|---|
| | % | (N) | % | (N) |
| 1830s and 1840s | 32.1 | 9 | 67.9 | 19 |
| 1850s | 26.3 | 15 | 73.7 | 42 |
| 1860s | 34.8 | 39 | 65.2 | 73 |
| 1870s | 29.1 | 39 | 70.9 | 95 |
| 1880s | 32.4 | 22 | 67.6 | 46 |

*Table 9.* Male and Female Suits by Decade of Complaint

| Decade of Complaint | Suits by Men % | (N) | Suits by Women % | (N) |
|---|---|---|---|---|
| 1850s and 1860s | 25.5 | 12 | 74.5 | 35 |
| 1870s | 26.3 | 31 | 73.7 | 87 |
| 1880s | 34.7 | 82 | 65.3 | 154 |

This county-level data reflected statewide patterns. In the period 1867 to 1886, women in California received two-thirds of the divorces.[29] A comparison with eighteenth-century New England data reveals that this preponderance of female plaintiffs in divorce court had not always existed. From 1692 until 1764, Massachusetts divorce petitioners were divided almost equally by sex (47 women, 51 men), but from 1765 to 1786 over 60 percent of the petitioners were women (82 women, 51 men). These findings, along with data showing greater sensitivity to women's sexual complaints, suggested to Nancy Cott that women's status rose in the late eighteenth century and that the Revolutionary years produced a more "modern" consciousness among women, an outlook characterized by increased self-assertion, confidence, and concern for the future.[30] The high percentage of female divorce seekers in nineteenth-century California suggests that women continued this move toward self-assertion and a sense of personal efficacy. As later analysis will demonstrate, women upset with their marriages were convinced that their fate was not sealed.

The stable percentage of men and women who requested divorces also suggests that expectations of men and women remained remarkably constant; if, for example, men brought 80 percent of the complaints in 1860 and women brought 80 percent in 1890, we would conclude that either marital expectations or legal tactics had changed fundamentally. That they did not implies the working out—over at least a century—of some accepted concept of roles and power within the family, a concept that had its roots in the companionate form of family life. This stability, it should be added, speaks well for the credibility of the records as historical documents. Wild fluctuations in the relative percentages of male and female plaintiffs would raise suspicions about the documents' usefulness in exploring family life.

Men and women were both remarkably successful in obtaining favorable decrees. In approximately 90 percent of the cases, the plaintiff—regardless of sex—either won the case or had it dismissed; thus, for all the emphasis placed on the sanctity of the nineteenth-century home, judges were by no means reluctant to grant divorces. Tables 10 and 11 show by decades the percentage of male and female plaintiffs who either received divorce decrees or dismissed their own complaints.

*Table 10.* Divorce Awards and Dismissals for Men by Decades

| Decade of Complaint | I Plaintiffs Receiving Divorces | | II Cases Dismissed by Plaintiff | | I + II |
|---|---|---|---|---|---|
| | % | (N) | % | (N) | % |
| 1850s and 1860s | 81.8 | (9) | 9.1 | (1) | 90.9 |
| 1870s | 75.0 | (21) | 10.7 | (3) | 85.7 |
| 1880s | 61.2 | (41) | 29.9 | (20) | 91.1 |

*Table 11.* Divorce Awards and Dismissals for Women by Decades

| Decade of Complaint | I Plaintiffs Receiving Divorces | | II Cases Dismissed by Plaintiff | | I + II |
|---|---|---|---|---|---|
| | % | (N) | % | (N) | % |
| 1850s and 1860s | 73.1 | (19) | 11.5 | (3) | 84.6 |
| 1870s | 89.2 | (66) | 9.5 | (7) | 98.7 |
| 1880s | 80.6 | (108) | 16.4 | (22) | 97.0 |

What stands out is the high rate of success that plaintiffs, but especially women, experienced in court. Despite the nineteenth-century emphasis on women's indispensable moral role in the family, the law did not force women to sacrifice their own happiness or peace of mind for the sake of family unity. Instead, women's presumed superior morality worked to their benefit in divorce court. One interesting difference in the two tables appears in the 1880s, when almost 30 percent of the men filing complaints withdrew them (a figure almost double that for women), suggesting that whereas men may have used the courts to improve their marriages, women more assiduously sought marital dissolution once they became convinced that happiness was impossible. Whatever the reason for the difference, these tables—when combined with those on the social class of the litigants, on the rise in the divorce rate, and on the constant sex ratio of plaintiffs—show that increasing numbers of men and women from all social classes were expressing dissatisfaction with their marriages, and that courts recognized the legitimacy of these marital complaints and in most cases awarded a divorce to the aggrieved party.

*The Setting: Rural California*

When couples did go into divorce court, when they finally made the decision to break one of the nineteenth century's most valued bonds, husbands and wives in San Mateo or Santa Clara County could in no way hide in the shelter of urban anonymity. Throughout the period 1850 to 1890, these two San Francisco Bay Area counties were rural communities with an economy dominated by farms and small shops.[31] The men in this study were farmers, agricultural laborers, carpenters, cooks, harness makers, blacksmiths, and small-town merchants. Just how rural these two counties were from 1850 to 1890 can be seen in population figures from the United States census (Table 12);[32] neither county ever reached a total population of 50,000 and San Mateo County barely rose above 10,000.

*Table 12.* Population of San Mateo and Santa Clara Counties, 1852-1890

| | 1852 | 1860 | 1870 | 1880 | 1890 |
|---|---|---|---|---|---|
| San Mateo | – | 3,214 | 6,635 | 8,669 | 10,087 |
| Santa Clara | 6,764 | 11,912 | 26,246 | 35,039 | 48,005 |

Only Santa Clara County had any town that even remotely resembled an urban center. San Jose, established in 1777, steadily rose in population from 9,089 in 1870 to 12,567 in 1880, and finally to 18,060 in 1890.[33] Aside from San Jose, the census included just six other villages in the two counties, (Table 13),[34] none of which met the census definition of a city, that is, a community with at least 2,500 residents.

*Table 13.* Population of Towns and Villages in San Mateo and Santa Clara Counties, 1870-1890

| | 1870 | 1880 | 1890 |
|---|---|---|---|
| Towns in San Mateo | | | |
| Redwood City | 727 | 1,383 | 1,572 |
| Millbrae | – | 195 | 243 |
| Pescadero | – | 238 | 221 |
| Towns in Santa Clara | | | |
| Santa Clara | – | 2,416 | 1,891 |
| Gilroy | 1,625 | 1,621 | 1,694 |
| Los Gatos | – | 555 | 1,652 |

Nineteenth-century historian J. P. Munro-Fraser described the towns and countryside of this area in breathless prose: "The farmers' houses, surrounded by gardens and orchards, appear like beautiful green islands in a golden sea."[35] Here in this ocean of wheat, farmers grew the crops and raised the livestock that comprised the backbone of the region's economy; in the towns, tradesmen produced the products and provided the services needed in a rural community. Agriculture dominated the economic life of both counties, a characteristic shared by the rest of the state as well.[36] In fact, from its start in 1777, the pueblo of San Jose was an agricultural center, and throughout the period from 1850 to 1890, agriculture and agriculturally related industries dominated the economy of Santa Clara County. As early as 1825, the mission of Santa Clara owned over seventy thousand cattle and eighty thousand sheep, and until 1860 the county's prevailing industry was horse and cattle raising.[37] By 1860 the cash value of farms was almost three million dollars and wheat production

*1.* San Jose, California in the 1860s. Although San Jose was the largest town in Santa Clara County, the 1860 population numbered less than 5000 people. Courtesy of the San Jose Historical Museum.

2. A San Jose street scene in 1866 showing several small shops. Courtesy of the San Jose Historical Museum.

3. Downtown Santa Clara, 1870. The 1870 census did not list the size of Santa Clara, but by 1880 it was the second largest town in Santa Clara County and had 2,416 people. Courtesy of the San Jose Historical Museum.

alone reached over one-half million bushels.[38] In contrast, manufacturers were limited and revealed an agricultural orientation; of the forty-seven establishments listed in the 1860 census, almost all turned out agriculturally related products—flour, bread, and liquor, for example—or nonindustrial products needed by both town and rural residents—wagons, saddles, and lumber. Aside from two mercury mines employing two hundred people, the fact that the largest concentration of nonagricultural workers was some fifty workers spread among nine sawmills highlighted the rural flavor of Santa Clara County; in 1860, it lacked anything resembling a genuine factory.[39]

Thirty years later, the county still exhibited a low level of industrialization. Two hundred manufacturing shops employed just three thousand workers, and though the aggregate statistics give no sense of the size of any one plant, figures a decade later from San Jose—the most likely town in the county to have large factories—reveal no single industry (let alone a single factory) employing more than 155 people.[40] The town of Santa Clara, the next largest in the county, had just thirty-six shops with only 248 workers all told. Men also monopolized the work force; in 1890 they comprised 98 percent of the officers and clerks and 87 percent of the operatives. Women's only inroads lay in piecework, where, along with children, they held 52 percent of the jobs—but this sector employed less than 250 people.[41]

If the statistics on agriculture and industry give a rural and small-town flavor to Santa Clara County, they give a positively bucolic flavor to San Mateo County. Recall, first, that Redwood City, the county seat and largest town, had just 1,572 people in 1890, a number suggesting that its claim to city status rested on future hopes rather than contemporary realities. In 1860, the entire county reported only three industries—flour making, lumbering, and shingle manufacturing—and they employed just sixty people in twelve different establishments.[42]

The next two decades showed little change. By 1870, the county supported two flour mills, a tanning shop that employed two people, and a handful of sawmills that provided work for less than two hundred men; moreover, lumber from the coastal mountains could not last, and by the 1880s, three sawmills had closed and the remaining eight employed just eighty men. Several small cheese and butter factories were the only other establishments listed in the 1880 census, and among them they employed thirty men. In all, two dozen shops employed 130 men (no women), figures that hardly signaled the arrival of industry in San Mateo County; rather, most people made

*4.* Redwood City, California in the 1880s. Redwood City was the largest town in San Mateo County and had 1,383 citizens in 1880; a decade later that number stood at 1,572. Courtesy of the San Mateo County Historical Association.

*5.* Redwood City, 1888. The population of the town at this point was about 1,500. Note the ships at the end of the street. Courtesy of the San Mateo County Historical Association.

their living as farmers, agricultural or general laborers, or tradesmen.[43] For those who did farm, life appeared to be less secure financially than for their neighbors in Santa Clara County. Whereas 77 percent of farmers in Santa Clara County cultivated land they owned, only 51 percent did so in San Mateo County; the other half either rented or sharecropped. However, like the farms in Santa Clara County, the San Mateo farms were not large; the average size in 1880 was 270 acres, similar to the 213 acres in Santa Clara County.[44]

As late as 1890, San Mateo County reported only twenty-one manufacturing businesses that together employed less than two hundred people, and unlike Santa Clara County, which had some small industries like canning, San Mateo lacked even the most elementary beginnings of industry.[45] The important point, in short, is that in both counties, most people owed their livelihood to agriculture, either directly, as farmers or farm laborers, or indirectly, as craftsmen or shopkeepers who supplied the products and services necessary in a rural economy. This, then, is the general background in which the four hundred couples who make up this study lived. Like most Americans, these Californians married, reared children, and went

6. Half Moon Bay on the Pacific Coast, San Mateo County, California, n.d. but probably 1880s or 1890s. Half Moon Bay was one of several small towns along the San Mateo County coast. It was formerly known as Spanishtown. Courtesy of the San Mateo County Historical Association.

about the business of earning a living. But at some point, domestic tensions became too acute, the disappointments too severe, and so they decided to end their marriages in divorce court. Their suits clearly signified discontent, but what was it that these male and female, rich and poor, literate and illiterate Californians expected from but did not find in their family life? How was it that they would not tolerate what earlier generations had endured? In the subsequent chapters, we will seek an explanation to these important issues by examining marital roles for men and women. From that examination will emerge the internal character of the nineteenth-century family and the range of problems, tensions, and failed expectations that drove an ever-increasing number of couples apart.

# 3

# *Ideal Womanhood in California*

Abigail Bennett was the wife of a Gilroy, California farmer and the mother of three children. After a hard day of washing and mending, she was unlikely to put her work aside, open a well-worn diary, and record her private thoughts for the day. When she reached old age, she was just as unlikely to sit down with pen and paper and reflect on the significance of her life by writing her memoirs. But thanks to her divorce suit in 1870, we know, by way of a relative, that she "was very industrious. I have known her for 16 years at least. She was never otherwise. She was very frugal. I think her character for chastity was the very best kind. I never knew anyone who was freer from guilt than she." A neighbor added her thoughts on Abigail's work habits: "As far as industry is concerned she has been considered one of the most industrious women in the county," and Abigail's seventeen-year-old daughter singled out the same qualities: "She has always worked very hard, was always very economical and saving."[1]

While the testimony of these three friendly witnesses may have overstated Abigail's virtues, it helps both to delineate social expectations (or sex roles) for women and to unravel some basic paradoxes of nineteenth-century womanhood. In the course of divorce proceedings, husbands and wives, supported by several hundred witnesses, discussed a wide range of topics—for example, female character, women's health, domesticity, motherhood, and sexual chastity—and in so doing illuminated the relationship between prescriptive demands and actual attitudes and clarified the connection between the emphasis on women's refinement and morality and their claims for greater respect and authority within the family. This chapter and the one that follows examine nineteenth-century womanhood from a variety of perspectives, but before proceeding to the California evidence, a general analysis of women's place in the nineteenth century is in order.

Some historians have argued that women's status declined in the nineteenth century. In the eighteenth century, so they argue, women played an indispensable role in the household economy and received respect and status commensurate with their contribution. As the economy changed in the early nineteenth century and women's work became less important in an increasingly urban, industrializing, and market-oriented society, their status likewise declined. What resulted was the doctrine of the spheres, the belief that men and women occupied two different, biologically determined worlds. Women were now cut off from the productive world, locked in the suffocating embrace of domesticity, and given special status as moral guardians rather "as a substitute for power than an acknowledgment of it."[2] Although recognized as morally and emotionally indispensable, married women in industrial society had lost their all-important economic function and had become either non-producers in the home or degraded laborers in the factories. Either way, women's status fell. They were now praised as angels but treated like China dolls; cheered for their domesticity but barred from public life; honored for their mothering but saddled with all the care of the children. Wives' duty to provide a moral refuge for their competitive-minded husbands only insured women's second-class status by denying them meaningful participation in nineteenth-century capitalism.

Dividing the social world into two spheres, the argument continues, did more than deny women a vital productive role. Relegating women to a secondary position left severe psychological scars. Alone and isolated in their domestic sphere, women experienced a lack of autonomy, a gnawing sense of self-doubt, and a deep sense of inadequacy.[3] Furthermore, in elaborating what became known as "the cult of true womanhood," moralists heightened such anxieties by underscoring women's allegedly innate nervousness, submissiveness, fickleness, diffidence, passivity, and dependence. These character traits, coupled with early socialization that instructed women to deny desires for self-assertion, meant that "the model nineteenth-century woman accepted that her husband's authority was sanctioned by God, nature, and tradition."[4]

Even women's role as moral guardian poisoned self-respect. A woman who took such duties seriously "obliterated her sense of self and virtually existed only in relation to others." Self-abnegation had become the female ideal.[5] Nineteenth-century education, by training women for the fulfillment of proper domestic duties, only exacerbated women's sense of inadequacy by providing an education "for the benefit of other, rather than for their own needs."[6] A nineteenth-century woman thus faced several riddles that left her perplexed but ultimately dependent: she was, in the words of Regina Morantz, "guardian of the race but wholly subject to male authority; preserver of civilization, religion, and culture, yet considered the intellectual inferior of men; the primary socializer of her children, but given no more real responsibility and dignity than a child herself."[7] Where women had once been respected, they were now dominated by men who, caught in social and economic changes they could scarcely fathom let alone control, channeled their impotency and frustration into a new control over their wives.[8]

In asserting that women's status declined as market-capitalism progressed, these writers propose what at first appears to be a logical and convincing argument. With industrialization, more and more women were indeed no longer vital cogs in the household economy. Surely their absence from the loom, the worktable, or the henhouse translated into a decline of status. The argument, however, is ultimately unconvincing. First, only sparse evidence is offered to show that women had high status in the eighteenth century. Aside from some weakly supported claims that Enlightenment thinkers recognized women's rationalism and that early nineteenth-century female lawyers, doctors, and midwives suffered under the onslaught of male-inspired professionalization, little solid evidence backs the claim that eighteenth-century women were better off than their nineteenth-century counterparts.[9] Nor is the claim of economic indispensability cogent. The labor of an individual or a group can be absolutely essential without that contribution translating into high status, as the experience of slaves and immigrant factory workers so graphically demonstrates. Finally, far more evidence reveals women's low status in the eighteenth century. In an earlier discussion of the companionate family, we found that eighteenth-century women lacked a positive self-image, lived as legal and political non-entities under the concept of coverture, and experienced repeated pregnancies and births that meant a lifetime of housework and child rearing.[10] Only the convergence of three developments—the Revolutionary War, domesticity, and the emergence of the companionate family—reduced patriarchal power, gave women vital social responsibilities, and created more expressive family relations.

The Revolutionary War, for its part, expanded women's opportunities for independent action and ultimately politicized the domestic sphere. Participating in economic boycotts to protest British taxation and in the homespun campaigns to free colonists from dependence upon British goods, raising funds to boost the morale of the soldiers, and managing farms and shops when husbands departed for the war brought women a new sense of importance and self-confidence. These changes, when linked with republicanism and its emphasis on independence, liberty, and non-coercion, laid the groundwork for more companionate, less hierarchical families: in the wake of the Revolution, children gained the right to select their mates, husbands and wives cooperated to prevent pregnancy, divorce became more easily obtainable, child governance assumed more rational, less authoritarian terms, women resisted traditional male slights of the female character, and the sexual double standard came under attack.[11] Liberty meant more than freedom from English rule.

After Independence, when men reasserted the principle of coverture and drew back from more far-reaching changes between the sexes, the impact of the war years remained visible. Concerned about the future of republican institutions, male and female theorists assigned women the crucial task of socializing the children to proper republican citizenship. If women were not to be men's true political equals, the Republican Mother could still exercise a political role by encouraging, as Linda Kerber explained, "her sons civic interest and participation. She was to educate her children and guide them in the paths of morality and virtue." The domestic sphere thus became women's poltical arena. Placing the future of the republic in mothers' hands, in turn, gave rise to demands for better female educational opportunities and an insistence that women's economic and political contributions to the nation be recognized. Thus, women's work was no longer unexamined drudgery but the foundation of civic virtue.[12]

Even as concern for republicanism waned, nineteenth-century womanhood retained its moral importance and added new, equally important tasks. As an aggressive commercial society replaced the older corporate economy of household production, as production became less home and family oriented and more individuated, and as regional economies became more diversified and urban, middle-class women organized voluntary associations to cope with these changes. In the process, and somewhat paradoxically, they established a new domestic ideology for women. These women, cut off from the corporate household economy of the past and faced with an uncertain economic future, worked, as Mary Ryan explains in her study of Utica, New York, to save the souls of their own families amidst the hubbub of a booming and boisterous canal economy. In churches, temperance societies, maternal organizations, and moral reform groups, women sought to stabilize society, arbitrate morality, and protect and shape their children's characters. As a consequence of such efforts, sororal bonds developed, women gained a sense of moral self-importance, and child nurturing assumed new significance. Then, as men's and women's spheres continued to divide under the impact of industrialization, as society became more heterogeneous, disordered, and impersonal, as economic problems beset old middle class residents and success increasingly depended upon "maximizing individual gain in a competitive market," women transplanted the values first nurtured in the associations to the privatized domestic sphere, now seen as a sanctuary against the outside world. The domestic sphere—woman's sphere—became the guarantor of morals and the incubator of character traits necessary for survival in a competitive world: hence the indissoluble link between domesticity and motherhood. In the eyes of some, women might even be the only hope for national unity: only they, with their superior morality and sensitivity, could bond together and stand against the disintegrating forces of early nineteenth-century America; only they could provide a moral refuge and sanctuary for husbands who spent their days in the immoral marketplace. Other commentators hoped women's natural morality, delicacy, and refinement would bring Christianity, civilization, and order to the untamed West. There is good evidence that frontier women accepted this heavy responsibility.[13]

Delegating such important responsibilities to women brought a simultaneous reevaluation of authority relations in the home. Nineteenth-century advice literature and personal documents reveal a clear shift to more equal, less hierarchical domestic relations. This change occurred in conjunction with another key development discussed earlier—the increasing importance of love and affection as the proper basis of family life. The two are closely linked: personal choice in mate selection, increasing emphasis on romance and courtship in marriage, and heightened emotional expectations for domestic life accompanied a move in the direction of more equality in the home. Such changes obviously redounded to the benefit of women. This does not mean that patriarchy eroded immediately or that men no longer monopolized many key family decisions, but it does mean that the direction of change by the early to mid-nineteenth century was clear: women were gaining status in the home; their expectations were increasing; their dissatisfaction with traditional male prerogatives was becoming more evident.[14] What all of this meant for the family life of most American women remains obscure. But the divorce evidence provides a clue. By mid-century, wives in California from all social classes described their emotional expectations, defended their character and work, and judged their husbands' behavior by the standards of domesticity and the companionate family.

If women like Abigail Bennett took the time to read local newspapers, they encountered advice that worked and reworked the soil of Victorian morality and the cult of true womanhood. In this view, women were innately more moral, emotional, and intuitive than men, but less intellectual, or, as the *Santa Clara Argus* wrote in 1866: "Men can better philosophize on the human heart but women can read it better."[15] The same idea appeared in the *San Mateo County Journal* in 1880: "The strength of women lies in their heart. It shows itself in their strong love and instinctive perception of right and wrong. Intellectual courage is rarely one of their virtues." The article asserted that women's "whole lives are bound up in their affections," then underscored the liabilities of their limited brain power and warned against venturing beyond the domestic sphere: "Without dwelling on the greater physical weakness of women in general, it is a fact that their brains are more easily deranged, and unless they change greatly are apt to deteriorate in essential womanly qualities, if thrown much or prominently before the world."[16] *The Weekly Argus* offered similar sentiments in criticizing women who worked for the vote: "When it gets to be a common thing for a woman to run around on the street electioneering, then she would have to depend on her power of reason, and there she would be at a disadvantage."[17]

Women's more emotional but less intellectual nature meant they were ideally suited for domestic life. The *San Mateo County Gazette* emphasized that women could be fairly evaluated only within their sphere: "It is only within the circle of her domestic duties that we can judge of the true worth of a woman, or make a correct estimate of her forbearance, her virtue, and her felicity. There are displayed all the finer feelings of which the pure heart of woman is susceptible."[18] There, too, happiness could be found even for the impoverished wife "who can be happy in the love of her husband, her home, and its beautiful duties without asking the world for its smiles or its favors."[19] The good wife centered her life on her husband: "The event of her day is his return from work. Her work is to make him comfortable and happy. His satisfaction and approbation are the standard of her success or failure."[20] The same article noted the essential reciprocity of the male and female spheres. Although different, each had something valuable to offer the other: "Woman is set in the household, and man is sent out into the world. He has to learn from her the household lessons of service and gentleness, and she needs to catch from him the larger outlook."[21]

This larger outlook, of course, was not to transcend the domestic sphere. Women's essence lay in fulfilling the responsibilities of domesticity, not in charting a course independent of the call of wifehood and motherhood. "Life is a failure," an 1880 article asserted, "to any woman who has not secured the love and adoration of some grand and magnificent man."[22] Self-satisfied spinsters came in for special indictment: "A female who has never felt at any period in her life a desire to engage in the duties or share in the delight of that state to which all human beings are drawn by force of nature and reason, must be utterly devoid of tenderness and the HEAVEN-BORN INSTINCTS with which all creation is rightfully endowed."[23]

The influence that women did possess stemmed not from public power but from nobility of purpose and moral righteousness. The *San Mateo County Gazette* described the essence of womanhood in redemptive terms: "There is a delicacy in female society which seems to check the boisterous, to tame the brutal, and to embolden the timid."[24] The *Weekly Argus* counseled young girls to create the right home environment. "Girls, you do not realize the extent of your powers and influence if you do not exert them for the benefit of the home circle."[25] Such power and influence was anything but derivative and trivial because "family and the home form the basis of a nation's civilization, and in their preservation should be enlisted every agency of custom and law and religion, at the service of the race."[26]

Family included children, and it was as mothers that women found fulfillment and sometimes apotheosis, as in this short rhapsody on motherhood: "There is nothing like it in this world of ours—nothing so morally beautiful: a self-fed, self-sustaining love . . . the one human love that spends itself wholly upon its object, and the roots of which even ingratitude cannot kill."[27] Such self-sacrificing rested on the bedrock of Christian humility and kindness, and by definition the good mother embodied Christian virtues, or as San Jose pastor T. S. Dunn preached in memory of a small child: "God alone, can fathom the depth of a mother's love, for He is its author." Later, Dunn emphasized that "Christianity differs from all the religions of the world in the honor it gives to women and children," and then concluded with a classic statement of Victorian optimism: "*As I look at this monument* [a new chapel] *of maternal affection, I am reminded that the world is getting better.*"[28]

This sampling of local newspaper advice confirms more general analyses of nineteenth-century prescriptive literature. Moralists ascribed to women an innate morality, sensitivity, and refinement beyond that of men's, insisted that women's duties were in the home but imputed to that sphere great moral and social significance, and underscored the almost religious significance of motherly love. To twentieth-century ears, much of this rhapsody about women sounds quaint if not a little silly, but that does not mean it sounded so to a miner's wife in 1865. In fact, as the divorce records make clear, such advice provided all women—not just those of the middle and upper classes—with a coherent set of values and a sense of personal worth that only recently, and not without opposition, have begun to erode. It was in the home that the married woman worked; here she found her purpose and exercised influence in family affairs, and here, too, she raised the children. That there were deleterious effects cannot be denied, but before equal rights and women's liberation would make sense to large numbers of women, their mothers and grandmothers had to gain a sense of self-respect, importance, and shared purpose. Domesticity and the companionate ideal provided that fundamental sense of worth.[29]

What emerges from the formal divorce complaints is a litany of virtues strikingly similar to that found in local newspapers. When lawyers drew up documents describing the general character of woman, they generally offered the court portraits that emphasized both affective and work-related contributions to the family: both functions were crucial dimensions of the domestic role. Catherine Court's complaint in early 1862 stated that throughout her marriage, she "conducted herself with propriety, managed the household affairs of her said husband with prudency and economy, and was to him at all times an industrious, frugal, and chaste wife."[30] Ellen Collamere's complaint contained a similar list; throughout her nine-year marriage, she was "a good, dutiful and loving wife" and was "affectionate, obedient, temperate, industrious, and economical."[31] Others' complaints emphasized the more emotional, affective side of the wife's behavior. Susan McMahill's answer to allegations of adultery insisted that she was "faithful, true and dutiful to her said husband and tender and careful of his feelings and interests."[32] Ann Warhurst, who worked as a domestic to support her family, tried to satisfy both the emotional and economic demands of the domestic role. Her complaint depicted her as "a true and faithful and affectionate wife [who] has continually endeavored by all means to promote his happiness and prosperity."[33] Julia Demartini and Katharina Wahl also had their husbands' happiness foremost in their minds: Julia maintained she was "dutiful to defendant and did all in her power to make the life of defendant happy and prosperous," and Katharina stressed her efforts "to make his home a pleasant and comfortable one." Nevertheless, her husband often left her for days on end, even missing the dinners she had "prepared with the greatest care and attention."[34]

Nellie Rathburn's 1873 answer to desertion and adultery charges went even further; not only was she "faithful and true," but she was a "devoted and loving wife and mother, economical and industrious in the administration and management of her household affairs," who tried to make their home "pleasant and their lives useful."[35] The vocabulary is strikingly modern and underscores the importance of women's domestic duties. Women did not simply "keep house" but rather "administered and managed" home life in an atmosphere of purposefulness and usefulness. Moreover, the performance of home duties required the correct attitude and disposition: May Stewart "endeavored in all sincerty [*sic*], love, affection, and kindness to discharge all the duties of wife and mother becomingly and to promote the happiness and welfare of her husband."[36] The court evidently agreed and dismissed her husband's charges of cruelty in 1883. Modesty and propriety also made their way into the formal complaints. Grace Weston, for one, claimed that she "conducted herself in a modest and ladylike manner" and Caroline White's complaint stated that she was "a modest and honorable woman and has always been a true and faithful wife."[37]

A Victorian image of women as redeemers emerges against this backdrop of female purity and decorum. Amilla Kelly's complaint ruefully admitted that her husband's cruelty was beyond redemption even though she "faithfully tried to be to defendant an affectionate and good wife and has earnestly sought to reclaim him but has been unable to do so and now feels that it is [in] vain to attempt it any more."[38] Ann Warhurst also admitted defeat; though she had tried "to mollify him and induce him to speak to her and treat her kindly," he continued his abuse and finally drove her away in November 1865.[39]

When we move from formal legal documents to the actual court testimony, we get a more personal, less legalistic sense of women's self-conceptions. Clearly, the moralists' emphasis on women's affective and moral contributions to the family struck a responsive chord with wives from all class backgrounds. Sarah Isbill, wife of an unemployed laborer, pictured herself as a determined redeemer of her wayward husband: "I always treated my husband as a dutiful and affectionate wife and did everything in my power to [give] him a [sense] of duty towards his family, and his responsibility." Isaac Wixam, Sarah's father, also emphasized that his daughter treated her husband "as a kind, affectionate, and dutiful wife; and I know that she did everything in her power to make him do otherwise."[40] Melissa Ray, the wife of a laborer, stressed her sense of duty, her tolerance, and her efforts to reform her indolent husband: "I was always and at all times a dutiful and affectionate wife, and bore patiently for years with his profligacy and misconduct." She added that she had "always been uniformly kind and affectionate to him and had hoped to make him do better, but my hopes and wishes in that respect have been blasted."[41] Like Melissa Ray, Ellen Havely, the twenty-three-year-old wife of an Illinois farmer, suffered various indignities though she considered herself a "dutiful, faithful, and affectionate wife who did all the household work and in addition assisted him in working the fields at all kinds of farm labor." His cruelty finally forced her to leave him and flee to California.[42]

Other women were more laconic, but they, too, stressed their belief that women had a sense of duty and responsibility. Julia Sabine admitted that her husband, a millhand, was difficult, sometimes even exasperating, "but I always tried to do my duty."[43] Annie Parker's one-year marriage dissolved even though she acted "always in a kind and affectionate manner, and I performed my whole duty as a wife," and Maria Estes's behavior, in her own opinion, was of "the kindest and most affectionate manner and never gave him any cause for his wickedness. I did my duty to him and kept my vow in every respect."[44]

These general virtues—duty, kindness, modesty, affection, industry—comprised the foundation of proper female character among nineteenth-century California women. Together they represented the fabric of nineteenth-century female morality, a fabric that maintained its strength and resiliency for decades and provided women with a set of meaningful values and standards. Moreover, what is clear from this evidence is the multidimensional quality of the domestic sphere. Lawyers, wives, and witnesses all focused on women's successful demonstration of expressive, redemptive, and work-related character traits. Embodying all three was at the core of proper womanhood, a difficult challenge that translated into respect for the responsibilities of the domestic sphere. This respect for domestic life helps to explain women's reluctance to move beyond the doctrine of the spheres, especially their suspicion of political movements that repudiated the very social structure that provided meaning for women like these Californians.[45]

### *Female Character*

The self-respect women gained by the high value accredited to domestic duties is no more clear than in discussions about proper female character. While women worked in the home, they were expected—at all levels of society—to embody the virtues of modesty, gentility, and decorum, a triad not to be confused with submissiveness. In fact, the place of submissiveness as a female character trait deserves some attention. Popular antebellum literature offered women contradictory advice on the role of obedience in marriage. Some writers clearly viewed it as a core character trait, leading Barbara Welter to include "submissiveness" among the four cardinal virtues of the cult of true womanhood.[46] That inclusion seems reasonable if the following from *The Young Lady's Book* (1830) is taken as representative: "It is, however, certain, that in whatever situation of life a woman is placed from her cradle to her grave, a spirit of obedience and submission, pliability of temper, and humility of mind, are required from her."[47] As late as the 1850s, the "Wife's Prayer," which appeared in the *San Mateo County Gazette,* besought God to "make me humble and obedient,"[48] But other writers, as Kirk Jeffrey has shown, emphasized the mutuality of marriage, the need for consultation, respect, and joint decision making.[49] Perhaps we can do no more than put one set of quotations against another or conclude with a feeble statement about the early nineteenth century's being a transitional period, but the divorce data suggest that by the mid-nineteenth century, people no longer emphasized female obedience. In real life, female submissiveness was undercut by the important position women held in the home, and though women certainly occupied a subordinate position in society, at home—where they spent most of their time—wives, ideally, were free from coercion and the compulsion to obey. In fact, husbands who treated their wives like servants might find themselves in divorce court.

The divorce records yield few references to the virtues of obedience or submission. Though one might appear in a formal complaint—Elaika Mattson, a miner's wife, was described as a "kind, faithful, and obedient wife"—rarely did a witness in court emphasize obedience as a quality worthy of special attention.[50] In fact, only *one* witness (out of 450) singled out obedience as a female virtue. Hannah Marrs described her daughter's behavior toward her husband as "in all occasions most respectful and as a dutiful, submissive, and obedient wife . . . [H]is will was her pleasure." It is noteworthy that Marrs was sixty-eight years old (born in 1797), and thus her views may reflect an older conception of marital relations.[51] Instead, what emerges from the divorce evidence is not a picture of submissive women at the beck and call of their husbands but rather one in line with the assumptions of domesticity and the companionate ideal: of purposeful women trying to perform important tasks while cultivating a character suffused with modesty, gentility, and decorum. While Mrs. Mattson's complaint did mention her "obedience," witness F. M. Hale took a more common approach and described her general character as "in every way becoming from a wife to her husband. . . . I saw her frequently while I was there. Her reputation was good as to peaceableness and friendliness."[52] Zenas Churchill's description of Ellen Havely likewise stressed her Christian virtues but made no mention of obedience. Asked about her character, Churchill replied that she was "industrious, neat, amiable and kind, modest and retiring in her disposition, and of a sensitively nervous temperment *[sic]* that harsh and ill treatment would greatly affect."[53] Others took a similar tack and emphasized women's efforts to make family life harmonious. C. D. Davidson, a farmer, praised the qualities of Sarah Forbes, who by nature avoided unpleasantness: "I have known her for fourteen years and she has always born [sic] a good character as far as any knowledge and information goes. She is peaceable and of a quiet disposition."[54] Martha Putman spent twenty-four years with an irritable laborer and tried, unsuccessfully, "not to cross him," and Grace Thomas, a farm wife, also tried to avoid provoking her husband. Asked if she in any way caused his outbursts of anger, she replied: "I never did. I always tried to do the best I could."[55]

These women, although not explicitly describing their homes as refuges, tried to create a harmonious home environment whose foundation would rest on proper female character traits. Criticisms of wives who failed to exhibit such traits offers another way to examine proper womanhood. What was missing in a wife's character suggests what was expected. Here, too, we see an emphasis on decorum and gentility but no specific references to disobedience. Though the following cases involved intransigent wives, the problem was cast not in terms of obedience but in terms of character. John Cardinell, a laborer, was happy when his wife, a woman of a "most ungovernable temper," vowed never to live with him again, "which I was very glad of because it was not pleasant or safe to live with her." He told the court that their arguments "usually began by me asking her to do something. She would refuse," words would follow, "and then she would fly into a passion."[56] Cornelius Paddock was another husband who faced a strong-willed wife. On several occasions, her sexual immodesty caused him great consternation, and though Cornelius tried to reason calmly with her about such actions, she simply told him to mind his own business, that she intended to "do as she pleases." He summed up her character by telling the referee: "She has a bad disposition, tantalizing and vicious."[57]

Though there is a hint of problems with obedience in the Paddock and Cardinell cases, the women's failures are set more in terms of character, as problems stemming not from simple disobedience—one party failing to recognize the other's legitimate right to command compliance—but from the absence of proper values. Other criticisms of wives took the same approach, which suggests that successful marriages were based on the good character and mutual respect of the couples involved and not on the wife's timid obedience to her husband's commands.[58] Joseph Tuers and William Stewart were faced with churlish wives, but neither chose to mention disobedience as a fault. Instead, Tuers stressed his wife's volatility and lack of decorum:

she was "excitable, peevish and annoying in the extreme," and Stewart saw his wife as "peevish, quarrelsome, jealous and fault-finding."[59] Samantha Kelly contrasted the shrewish behavior of Arena Gardner with the restraint of her husband: "I have frequently heard her abuse him in the presence of company and seen him much embarrassed by her abuse—once or more I knew him to rise and leave the table on account of her language to him."[60] Edwin Parker even indulged in a little psycho-history in arguing that his wife's current misbehavior was rooted in her past. In a letter of 1882 to his estranged wife, Edwin groped for an explanation as to why she was divorcing him. The trouble lay, in his view, with his wife's unladylike character, and her faults could be traced back to her childhood. Despite admitting that he knew "but little of the halcyon days of your youth," Parker plunged into her past life with relish, pointing out that he knew she used to quarrel with her two brothers, that she had been "at loger *[sic]* heads" with her father, and that she was "overbearing and vindictive with both your husbands for both enjoyed the rich blessings of unrequited love."[61]

The point is that all of the above cases contain a litany of character defects in which mention of disobedience is conspicuously absent. Surely if male–female relations were generally conceived as a superordinate–subordinate relationship, someone would have cast a wife's shortcomings explicitly as a failure to obey. That no one did suggests that marital relations entailed a good deal of mutual respect and even equality within the domestic sphere.

### *Women and Health*

The respect for women and the move beyond hierarchical relations in the home meant that even an apparent weakness like female invalidism could be turned to women's advantage. Power relations between husbands and wives did not change immediately or without struggle, but the movement toward domestic equality gave women leverage they lacked in the previous century, leverage in this case that expanded the social uses of ill-health: women could now use invalidism to check a husband's power, to rationalize withdrawal from a job market that offered only menial work opportunities, and to help end an insufferable marriage.

Although scholars agree that bad health (whether real or imagined) was common among middle- and upper-class females, they disagree over the meaning of widespread invalidism. For some, the high incidence of poor health and the belief in women's gender-based debility functioned to confirm and legitimate nineteenth-century attitudes about women's dependence and inferiority. In this view, prejudiced biologists and doctors presented as scientific fact what were in reality only bold-faced attempts to legitimate women's secondary position in the home and society. Some doctors, for example, attributed women's poor health to misguided intellectual, sexual, or work-related aggressiveness. So great were physicians' suspicions of women, so great their fear that women might rebel against domestic duties, that doctors engaged in psychological (and surgical) warfare with their female patients. Such fears led these doctors to see moral depravity behind female ills, to suspect their patients of malingering, and, most regrettably, to practice needless and cruel medical techniques on women's reproductive organs.[62]

This theory of victimization has been challenged from a variety of perspectives. Doubts about the frequency of gynecological surgery, especially in light of the well-documented opposition to it, suggest that clitoridectomies and the like represented not generalized male hostility but seldom-used and little-respected surgical techniques. It is also unlikely that more frequently practiced barbarities (leeches, injections, and cauterizations) symbolized deep pathological suspicions and anxieties about women—more likely (given their use with men, too) they represented nothing more malevolent than simple medical ignorance. Nor, it appears, were doctors engaged in psychological warfare with female patients in an effort to render women still more submissive and weak: on the contrary, the doctor most heavily criticized in this regard (S. Weir Mitchell) actually respected intelligent and capable women, advocated vigorous physical activity for females, and practiced "in accord with the most advanced neurological thinking of his day."[63]

The most fruitful reinterpretation of female ill health focuses on the social uses or functions of invalidism. Hysteria, to take one common debility, may have been a reaction to the paradoxes of nineteenth-century womanhood: women, instructed on the one hand to renounce independence, self-assertion, and aggression, and, on the other, to be strong, self-reliant, protective, and efficient household managers, perhaps buckled under the pressure of the contradiction. Coming to adulthood with significant ego weaknesses, many nineteenth-century women found themselves overwhelmed by the responsibilities of wifehood and motherhood. Hysteria resulted. But the twitches, trances, paralysis, and sobs came not without rewards, and as Carroll Smith-Rosenberg explained, despite the real pain, a stricken wife now became the center of family life, her frequent petulance only reminding all of her needs and debility. She also received elaborate sympathy and gained the right to be seen and treated by a physician who more than likely advised that she rest in bed, welcome advice to a woman worn down by her endless duties.[64] If her condition required it, she might even be sent to a special facility where the "rituals of invalidism" provided companionship, consolation, and affection.[65]

California wives were not immune to the widespread invalidism observed by Catharine Beecher and other nineteenth-century commentators. The sallow, fainting, feeble, coughing, nervous denizens of urban middle-class parlors had their counterparts on the farms and in the small towns of rural America, a point of some importance given the usual emphasis on middle-class city women. Before exploring the social uses of ill health, the relationship between health and social class deserves elaboration, beginning with a comparison between the class background of sickly women and the class composition of the entire sample. Among the divorce seekers, 75 of 401 cases mentioned poor female health, and of that number, 54 included the social class of the husband. Table 14 clearly shows that poor health was not concentrated at the middle and upper levels of society but, on the contrary, closely parelleled the known class composition of the entire sample. In fact, the results suggest a slight skewing among lower-class occupations; that is, the percentage of women reporting poor health among the lower classes was slightly higher than their total percentage in the sample.

*Table 14.* Social Class and Female Health

| Social Class of Wife | Class Breakdown of Entire Sample | | Class Breakdown of Sick Women | |
|---|---|---|---|---|
| | % | (N) | % | (N) |
| Upper Class | 17 | (35/203) | 16.7 | (9/54) |
| Middle Class | 17 | (34/203) | 13.0 | (7/54) |
| Farmers | 14 | (28/203) | 9.3 | (5/54) |
| High Trades | 19 | (38/203) | 20.4 | (11/54) |
| Low Trades | 9 | (19/203) | 14.8 | (8/54) |
| Laborers | 24 | (49/203) | 25.9 | (14/54) |
| Total | 100 | | 100.0 | |

When we shift from the class composition of the sickly women to the percentage of unhealthy women in each class, we again see no clear relation between class and health. The percentage of wives reporting bad health in each class is given in Table 15.

*Table 15.* Percentage of Wives in Each Class Reporting Poor Health

| Social Class | % of Women in Each Class Reporting Bad Health | (N) |
|---|---|---|
| Upper Class | 25.7 | (9/35) |
| Middle Class | 20.6 | (7/34) |
| Farmers | 17.9 | (5/28) |
| High Trades | 28.9 | (11/38) |
| Low Trades | 42.1 | (8/19) |
| Laborers | 28.6 | (14/49) |

The only dramatic figure in this table is found among the low trades, where over 40 percent of the wives reported poor health, evidence that in no way supports an interpretation of female sickness as being particularly common among the upper and middle classes.

Does the same absence of relationship hold between female health and the type of job a woman held? Perhaps sickness was associated only with particular kinds of work done by women. Because of the limited range of female occupations, the known occupations of women have been separated into just two divisions—menial and non-menial—but here, too, as shown in Table 16, we see no bias in favor of upper- and middle-class women.

*Table 16.* Women's Work and Health

| Women's Occupation | Occupational Breakdown of All Women in Sample | | Occupational Breakdown of All Sick Women | | % of Women in Each Class Who Complained of Bad Health | |
|---|---|---|---|---|---|---|
| | % | (N) | % | (N) | % | (N) |
| Non-menial | 15 | (14/96) | 13.8 | (4/29) | 28.6 | (4/14) |
| Menial | 85 | (82/96) | 86.2 | (25/29) | 30.5 | (25/82) |

The percentage of sickly women working at menial jobs closely approximated the percentage of women working at menial tasks in general, and the same held for women working in non-menial tasks. The percentages alone make the point; 28.6 percent of women working in non-menial jobs and 30.5 percent of women working in menial jobs mentioned bad health.[66]

When specific Victorian infirmities—in this case "nervous" problems, a "delicate" constitution, or uterine ailments—are checked against class background, we find no clear connection between class and health. For example, of the four women who suffered uterine problems, one was a farm wife and three were laborers' wives; of the five who declared themselves delicate, one came from the middle class, one from low trades, one from high trades, and two from laboring households. Among the twelve wives with nervous problems, five came from the upper and middle class, three from laborers, and four from high trades and farmers. All of these figures suggest that sickliness was a characteristic of nineteenth-century womanhood in general. In rural and small-town California, the wife of a laborer and the wife of a merchant were equally likely to complain of their delicate health or of their nervous problems.

On some occasions, poor health was linked with the inability of women to exercise independent judgment, a combination that would warm the heart of Victorian moralists who argued that female refinement and rectitude stemmed, in part, from their great intuition but limited rationality. H. F. Thurston, a hotel keeper and carpenter, defended himself against his wife's charges by asserting that she was "a good woman but of exceedingly nervous temperament and easily led by other parties."[67] Katharina Wahl's self-description also stressed her poor health and consequent vulnerability to outside manipulation. She claimed that her husband tricked her into signing a document which she thought dismissed her divorce suit but which in actuality made him co-owner of her land, and the reasons she was so deceived illuminate the relationship between female health and the perils of venturing beyond the domestic sphere. First, her general health suffered due to the "misfortune, disgrace and annoyance" of the divorce suit; second, she was of "nervous and excitable temperament and easily affected by cares and troubles and [wa]s of a trusting and confiding nature"; finally, she hoped "they could and would live in harmony and quiet."[68] In short, she was in no condition to transact business; her basic trust, her hope for domestic happiness, and her sensitivity all weakened her ability to live in the public sphere.

Relatives might even shield a woman from litigation if they believed that her poor health and Victorian sensibilities could not stand the pressures of court action. Initially, Ellen King was not told of the divorce complaint against her for fear that the "mental anguish" produced by such knowledge might rekindle her "brain fever" and because she was "utterly inexperienced in business or litigation." Her father also kept her in ignorance to protect her reputation: "It was better to arrange matters so that there could be no publicity," and his fears may not have been groundless. Ellen later claimed that she had no idea her youngest child would be taken from her because at the time of the divorce suit, she "was in great distress of mind." In addition to taking her child, Ellen's husband had also defrauded her of land by convincing her to sign what she thought was a mortgage request but turned out to be a land transfer; she did so "in utter ignorance of the nature or the contents of the paper signed by her."[69]

The trial testimony of both men and women shows a strong

preference for Victorian diction in describing female health, as in the case of Nellie Jones, who convinced the court of the absurdity of her husband's cruelty allegations: "I am delicate and do not exceed 110 pounds in my best health, and at the times these acts of cruelty are alleged, I weighed about 95 pounds."[70] E. F. Wilcox neatly linked Vicenta Wilson's poor health with other desirable Victorian qualities in his description of the rancher's wife: "She is a weak, nervous woman, amiable in her disposition and modest in her deportment."[71] In an 1883 case, William Duncombe wrote to his lawyer that his wife "has medium health, though subject to hysteria and hereditary scrofula in a mild form." Rarely did physicians testify, but Dr. A. B. Caldwell did speak on behalf of Antoinette Johnson, wife of an unemployed clerk: "She is of a nervous temperament; any shock or dislike would have [a] very strong affect [sic] upon her producing great nervous excitement." He added that for three years she has been "rather an invalid. . . . I have considered her rather frail and not very healthy." Caldwell concluded by again stressing Mrs. Johnson's vulnerability and cautioning that further accusations of adultery would "terribly shock her mind and body and have a very bad effect upon her general health."[72]

It is not surprising, in light of women's predisposition to nervousness and frailty, that husbands were sometimes accused of causing female illnesses—or, more precisely, of bringing to the surface the wellspring of infirmities that characterized nineteenth-century womanhood. The imbalance between healthy, "robust" husbands and sickly, "delicate" wives meant that husbands had to be cognizant of their wives' limitations or face the consequence in divorce court, and though women's claims of "nervousness" and "frailty" symbolized female dependence, they also provided one way for women to check the behavior of their husbands. The close relationship between poor health and accusations of cruelty becomes clear when healthy and unhealthy women are compared with the likelihood of whether or not they brought divorce charges on grounds of cruelty. What we find is a clear statistical relationship between women who complained of poor health and their tendency to sue on grounds of cruelty: among unhealthy women, 60.9 percent sued on grounds of cruelty (total N = 64), whereas only 41.2 percent (total N = 212) of healthy women brought similar charges.

Evidence from specific cases reveals how claims of poor health, when linked with assumptions about women's refinement, sensitivity, delicacy, and moral superiority, functioned to increase the power of cruelty complaints and to erode the arbitrary power of husbands. The experience of these unhappy couples also showed that the move to less hierarchical relations and more respect for women did not come without struggle, that some men resisted or were oblivious to the change, and that wives could use the high status of women as a source of power against husbands. It would be surprising if some men did not resist, if some marriages were not out of phase with the companionate ideal, but the following cases reveal just what form conflicts took between husbands and wives. In 1884 Annie Semenoff added weight to her cruelty complaint by noting that her husband's acts came despite the fact that she was "nervous and modest in her deportment and amiable in her disposition," here linking "nervous and modest" as if one naturally followed from the other.[73] Jennie Moulton's cruelty and adultery complaint underscored the damage caused by her husband's adultery, especially because she was "of a nervous temperament and used to the kind attention of friends and relatives."[74] Many other cruelty allegations cast the husband's transgressions against the backdrop of his wife's delicacy: Antoinette Johnson was "a person of delicate health and constitution"; Maria Schwab was "naturally bodily weak"; Martha Rinehart was "a weak and delicate woman"; Alice Kilday was "a delicate lady of refinement and education"; and Caroline Planer was a "sickly woman, and of a nervous temperament."[75]

Many allegations did more than juxtapose male abuse and female delicacy and insisted that husbands directly caused wives' debility. Husbands who abused healthy wives were bad enough, but a husband who caused his wife's illness, who cruelly treated the moral center of the family and violated the companionate basis of marriage, found himself beyond the pale, especially in light of the ever-broadening legal definitions of cruelty noted earlier. In 1869, Ellen Havely's complaint noted her "nervous temperament," then argued that her husband's adultery had produced "frequent attacks of illness.[76] Eleanor Chesley charged that her husband's cruelty caused her great "mental suffering," especially given her "tender, nervous, sensitive, and refined nature," and Louisa Koppell accused her husband of causing a "paralletic *[sic]* stroke" because he insisted she *"keep boarders and cook for them"* despite her poor health.[77] The complaint of Annie Semenoff contrasted her husband's "strong build" and "robust constitution" with her nervousness and then stated she could not withstand, either "physically or mentally," any further abuse.[78] Martha Brisbine's accusations included a story in which, soon after she had given birth and "being weak in body and mind," her husband forced her to move with the infant to Reno, Nevada, and then temporarily abandoned them; so callous a disregard for her health and the prerogatives of motherhood brought Martha a divorce in 1874.[79]

Further testimony reveals the close relationship between male cruelty and female depression and anxiety. It is plausible that much of the chronic and widespread ill health of American women, so often mentioned by contemporary commentators, can be traced to real domestic discord and the disjunction between the ideal and the reality of marriage. A young woman, convinced that a loving, lifelong marriage held the key to her future happiness, might understandably come apart when her husband treated her unkindly. The ensuing "nervous debility" thus symbolized her dependence and disappointment, but, paradoxically, gave her power in the divorce suits. In the cases that follow, women used cruelty-inspired poor health to help gain freedom from their husbands. Testifying in 1866, Sarah Wilcox informed the court that Vicenta Wilson "was confined to her bed by sickness for about six or eight weeks." Asked the cause, Wilcox replied: "I think mental pain had much to do with it, and but for that she wouldn't have been prostrated in bed. . . . I think his presence worried her and retarded her recovery." Another friend of Vicenta's added her own explanation: "I should say from appearances it was caused by mental excitement and pain," and she, too, thought Vicenta would recover more quickly if her husband were gone.[80] In a different case, Eunice Bennett claimed that her sister-in-law, a farm wife, literally wasted away because her husband's false accusations of adultery caused her "loss of appetite. She had more the appearance of a petrified person than of a living person. It affected her health so much that people would ask me what was the matter with her. Was she sick? She feared the loss of reason."[81] In 1883 Esther Philbrick testified on her own behalf and stressed the direct connection between her nervousness and her husband's abuse: "I am of a very nervous temperament aggravated by the extreme cruelty of said defendant." Pressed for details, she said that in 1874 her husband hit her on the head with a milkpail when she refused to milk the cow, and since then she had suffered continual anxiety: "It seems to be a nervous fear which I attribute to the effects of that blow."[82] The mental health of Antoinette Johnson withered in the heat of her husband's assault on her Victorian sensibilities; first, he insinuated that she paid for some groceries with sexual favors, an accusation that put her under a doctor's care for a week; then, he continued to drink heavily, and the two together "shattered my nevous system so it unfitted me for my duties altogether."[83]

Antoinette Johnson's "duties" referred to housekeeping, but poor health could also prohibit women from working at outside jobs, a situation, perhaps, in which female "delicacy" legitimized dropping out of an economic situation stacked against them in the first place.

Faced with bleak economic opportunities—and crippled by a supposedly weak musculature and sensitive nervous system—the deserted, estranged, or unsupported wife could plead poor health, leave the labor market, and seek direct assistance from relatives and friends. Three things were thus accomplished: first, the woman was spared the drudgery of menial wage work; second, domestic values were preserved because the woman remained in a "home" setting—by falling back on the resources of the community, women did not have to face the vicissitudes of the marketplace or its dubious morals; third, the integrity of the female life cycle was preserved. Ideally, women worked outside the home prior to marriage and labored in the household thereafter. A married woman deserted by her husband, however, faced a return to menial outside labor (especially if she had children), unless she could gain assistance from friends and relatives. Claims of poor health could function to keep the life cycle intact by legitimating the rejection of work outside the home.

Among women who reported both poor health and their means of support, 68 percent supported themselves (in part) by their own labor; 42 percent received some assistance from friends and neighbors; 18 percent got help from relatives; 16 percent received help from their children and 12 percent from parents; and 4 percent obtained some help from siblings (total N = 50).[84] When these figures are compared with those for healthy women, the one significant difference lies in the support that children provided for their ill mothers. Sixteen percent of unhealthy women relied, in part, on their children for help, compared with only 2.5 percent of healthy wives. One explanation for this finding is that unhealthy women were long-term economic liabilities, and whereas friends and relatives might willingly help a healthy woman temporarily, the financial support of children was required in cases where lengthy financial assistance might be needed.

Those unhealthy women who did work, if offered alternatives, seldom continued to support themselves for long. Mary Dale entered domestic service after her husband deserted her in 1866, but her poor health prevented her from gaining self-sufficiency, and she told the court that she was dependent on the charity of her sister for support; at the time of her divorce suit, she had lived with her sister's family for three years. Albert Vincent supported Dale's testimony and said that Mary had "worked out from place to place . . . but at times was in febel *[sic]* health and had to depend in a manner upon friends."[85] The wife of mechanic David Shupe found security in her parents' house. She did some sewing and housework after her husband left her, but her chronic poor health forced her to live with her parents and depend upon them for charity.[86] When laborer Fred Sayers ran off in 1865, his wife immediately turned to her mother and brother for support, support readily given because of her poor health and her duties of motherhood. Jane Sayers's mother explained why her daughter could not support herself: "She was in rather delicate health the most of the time and with the care of those children on her hands, it would have been impossible to support herself."[87] The warmth of a sibling's home provided for Mary Glover's domestic comforts. Left destitute, hungry, and "poorly off" for clothing, she worked briefly in a San Francisco shoe factory, then moved in with her sister's family in Santa Clara County, where she lived for almost four years before filing for divorce.[88]

Other unhealthy women in need of financial help turned not to relatives but to friends and neighbors for support. The cult of domesticity and the emphasis on the "sanctity" of marriage pressured couples to remain together, but when a split occurred, neighbors lent financial assistance to the wife. Support, however, varied widely and depended on whether or not the woman was viewed as an innocent victim or the culpable party. In those cases where the source of the unhealthy wife's support was known and the wife brought suit against her husband, 51.2 percent (total N = 41) of the wives mentioned receiving some help from neighbors and friends. On the contrary, when the husband brought suit and the case included information on the wife's source of support (generally supplied in her answer or cross-complaint), no cases mentioned a wife getting help from the community (total N = 9).[89] Neighbors stood by the wronged wife, but no support went to those women charged with causing the breakup—apparently financial assistance was dictated by moral judgments about the sickly woman's behavior.

Several cases reveal that in these rural communities and small towns, the limited range of economic opportunities for women made the receipt of private charity necessary and almost inevitable. Yet, each of the following women, who tried but failed to make a living, explained her failure not in terms of limited economic opportunities—egg selling, sewing, laundry, housework—but in terms of poor health. To convince the court of their virtue, women felt obliged to argue that they had tried mightily to support themselves and that only poor health had driven them into a state of dependence upon friends and relatives. Such dependence, it appears, was not considered acceptable without some kind of explanation. The experience of Margaret McClelland was representative: after her husband, a teamster, left, she eked out a living selling eggs and doing laundry until a "rupture" made her dependent upon the generosity of friends and relatives.[90] Susan Gilbert's career as a domestic and seamstress was cut short by poor health, and eventually the laborer's wife received some help from friends plus a small alimony. Her doctor could hardly have sounded more Victorian when he described Susan as unable to work because she was "affected with ailments peculiar to her sex which have become chronic in form."[91] Elizabeth Etts's testimony revealed the limited opportunities available to the wife of an unemployed laborer and self-styled hunter:

> I provided for myself as far as my health would permit. I worked round amongst the neighbors, took in washing and went out working by the day, and sometimes worked out by the week, and sometimes I took one or two boarders and managed any way I could to get a living but some of the time I was in bad health and was obliged to depend upon the charity of my friends for means to live upon.

Her neighborhood grocer, A. R. Sansman, noted Elizabeth's determination: "A part of the time she was keeping house as well as she could, and a part of the time she worked amongst the neighbors. She would go out washing and do anything she could get to do." Other times, Sansman explained, "when she was sick which was considerable during the time they lived there, the neighbors would get things for her and pay for them themselves."[92] May Short, Ann Warhurst, and Harriet Shupe all did housework until health problems made them dependent on private charity, and not even menial work was open to Ottilia Kottinger, who testified, "I am over fifty years of age and in feeble health, and I have not been able to earn anything."[93] Martha Lucas's condition was much the same: she was "a feeble and weakly person and not physically able to do any hard work . . . and has required care, nurture, and attendance and strengthening food and nourishment."[94] Mrs. H. S. Hanover revealed that her belief in the connection between poor health and economic dependence could withstand some pointed questioning. The court asked Hanover if she thought that her neighbor, Vicenta Wilson, could support herself and family without risking damage to her health. Hanover answered, "I shouldn't think she could." The defense counsel then asked if it were not true that Mrs. Wilson had already supported herself for some time, but Hanover successfully parried by admitting that indeed she had, but "her health has been failing ever since."[95]

The general portrait of ideal womanhood included modesty, decorum, and gentility, but few in court—even among those with a vested interest in placing a wife in the most favorable light possible—singled out obedience and submission as a cardinal female virtue. Nor did the views of the presiding superior court judge—who argued in 1886 that the husband "is the head of the and the MASTER OF THE HOUSE"—bring these Californians either to emphasize the presence or bemoan the absence of a woman's submissive qualities.[96] The reason is that domestic relations were moving away from such hierarchical relations, and these rural Americans reflected that fact. Moreover, even female sickliness, which on the surface epitomized female dependence, could be turned in positive directions, both in helping women gain divorces and in justifying their reliance on friends and relatives for support. Domesticity and appeals for more egalitarian relations, then, did have behavioral consequences, and although many couples did not measure up to the ideal, more significant is the fact that husbands and wives (along with friends and neighbors) judged marriages against these two standards. This point will become more clear in the next chapter, where we examine women's work in the home, chastity, and female independence.

# 4

## *Dimensions of Womanhood: Domesticity, Chastity, and Independence*

Women and men worked in two worlds in nineteenth-century America, but each performed labor that society recognized as necessary and important. Women's housework assumed a moral importance it had not had in the previous century, and the most routine tasks took on new meaning. Housewives, far from being considered either ornaments or drudges, were seen as important workers laboring at a task deserving respect and admiration. Moreover, both sexes adhered to similar work values, and while women may have labored in the private realm, their work did not go unnoticed. The testimony of neighbors and lodgers plus that of wives themselves reveals the purposeful nature of housework. The moral elevation of work in the home—the "cult of domesticity"—brought social recognition to women's work and helped create meaning and purpose in women's lives. Among these rural and small-town Californians, housework offered a sense of fulfillment with its own standards: domestic chores were serious business, and to do them well was important for a woman's self-esteem.

### *Domesticity*

The emergence of domesticity, with its emphasis on women's special moral role and the home's function as a refuge from society, has been described but needs some elaboration. As early as the seventeenth century, some of the appurtenances of domesticity began to be evident. Probate inventories from England reveal that commoner's homes began to improve in the late sixteenth and early seventeenth centuries: fireplaces, room partitions, glass windows, and beds appeared, additions that signified more concern with the home and that encouraged people to spend more time there. Yet, at this early date, few signs of the affective or sociable side of domesticity were evident—the home was still far from being "the center for most nonmarket interaction."[1] Household goods that promoted social interaction—tea sets, for example—were not listed in the inventories, and meals were not occasions for family togetherness; in fact, many working people ate at the table of their employer or at the local alehouse. However, such indifference to home life did not last, and by the eighteenth century, "a whole group of commodities that promoted domesticity began to surface in ordinary households."[2] The presence of knives, forks, glassware, china, and tea equipment in the inventories suggests that family meals were becoming more sociable and leisurely, that life in the home was assuming new importance.

One should not make too much of this evidence. At best, it suggests that people's interest in the sociable and affective side of home life rose in the eighteenth century and that the preconditions for domesticity were being established. (At worst it means only that a rising standard of living allowed people to buy more forks and tea sets.) But we have already seen from other eighteenth-century evidence that there was little self-consciousness about the meaning of women's domestic duties or of home life in general. If some of the appurtenances of domestic comfort were appearing, domesticity had not yet reached the level of social theory, and women's duties in the home were still considered self-evident and in no need of theoretical embellishment.[3]

Not until the Revolution was the role of domesticity thoroughly reevaluated, a development that "would eventually culminate," in Mary Beth Norton's words, "in nineteenth-century culture's glorification of woman's household role."[4] By politicizing the household and making motherhood crucial to the future of the republic, the domestic realm became central to the social theory of the new republic. Writers now urged women to make the home an efficient work place free from the distractions of frivolity, and school reformers likewise shaped curricula to meet the elevated status of domestic life: domesticity had become a vocation and motherhood a profession.[5] Meeting the challenge of self-government required the contributions of both sexes—men to work in the economic and political realms, women to rear virtuous children and manage well-ordered households. Associated with this mutual republican endeavor came a rising status for women, as evidenced by the erosion of the sexual double standard (a clear violation of republican equality), the rising success rate for women seeking to end unhappy marriages, and the expansion in women's educational opportunities.[6]

Domestic life's heightened significance continued into the nineteenth century, no longer because of the Revolution but in response to economic and social changes. Economic growth, market rationalization, industrialization, the increasing importance of wage contract relations, and the separation of home and work prompted women, in Mary Ryan's analysis, to organize voluntary associations to mitigate the impact of these changes. Within temperance, religious, maternal, and moral reform groups, a new ideology emerged that inflated women's moral importance, elevated their role as child nurturers, and drew more tightly the bonds of womanhood. As economic change continued to divide the sexes, women transferred these values to the increasingly private family, thus forging what became the "cult of domesticity." At the same time social thinkers responded to this development by drawing an ever sharper distinction between male and female roles, a distinction that became known as the "doctrine of the spheres."[7] Women's sphere—the home—functioned as a "haven in a heartless world" and as a moral anchor and source of national unity in an increasingly complex, divided society.[8] That this new ideology struck a resonant chord among the literate (especially urban) middle class has been amply documented. New England reformers, ministers, and female diarists all bid allegiance to its assumptions, and Southern wives, though subjected to a "fanatical idealization" of their role, exhibited a belief in the moral and intuitive superiority of women. Like their Northern counterparts, Southern women also engaged in purposeful work that was crucial to the well-being of the family.[9] Even frontier women, far from the urban and industrializing areas that had given rise to the doctrine of the spheres, found meaning in the domestic ideal. School texts in fontier towns carried the message of women's moral superiority, and Midwestern periodicals advised farm wives of their special mission and role. In fact, the frontier offered women a special challenge, a place to translate the theory of women's civilizing and unifying mission into the reality of combatting the lawlessness, ignorance, and intemperance of the west. Women's support for education, churches, Sunday Schools, temperance and Sabbath societies, and anti-prostitution campaigns attests to their efforts in this direction. Even Mormon women, some of whom were involved in polygamous marriages, subscribed to the tenets of domesticity, and, by the 1870s, census takers found Mormon wives "keeping house" rather than working outside the home as the church encouraged them to do. Julie Jeffrey concluded her study of Mormon women by arguing that "despite unique religious and social conditions, once again women found that domesticity gave their lives meaning."[10] The same was true for women on the overland trail who tried, often in vain, to maintain domestic proprieties and familiar household routines during the journey west.[11]

Elevating the status of domestic work and accentuating the differences between the two spheres, however, did not mean that male and female work values were different. The purposes were different to be sure: men worked to support their families and because labor was virtuous, women to bring morality and stability to the home and society. But the work values were similar. Resourcefulness, purposefulness, diligence, and efficiency formed the core of male and female labor despite their different settings, a point demonstrated by Santa Clara County Judge David Beldon in 1886. In rejecting a request for a large alimony settlement, Beldon opined that the woman was entitled to no more than what "usually rewards the efforts of a lifetime of industry, thrift, and economy." He then added that she should not be maintained in idleness: "It is not the condition of useful and deserving wives throughout the community."[12] Some moralists, as Nancy Cott found, even described women's work using business metaphors, thereby making the two spheres analogous. A *Godey's Lady's Book* story in 1841 described a businessman's displeasure with his wife's management of the household, a problem he believed could be corrected if only she would give to her tasks the same attention and devotion that he gave to his business interests.[13]

Domesticity brought new meaning to housework as the unexamined drudgery of the mid-eighteenth century became the morally redemptive set of duties of the nineteenth. For divorce seekers, domesticity provided a standard against which to judge a woman's performance, functioning as either a source of strength or a point of vulnerability depending upon whether the witness was friendly or hostile to the wife's position. Regardless, domesticity established the contours of proper behavior, a point made by Frances Cory in 1871. A mother of five, Cory sued her husband on grounds of desertion and non-support and described in her complaint her struggle to overcome her family's poverty by managing her household "with prudence and economy." When he deserted her, she continued "to manage an efficient, well-ordered household."[14]

Friends and neighbors routinely passed judgment on women's housekeeping standards, and in their comments we see the seriousness with which they appraised domestic labor. For example, Margaret Peterson, a forty-five-year-old San Jose housewife, spoke approvingly of her friend Annie Holden's efforts at home: "Yes sir, she has been a hard working tidy housekeeper." Elaborating slightly, Peterson added that Annie "has always been a prudent, economical, and industrious housekeeper and wife." On her own behalf, Annie singled out her frugality, noting, with some pride, that she had managed her household on six dollars per week for five years. Another neighbor told the court that Annie, a plumber's wife, was a fine homemaker. When asked under cross-examination how she knew this, given her infrequent visits, she replied confidently, "because my own judgment teaches me to know. When I go into a person's place I can tell."[15] The praise for Mrs. Holden paled compared to that offered Antoinette Johnson, wife of an intemperate, unemployed clerk. Her neighbor, Dr. A. W. Saxe, had few reservations about her housework and no modesty about the scope of his judgment when he pronounced "her to be industrious and one of the best housekeepers in the state."[16]

The testimony of lodgers and resident farm hands reveals that women's work was not taken for granted by those who lived, even temporarily, in the household. Perhaps, in fact, the presence of lodgers or hired hands brought a degree of recognition to domestic labor that diminished when lodging died out in the early twentieth century, thereby depriving women of an "audience" save that of their husband and children. Prior to that time, as the experience of Sarah Simonds suggests, women's labor was neither so private nor so unrecognized. In 1864, a former lodger of the Simonds family described Sarah's behavior while he lived with them. According to Abner Colburn, Sarah was "a virtuous, good woman," but what impressed him the most were her domestic abilities: "She was a good, industrious wife, and one of the best and neatest housekeepers in the county." Neighbor George Troop was less effusive, but he declared that Sarah "was a good housekeeper—better than ladies in general."[17]

The observations of resident hired hands of Joseph Tuers attest to the social nature of female labor on many nineteenth-century farms and to women's responsibility for maintaining the proper "peaceable" atmosphere at home. Although most scholars associate the duty to maintain a refuge from the maelstrom of nineteenth-century society with urban life, this California evidence demonstrates that farm wives, too, were obligated to create a peaceful domestic milieu. Joseph Winterbarn, a fifty-six-year-old laborer, worked for Tuers in the early 1860s, and when Emma Tuers sued her husband for divorce in 1865, Winterbarn spoke on her behalf: "I consider her a very neat and industrious woman in going about her work and in keeping things neat and respectable, so far as I saw." Another field hand, John Patterson, noted that Emma waited the table when the hands ate dinner: "She seemed to be very particular to have everything right and pleasant." Hired hand William Stewart added a similar observation: "I never saw plaintiff but that she seemed to be pleasant and cheerful and talkative and made everything pleasant about the home." C. D. Rodgers, a former laborer on the farm and now a justice of the peace, described Emma as "industrious and everything went on as peaceable and quiet as in families usually." Laborer William Spencer also respected the industry of Mrs. Tuers: "I have seen her at it—she was up and got the breakfast early, always." She "generally was up about six o'clock in the morning and sometimes earlier. I would lay until I heard a noise about the stove and would get up and go feed the work horses. I have seen her feeding the poultry."[18]

The repeated mentions of "industry," "frugality," and "economy" suggest that Calvinist virtues were as entrenched in the private sphere as in the public one. Men and women worked in vastly different realms, but the nineteenth-century gulf separating women's and men's work was bridged by a shared understanding of basic work values; despite the moralists' emphasis on women's gentleness and "softness," wives were expected to work hard and to apply the same values to housework as their husbands did to farming or tanning. For example, Abigail Bennett embodied classic Victorian virtues, at least in the eyes of her neighbor, who considered her "one of the most industrious women in the neighborhood." The neighbor's husband repeated his wife's praise of Abigail's habits and also commented on her sexual decorum, a linkage of virtues that was probably not accidental: "I have considered [her] as industrious and as chaste a woman as there is in the county." And the young daughter of Mrs. Bennett drew attention to her mother's work habits when asked about her mother's character: "She has always worked very hard, was always very economical and saving."[19]

Other women were praised for their orderliness and sense of duty. Kate Weller, the thirty-five-year-old daughter of Catherine Cleal, recalled her mother's domestic Calvinism: "She conducted her household affairs with prudence and economy. She was industrious and kept everything about the house neat and in proper order."[20] Mary Wixam lamented her son-in-law's laziness, blamed his unemployment on sheer indolence, and then defended her daughter's character: "She was always a good and dutiful wife—too good for him and did her duty and her whole duty as a wife and mother."[21] Like Mary Wixam, Alice Crane affirmed the sense of duty and industry of her daughter, Mary Sharp: "She was always a dutiful and affectionate wife, and was never remiss in her duty. When well, she always did her share of the work of providing; in fact for the last seven years about all of it. She is very handy and industrious and can turn her hands to anything in the way of work."[22] Timeteo Sierra, an illiterate farmer, depicted his neighbor, Grace Thomas, as "an industrious, quiet and peaceable woman," and Tadeo Lopez described the character of Maria Alviso in much the same way: "She behaved herself as a good wife and since he left her, she has been honest and industrious."[23]

Women's sphere was unquestionably in the home—here she worked, managed, nurtured, and saved. If she did the job well, friends, neighbors, and lodgers commended her effort, but if she worked poorly, if she failed as a home-bound Calvinist and disregarded the moral importance of the home, she invited censure. Criticisms of slovenly, lazy, or improvident wives buttress the argument that the values comprising the "spirit of capitalism" also resided in the well-run home. More important, they also show how the moral elevation of domestic tasks—and with it the assumption that the two spheres were equal but different—provided leverage for husbands seeking divorces: with the insistence that women's opinions, judgments, and work be respected came the corollary responsibility that women perform in a manner deserving of such respect. Heightened expectations and rising responsibilities, while increasing women's self-esteem and autonomy, also brought increased marital instability. The shortcomings of Martha Lucas illustrate the point. In 1866 Robert Lucas, an unemployed laborer, denied his wife's charges of non-support by insisting that he had supported her for one and one-half years, and only stopped because "her management of the household became so improvident and slothful that he became entirely discouraged." Lucas gave his wife an ultimatum: he would not work unless she conducted "herself towards him as an affectionate and dutiful wife," cut down on her beer consumption, and ceased being "untidy and filthy in her person and in and about her household affairs."[24] Louis Franklyn lodged a similar complaint, alleging that he had indeed left his wife, but only because she "refuses to assist him in the conduct and management of his home."[25]

Other men also emphasized women's shortcomings as housekeepers and thereby revealed how important industriousness among wives was to these people. William Gray successfully characterized his wife as an incompetent homemaker, no doubt helped by the testimony of his daughter, who characterized her stepmother as a woman who was "disorderly in her household, neglected her family, was quarrelsome with her neighbors and she was heartless and irritable in her conduct toward children."[26] Henry Conner's grief came because his wife preferred the excitement of saloons to her obligations in the kitchen, and for two years he either had to make his own breakfast "or go to work without it."[27] If Conners had to go without breakfast, J. C. Koppel, a San Jose cigar seller, was forced to miss lunch, all because his wife "neglected most of said time to send him his lunch or any refreshments whatever, although requested by defendent so to do."[28] In an 1865 case, Emma Tuers was accused of shirking her domestic obligations, accusations that sparked a sharp debate over domestic performance. On one side were several former hired hands who applauded Emma's industry, and on the other side were two stepsons, both critical of her housework. The favorable testimony has already been quoted, but in rebuttal William Tuers testified that most of the housework was actually done by his sisters: "I never saw her do any washing unless it was for her child." John Tuers, a wandering minstrel, stopped in Santa Clara County long enough to notice his stepmother's distaste for cooking: "Sometimes I did the cooking, sometimes Defendant [Emma's husband], sometimes plaintiff [Emma], probably once a week when she took a notion."[29] Clearly, taking a "notion" fell far short of dutiful and responsible domesticity. The point is not whether Emma actually did or did not perform her housework but that both sides obviously agreed that it was an important task, argued at length over the accomplishment of these duties, and accepted the legitimacy of this issue in helping to determine whether or not a marriage should be dissolved. It is noteworthy that divorce data from the previous century made no mention of such disputes, a point in keeping with the absence of a developed domestic social theory in eighteenth-century America.[30]

### *Female Chastity*

The heightened significance of domestic work and the belief that women provided the moral foundation of the nation grew out of assumptions about the moral superiority of women, assumptions, in turn, that developed, at least in part, from the belief that women were less carnal and sexually passionate than men. By the late eighteenth century, increasing numbers of moralists, especially evangelical ministers, insisted upon women's basic disinterest in sex, and by the nineteenth century, sexual purity had become enshrined as a fundamental component of ideal womanhood, "the everlasting barrier against which the tides of men's sensual nature surge."[31] Standing opposed to such lust, women sought to check male sexuality while simultaneously exerting moral pressure in a socially beneficient way.

That nineteenth-century culture considered female chastity a basic element of true womanhood is beyond dispute. What chastity meant, however, is a matter of contention. The most straightforward explanation sees sexual purity as part and parcel of the idealized cult of true womanhood, as intensifying "the image of a passive, porcelain being whose immaculate delicacy made her willing to submit to the superior wisdom of her worldly, knowledgeable husband or father."[32]

Nor was this all. In arguing that only the most depraved females had sexual desires, "antebellum males," contends Barbara Berg, "made certain that their women remained at home, malleable and immobile."[33] Chastity was thus a means of control, a way to divide the world into the virtuous and the depraved, and woe to the woman who tottered on, much less fell into the abyss of sexual immorality. She then became a "fallen angel," a pitiable creature who, having succumbed to the predatory sexual drives of passionate men, became a social outcast. Men, by contrast, continued to exercise a range of sexual freedom unavailable to women.[34]

Other interpretations of the meaning of chastity are not so negative and appear more convincing. They begin by asking why the ideal of purity appealed to women? Surely women would not knowingly contribute to their own oppression, nor were women simply ground beneath the heel of malevolent male power. Instead, Nancy Cott has suggested that "passionlessness"—the belief that women lacked even an interest in sex—served several useful functions: first, it "allowed women to retrieve their identity from a trough of sexual vulnerability and dependence" brought on by social changes in the late eighteenth and early nineteenth centuries; second, passionlessness supported women's claims to be society's moral guardians, a role they took seriously as evidenced by their work in temperance, charity, Sabbatarian, and anti-prostitution campaigns; third, the ideology elevated in an obvious way women's status by replacing a "sexual/carnal characterization of women with a spiritual/moral one, allowing women to develop their human faculties and their self-esteem"; fourth, it functioned to check the predatory sexuality of husbands, thereby enhancing the power of women in the sexual arena; fifth, passionlessness functioned to reduce the frequency of coitus and hence the frequency of pregnancy.[35]

If the California evidence is an accurate gauge of the nation's attitudes, Cott's analysis of the meaning of nineteenth-century chastity is more cogent than those depicting purity as a symbol of female dependence. Victorian sexual morality, as it emerges from the divorce records, provided women with a way to check their husbands' powers and a means to increase the respect society owed women. By the same token, the ideal also provided husbands measurable leverage when their wives transgressed the sexual ideal.

Women's complaints contain many references to Victorian sexual mores, and when lawyers drew up allegations, women of all social classes were defended in terms that can be called Victorian. Louise

Butchart's complaint described her as "a maiden of good repute and unblemished character" who was deceived by her bigamous husband into "the submission of her body to his embraces and lust." She also claimed that the bigamy scandal meant she was "greatly injured in her good name and fame" and "her prospects in life have been blasted, and she hath been damaged in the full sum of twenty thousand dollars."[36] Other complaints were less dramatic, but they, too, defended wives' sexual decorum. Both the complaints of Maria Quentin and Jennie Hammond mentioned that the plaintiff was "ever mindful of her marriage obligations and had conducted herself as a chaste and dutiful wife."[37] Less stilted language appeared in Grace Weston's allegations; she "conducted herself in a modest and ladylike manner" and was "a kind, affectionate, and devoted wife."[38]

Aside from these somewhat formal descriptions of female purity, the female complaints offer another angle of approach by showing how domesticity, the companionate ideal, and the law effectively blunted a husband's power to shame and verbally humiliate his wife. Legal interpretations of the nature of cruelty, as we noted earlier, reflected the moral assumptions of the companionate ideal, and by 1857 cruelty sufficient for divorce could be proved on the basis of simple character defamation and false imputations of infidelity. California women used this broadened interpretation of mental cruelty to end onerous marriages, thereby revealing the behavioral implications of women's elevated moral status: they simply would not and did not have to tolerate behavior that earlier generations of women had been forced to endure. An enraged husband might, for example, recklessly call his wife a "God damned whore" as laborer Egbert Etts did, only to find his epithet used as evidence against him in a divorce court. The same thing happened to Edward Evans, who accused his wife of giving him venereal disease—"about three years ago I caught something from you"; and to Daniel Wilson, who charged that his wife "had whored with a nigger in a haystack"; and to Isadore Keller, who humiliated his wife by calling her a "whore, not as good as a whore, a common woman, an animal, and a woman of the town." All of these men's wives received divorces.[39]

Accusations of infidelity in the presence of other people were especially cruel, and women used the courts to defend their honor and self-respect in the face of such charges. For who could be a pillar of virtue if such accusations went unanswered? Who could insure the nation's morals with her own under attack? To redeem themselves, women turned to the courts, where they found a sympathetic hearing. The experience of Antoinette Johnson suggests how shocking false accusations of adultery could be to a woman of Victorian sensibilities. When Antoinette learned that her husband had insinuated to her butcher that she paid for her meat bills with sexual favors, Mrs. Johnson was distraught and under a doctor's care for a week: "It made me sick and I couldn't do anything and I endured it as long as I could and I could not stand it any longer and I at last stated to him that I should apply for a divorce." Dr. A. B. Caldwell testified that Antoinette collapsed from "nervous prostration" and did not recover for four days. In Caldwell's judgment, further accusations of infidelity would "terribly shock her mind and body and have a very bad effect upon her general health." One index of Victorian sexual sensitivity is the fact that Antoinette endured her husband's intemperance for two and one-half years, but she could stand the infidelity charges for no more than two weeks.[40]

In a similar case, Abigail Bennett managed to maintain her health, but she lost her happiness when, in the fall of 1855, her husband accused her of adultery with his brother: "I have never," she testified, "seen a happy day since then." In 1857 William again accused her of infidelity, and later testified that on this second occasion she had sex with a field hand in the barn: "He asked her for some and she said oh no, as they always do you know, and he said he had some, a standing up, with her back to the manger." Abigail pleaded with her husband for a chance to clear her name and defend her reputation: "I [did] beg of him for the sake of the family around him to allow me to prove that I was innocent." Finally, Abigail defended her honor in court, and her brother-in-law, called in her behalf, described her as a model woman: "She was very industrious. I have known her for sixteen years at least. She was never otherwise. She was very frugal. I think her character for chastity was the very best kind. I never knew anyone who was freer from guilt than she."[41]

Abigail's case was certainly helped by the fact that in 1870 several citizens of Gilroy, California, had William Bennett declared insane because of his accusations of adultery. Though Bennett did not remain at the asylum for long, the mere fact of his commitment suggests how strongly the community felt about the sanctity of virtuous womanhood. The judge in the sanity hearing explained at the divorce trial why he decided William was insane. First, he admitted that he personally had found Bennett "clear headed and distinct," but he signed the order on the doctors' recommendations. The judge recalled that the physicians said the question of sanity hinged on the truth or falsehood of the adultery charges, and because Judge Archer believed they were false and had probably arisen from hallucinations "fixed in his mind," it therefore followed that Bennett was insane. That false accusations of adultery could mean commitment to the local insane asylum speaks volumes for the importance of chastity and sexual reputation for women in the nineteenth century.[42]

Many other cases included allegations that husbands had publicly questioned their wife's chastity, thereby ruining latter's standing in the community. The social and legal significance of female chastity is underscored by the fact that although men accused their wives of cruelty, they rarely claimed that their wives publicly humiliated them by false charges of sexual immorality. Thus, although nineteenth-century women reformers tried to hold men and women to the same sexual standard and vehemently opposed the double standard, the actual marital tensions between men and women suggest women's greater psychological and social vulnerability to sexual epithets. Husbands surely realized that such charges disgraced their wives and challenged the very essence of ideal womanhood. Women had little choice but to fight back and clear their name in court, in the process revealing the paradoxical relationship between emotional vulnerability and the simultaneous presence of considerable legal power. Dressmaker Mary Gray, for example, received a divorce after her husband accused her of adultery "upon the public streets in loud tones of voice, both in the daytime and the nighttime" and in so doing caused her great mental pain.[43] While in a store in Santa Cruz, Sarah White's husband abused her by saying she was "too damn thick with other men," and in a different case, Greenburg McMahill accused his wife in the presence of neighbors of having abortions to conceal her adultery.[44] Archibald White's cruel public offer to set his wife up as a prostitute disgraced her in 1878, and laborer Michael Fay had the same low regard for his wife when he called her a prostitute. Asked whether her neighbors knew of these calumnies, Winnifred Fay answered: "Yes. It has become the talk of the whole neighborhood."[45]

Both sexes agreed that chastity and fidelity were central to ideal womanhood: irate men tried to shame their wives with sexual epithets and false accusations of adultery, and women defended themselves by asserting their sexual purity. Even on matters far less weighty than adultery, husbands and wives agreed on general social proprieties for women. Take Susan Gilbert, another woman who found her sexual reputation, and hence her very character, attacked by her husband. She defended herself, not by repudiating her husband's moral position, but by claiming that she steadfastly embodied the moral values he charged her with violating. Frank Gilbert, a lumberman, claimed that his wife ruined his Thanksgiving Day dance of 1873, particularly because she allegedly left the ballroom on several occasions in the company of an unknown gentleman; moreover, throughout the evening, she "carried on to such an extent as to attract the attention of persons present and cause remarks to be made."[46] Gilbert believed he had built a successful case against his wife, but she defended her virtue and insisted that her character met Victorian criteria of excellence. She was not "in the habit of playing, or did play cards alone with men until late and unusual hours of the night," and when she left the dance floor, she did so "in company with a lady friend whose escort, unlike plaintiff on that occasion, was sober." In fact, she never left the room "unless also accompanied by one or more ladies."[47] It is worth noting that both Frank and Susan agreed that propriety dictated that respectable women leave dance floors with their husbands or protectively accompanied by upstanding women.

Just as the Gilberts agreed that sexual modesty was central to proper womanhood, Michael and Mary Barney both observed and condemned the moral laxity of their next-door neighbor. Michael even took it upon himself to shield his wife from the sexual licentiousness of the neighbor, but not before convincing himself that the neighbor was a woman of questionable virtue. Having seen a man visiting his neighbor's wife "as late as nine and ten o'clock at night," Barney "went to their bedroom window to satisfy myself with regard to the reports that I had heard in regard to her character—reports were that she was a bad woman, and was living with another man." With his curiosity satisfied and certain that "no man would be going in and out of a residence of another man's wife without there being something wrong," Barney proceeded to warn his wife: "I thought it was very suspicious and cautioned my wife about associating with Mrs. Rathburn under the circumstances . . . for I did not think it prudent for my wife to associate with her." Part of his concern stemmed from a desire to protect his family's image in the eyes of the community because Mrs. Rathburn's immorality was widely known and discussed: "I have heard it in different places and from different parties; it was very common talk in Gilroy." In fact, Barney himself had discussed the situation with several local men.[48]

Mary Barney's testimony echoed her husband's, but she offered an interesting comment on the limits of community outrage. She, too, had seen Daniel Shackelford visiting Nellie Rathburn at dubious hours, and for that reason she dutifully avoided seeing her neighbor socially; in addition, she even forbade a girl who worked for her to associate with Mrs. Rathburn. Nevertheless, Mrs. Barney, a seamstress, continued to make dresses for her neighbor and testified that despite her neighbor's bad reputation, "I have no hard or ill feelings towards her, none at all."[49] Mrs. Barney's comment suggests that social and business morality could be separated, that economic ostracism and personal animosity did not necessarily follow social rejection;

mere social separation—as if from a contaminant—was enough. At least in this case, the channel of nineteenth-century sexual morality cut deeply but also rather narrowly.

Part of sexual modesty was simply restraint and decorum, but part was something more, something spiritual and ennobling. If the "strength of women [lay] in their heart" and if their "whole lives [were] bound up in their affections," then correct female behavior should reflect this moral attitude.[50] Unfortunately, Annie Parker's actions were far too worldly to satisfy her husband, Edwin, an unemployed school teacher. In a letter to his wife, Edwin scarcely concealed his concern with her excessive sexuality: "Your love was, as was expressed a year ago by a person that I never told you about, but an animal love, that subsiding you also subsided and you then had no farther [*sic*] use for me save to torment and annoy." He then linked her "animalism" with other faults and provided a portrait of a woman who was not a lady: "Your ideas of the duties of a wife before and after marriage were sadly at variance. Your neglect of home duties, your flattering remarks to other men, receiving both insults and vulgarity from them without retorting in any way, your constant coldness towards me will all be transmitted to your home although out of deference to your wishes I have concluded to refrain from letting them [her parents] know."[51]

Tensions like those between the Parkers reveal the importance of chastity to proper womanhood. Statistical evidence from the records also reveals the importance of female purity. Women were charged with adultery in 20.8 percent of the male complaints, whereas men were charged with infidelity in only 10.9 percent of the female complaints; moreover, women were found guilty of adultery in 16.8 percent of the cases, whereas men were believed by the court to be unfaithful in only 6.5 percent. It is doubtful that women committed adultery at a rate double that of their husbands. More likely, the disparity reflects a version of the double standard. Given the importance of female chastity, women were particularly vulnerable to allegations of infidelity, and though men were also expected to be chaste, their transgressions were less subject to legal action than were those of women.

Some suggestive patterns emerge (though the numbers are admittedly small) when we compare adultery accusations among classes. The upper and middle classes had a low incidence of adultery accusations against women; only 2 of 25 (8 percent) included charges of infidelity. The comparable figures for the blue-collar occupations (farmers, high trades, low trades, and laborers) was 9 of 30 (30 percent). Again, the disparity is probably less a fact of behavior than of morality. All classes adhered to Victorian notions of female purity, but the upper and middle classes—as self-styled conservators of public morals—avoided bringing public attention to family scandals.

Finally, adultery required immediate court action. Husbands might endure a year or two of desertion or cruelty, but adultery—"criminal connection" as it was called—was a sin of a different magnitude and required prompt action. (Women, too, brought adultery accusations soon after the transgression, suggesting that men were subject to the same standards of marital fidelity as were women.) Comparing the elapsed time between the woman's alleged act of adultery, desertion, intemperance, or cruelty and the filing for divorce reveals the threat adultery posed to marriage.

*Table 17*. Elapsed Time between Violation of Marital Bonds and Divorce Filing

| Basis of Male Complaint | Percent of Complaints Filed within Less Than One Year | | Percent of Complaints Filed within 3 Years or Less | |
|---|---|---|---|---|
| | % | (N) | % | (N) |
| Adultery | 58.3 | 14/24 | 91.7 | 22/24 |
| Desertion | 3.9 | 3/77 | 63.6 | 49/77 |
| Intemperance | 0 | 0/11 | 72.7 | 8/11 |
| Cruelty | 5 | 1/20 | 35.0 | 7/20 |

A husband might await his deserted wife's return or tolerate her excessive drinking for a time, but adultery was an act of dramatic finality, a single act by which a woman surrendered all claims to virtuous womanhood. In committing adultery, a woman cut herself off from a moral world built on domesticity, proper character, and female chastity.

### *Female Independence*

Although the ideal wife may have been modest, genteel, decorous, and chaste, these character traits did not prevent women from acting with considerable independence. The idea that wives were without options, prisoners to domestic drudgery, ignores the real independence open to women who either relied on their own abilities or on friends and relatives for support. Nor were women ill-equipped ideologically to meet the demands of living without husbands. Despite the limited economic opportunities for women, the values central to domesticity—frugality, industriousness, efficiency, orderliness—could be put to good use outside the home. In fact, the whole thrust of domesticity and the companionate ideal pushed women toward hard work, purposefulness, decision making, and autonomy; moreover, sororal ties, educational opportunities, legal gains, and reform work all enhanced women's self-respect and confidence. It should come as no surprise, then, that some of these California women acted with considerable independence.

Simply filing for a divorce is, of course, an independent action, and as Nancy Cott revealed in her study of the relationship between divorce and the status of women in eighteenth-century Massachusetts, an increasingly large number of women were exercising such an option. She also argued persuasively that the disproportionate growth in women's divorce petitions "suggests that they, even more than men, had rising expectations in marriage" and that women's increased success in gaining favorable decrees meant that the status of women improved during that century. Cott found that between 1692 and 1774, only 49 percent of the wives bringing suit received favorable decrees, but that between 1775 and 1786, 70 percent were successful petitioners; moreover, in that Revolutionary decade, 62 percent of the petitioners were women, in contrast to earlier decades when the proportion of husbands bringing suit was either equal to or higher than that of wives.[52] The divorce evidence from California shows that this trend extended into the nineteenth century and that the divorce court had become an effective means by which wives could gain independence from their husbands. In the 1850s and 1860s, women brought 75 percent of the suits; in the 1870s, 74 percent; and in the 1880s, 65 percent. When the analysis shifts to actual decrees of divorce, the data reveal that women in approximately 90 percent of the cases either won the case or had it dismissed; thus, for all the emphasis placed on the sanctity of women's place in the nineteenth-century home, judges were by no means reluctant to grant divorces. Table 18 shows by decade the percentage of female plaintiffs who either received a divorce or dismissed their own complaints.

*Table 18.* Divorce Awards and Dismissals for Women Plaintiffs by Decades

| Decade of Complaint | I Plaintiffs Receiving Divorces | | II Cases Dismissed by Plaintiff | | Total I + II |
|---|---|---|---|---|---|
| | % | (N) | % | (N) | % |
| 1850s and 1860s | 73.1 | 19/26 | 11.5 | 3/26 | 84.6 |
| 1870s | 89.2 | 66/74 | 9.5 | 7/74 | 98.7 |
| 1880s | 80.6 | 108/134 | 16.4 | 22/134 | 97.0 |

Far from being hostile to women's desires, the divorce court was an effective institution enabling women to start new lives. Community and family pressure certainly kept many women from filing for divorce, but when they finally summoned the courage to face economic uncertainty and social stigma, wives could expect a favorable disposition by the court.

But despite the increasing number of women in divorce court and the success they encountered there, many women chose a more direct and cheaper way to gain independence from their husbands. Perhaps the boldest display of independence from a wife came when she simply deserted her husband and made no attempt to obtain a divorce. Desertion was by far the most common complaint levied against women, and women were also more likely to be charged with and found guilty of desertion than were men; women were charged with desertion in 64 percent of the cases brought by men, but men were so charged in just 37.7 percent of the actions brought by women. The bases of divorce judgments showed a similar pattern; a finding of desertion appeared in 40 percent of the judgments against husbands and in 64 percent of the judgments against wives. The following two tables compare both the incidence of different legal complaints brought against men and women and the bases of divorce judgments by sex.

*Table 19.* Divorce Complaints against Men and Women

| Type of Complaint | Brought by Husbands against Wives (total N = 125) | | Brought by Wives against Husbands (total N = 276) | |
|---|---|---|---|---|
| | % | (N) | % | (N) |
| Desertion | 64.0 | 80/125 | 37.7 | 104/276 |
| Intemperance | 9.6 | 12/125 | 21.4 | 50/276 |
| Adultery | 20.8 | 26/125 | 10.9 | 30/276 |
| Non-support | 0.0 | 0/125 | 48.2 | 133/276 |
| Felony conviction | 0.0 | 0/125 | .4 | 1/276 |
| Cruelty | 20.8 | 26/125 | 45.7 | 126/276 |

*Table 20.* Divorce Judgments against Men and Women

| Basis of Divorce Judgment | Against Wives (total N = 75) | | Against Husbands (total N = 197) | |
|---|---|---|---|---|
| | % | (N) | % | (N) |
| Desertion | 64 | 48/75 | 40 | 78/197 |
| Intemperance | 5 | 4/75 | 20 | 39/197 |
| Adultery | 28 | 21/75 | 9 | 18/197 |
| Non-support | 1 | 1/75 | 45 | 88/197 |
| Felony conviction | 0 | 0/75 | 1 | 1/197 |
| Cruelty | 13 | 10/75 | 34 | 66/197 |

These tables suggest that desertion was the major way in which women escaped an intolerable situation in which husbands had the preponderance of physical and economic power. While husbands might turn to cruelty, drink, or general indolence to vent their frustrations, women more often simply abandoned the home when marriage soured.

This preponderance of complaints based on desertion continued a long-standing trend dating from the eighteenth century. Linda Kerber found that Connecticut men prior to the Revolutionary War rarely based their complaints on desertion but that after the war such complaints became much more common. From 1789 to 1793, 35 percent of men's petitions (14 of 40) accused their wives of desertion, a fact that suggested to Kerber "a growing degree of physical mobility in postwar New England." Compared to the years before the Revolution, unhappy wives no longer dutifully remained at home but chose to physically remove themselves from their households.[53] Although the percentages of male desertion complaints in this study were irregular over time—50 percent of male complaints in the 1850s, 90 percent in the 1860s, 52 percent in the 1870s, and 66 percent in the 1880s included desertion allegations—the essential point is that in all four decades, at least 50 percent of male complaints included allegations of desertion. The physical mobility available to women in eighteenth-century New England paled in comparison to that afforded wives in nineteenth-century California.

Significantly, women from all class backgrounds were willing to incur the risks that came with desertion. The percentage of women found guilty of desertion showed no dramatic skewing at either end of the social scale: 34 percent (12/35) of upper and middle class women were found guilty of desertion while 33 percent (10/30) of blue-collar wives (wives of small farmers, skilled tradesmen, unskilled tradesmen, and laborers) deserted their husbands. Whatever their specific reasons for leaving, women from a wide variety of social backgrounds believed that the advantages of leaving their husbands outweighed the obstacles they would surely face once free of their spouses.

One of the major obstacles women encountered was the limited range of job opportunities. The economic situation of wives who deserted their husbands is unknown—in these cases it is the husbands, not the wives, who appeared in the divorce records—but the economic situation of wives deserted by their husbands or wives forced to leave cruel, intemperate, or financially non-supporting husbands can be analyzed. There is little reason to doubt that deserting wives faced similar economic hardships, and either situation required a woman to support herself or to turn to the community for help. The occupations of the wives in this study are shown in the following table.

*Table 21.* Occupations of Wives

| Nonmenial | (N) | Menial | (N) |
|---|---|---|---|
| Actress | 1 | Domestic | 37 |
| Bookkeeper | 1 | Seamstress | 17 |
| Clerk | 1 | Prostitute (alleged) | 7 |
| Hotel keeper | 1 | | |
| Doctor | 1 | Cook/servant | 4 |
| Storekeeper | 2 | | |
| Nurse | 2 | | |
| Teacher | 6 | | |
| | 15 | | 65 |

Menial occupations comprised 81 percent (65/80) of the work mentioned in the records, and nonmenial work made up the other 19 percent (15/80). The high percentage of women doing menial work, especially domestic work, reflected the low level of employment opportunities for women in general and the low level of industrialization in these California counties in particular. Although women preferred factory work to domestic service, 45 percent of gainfully employed American women in 1880 worked in domestic and personal service, and the vast majority of these women were single. (In 1890, only about 25 percent of gainfully employed women worked in manufacturing.)[54] In San Mateo and Santa Clara Counties, the low level of industrialization meant that women's opportunities were even more restricted: the 1890 census listed *no* skilled or unskilled female operatives and no female pieceworkers in San Mateo County and only 291 women operatives and 85 pieceworkers in Santa Clara County.[55] The rural character of these counties left women few alternatives—they could either work in personal service or leave the area in search of factory work.

Despite their sorely restricted economic opportunities, these wives knew the meaning of hard work. The "habits of industry, frugality, and orderliness," so central to domesticity, offered a functional set of values for work outside the home, and in this sense, at least, women were not ideologically crippled when forced to support themselves. In addition, most of the menial jobs kept women in a domestic setting. Domestics, seamstresses, cooks, and servants spent their days not in the hurly-burly of the marketplace but in the protective confines of the home. Even among the nonmenial workers, the two nurses and six teachers worked in jobs thought particularly appropriate for women. For the great majority of these wives, then, self-support entailed no severe displacement from one sphere to another but merely a transfer of skills within a familiar setting. While such narrow job opportunities surely discouraged some wives from supporting themselves, the fact that women could use their domestic skills to earn an income must have encouraged others.

Specific cases reveal the determination and self-confidence of wives despite the economic obstacles they faced. J. W. Landon twice overheard William Hendrickson urge his wife to return home, but on both occasions she adamantly refused, telling him "to take care of himself and that she would look out for herself."[56] Annie Parker showed similar determination and self-confidence. When her husband deserted her in Linden, California, Annie testified: "I came to San Francisco to find employment and better my condition." By her own labor and with the help of friends, she succeeded.[57] Susan Battey and Mary Gray did the same. When Battey discovered that her husband expected her to live in a decrepit flophouse, she became a laundress and secured decent quarters. Gray, who left her husband because of his cruelty, worked so profitably as a dressmaker that she bought property in Redwood City.[58] Elaika Mattson, a miner's wife, possessed similar determination. She endured a year of wife beating and then, at the age of nineteen, escaped the cruelty and earned her own living. After five years on her own, she filed for divorce. When asked why she had waited so long to bring suit, she replied that she had had to save enough money to bring a case. Her diligence was rewarded in 1881 when she received a divorce.[59]

An estranged wife's economic situation did not depend solely on her ability to support herself. Wives left in financial straits by indolent or departed husbands could turn to neighbors, friends, or relatives for help. Table 22 summarizes the sources of such aid for those women who provided this information in the divorce proceedings. The table reveals that women depended primarily on themselves for support.[60] Despite the poor job opportunities, three-fourths of the wives earned at least part of their own livelihood. The other sources of help were split almost evenly between kin (parents, children, siblings, and other relatives) and friends or neighbors.

*Table 22.* Sources of Support for Wives

| Source of Support | Women Who Mentioned Receiving Such Support (Total N = 172) % | (N) |
|---|---|---|
| Self | 75.0 | 129 |
| Friends/Neighbors | 37.8 | 65 |
| Parents | 15.6 | 27 |
| Relatives | 15.1 | 26 |
| Children | 6.4 | 11 |
| Siblings | 5.2 | 9 |

Unfortunately, the records do not indicate the size of the contributions, so the absolute numbers may be deceiving. Parental help, for example, was probably more substantial and of longer duration than neighborly aid. Nevertheless, the number of wives receiving community charity is striking. Women who "failed" in marriage were obviously not social pariahs avoided by their friends.

However, this community support was not automatic but usually came only after the wife's innocence or guilt had been established in the eyes of the community. When income sources for female plaintiffs (the innocent party) are compared with sources for female defendants (the accused party), sharp differences emerge, particularly in the support offered by friends and neighbors. Wives bringing suit received help from the community in 46.3 percent of the cases (62/134); but the same figure for women accused of destroying the marriage was a mere 7.9 percent (3/38). Community assistance was an accurate barometer of wifely morals; it was high when her actions were judged morally correct and almost nonexistent when her character was in question.[61]

For Victorian wives, life without a husband was hard but not impossible. Friends and relatives were willing to help, and their aid, coupled with the wife's own labor, meant that a husband's desertion or non-support was not catastrophic. Certainly the transition from domestic duties to work outside the home was eased by the domestic nature of much of the work, but the high percentage of women who supported themselves speaks well for their ability, when necessary, to move beyond dependence on their husbands.[62]

Economic support from relatives and friends was not the only kind of assistance wives received. Women also relied on other women for moral and sororal support. The "female world of love and ritual," so perceptively analyzed by Carroll Smith-Rosenberg, was a world of intense, lifelong, and special friendships in which women shared their sorrows, anxieties, and joys. Evolving from the separation of men's and women's experiences into two distinct spheres, this homosocial world of love and mutual support revealed the "essential integrity and dignity" of women's domestic world. In letters and diaries, women wrote of their profound love for each other, a love nurtured first by the closeness of female kin relations and later by the lifelong friendships women made as adolescents.[63] These friendships, women believed, were more ennobling than those between men and women because they were founded not on carnal passion but on the spiritual, moral, and emotional affinities between women.[64] Even women on the overland trail did their best to maintain lasting ties with other female migrants and dreaded those times when they traveled without female companionship. Once settled, they wrote to their female friends in the East and urged them to move West; some added that if they could not see each other in the West, they would at least meet again in heaven. Such friendships were, indeed, eternal.[65]

Although these ties did not directly challenge domesticity (in fact they were a corollary of it), they could function as an important resource for unhappy wives. While the following evidence is only suggestive, it does indicate that the bonds of womanhood provided assistance in times of crisis. This is dramatically revealed in the case of Samantha Hughes, a farmer's wife, who in 1863 was accused by her husband of desertion. Sometime earlier Elisha Hughes had written her a letter asking her to return and suggesting that she must be miserable now that they no longer lived together. Her reply appears in the divorce records. "You are very much mistaken," she told him. "I *am not* sad and lonely. I am only in bad health." She then thanked him for his offer of assistance but quickly added, "I do not neede *[sic]* anything. I am as happy as any one can be who is in bad health. I have a good home with Julia and plenty of good kinde *[sic]* friends." Samantha's language became even bolder and more resolute: "I would beg, starve, and die rather than live with you againe *[sic]*. I do not want a husband. All I want is a good home and that I have with Julia and will have as longe *[sic]* as she lives. . . . I never will live with you againe *[sic]*. Do you understand, never NEVER."[66]

Although perhaps not as dramatic or emphatic as Samantha Hughes in rejecting her husband, Margaret Tanner, a druggist's wife, was determined to remain separated from her husband and equally dependent on a longtime friend for help in this task. When in 1886 she decided to leave her husband, Margaret first went to a real estate agent in Santa Cruz, who recalled, "She gave me her property to sell. I asked her if she was not coming back anymore and she replied she did not intend to live with John anymore." With the money from the sale,

Tanner left for Arizona, where she joined a longtime friend, Louise Ord, but Ord dutifully convinced Margaret to return to her husband: "She said," recalled Ord, "she had determined not to live with him again. . . . I persuaded her to go back. She said it was distasteful to her and that she had made up her mind not to go back." Initially, Ord prevailed and Tanner returned to Santa Cruz in late 1886, but she soon left for San Francisco. Later, she rejoined Ord in Arizona, once again returned to her husband in the summer of 1887, and then, in late 1887, left him permanently. At this point, recalled Ord, Margaret was determined to remain apart from her husband: "She said repeatedly that her life with him was distasteful to her, and she wished to be released from living with him." In 1887 her wish was fulfilled when the court granted her husband a divorce. It is significant that Ord, who first convinced Mrs. Tanner to return to her husband, did not break with Margaret but continued to help her. At the time of the divorce suit, the two women were living together in San Jose.[67]

Such sororal assistance threatened men who feared an independent wife. In 1882 Edwin Parker, an unemployed school teacher, was accused of cruelty and failure to support his wife. He attributed his wife's charges to her association with a group of women in San Francisco whom he disparaged as a "batch of low bred scandal loving women . . . who kneel at the shrine of a religion which teaches its devotees that they ought to leave their *undeveloped husbands* and seek their affinity elsewhere." Chief among the "low bred" and the woman responsible for convincing his wife to search for a rich husband (in contrast to an "undeveloped" one) was a "medium, Mrs. Wilson, No. 675 Mission Street, [who] received a communication from some one purporting to be her first husband that she ought to leave that undeveloped man." Edwin, often unemployed and anything but wealthy, saw a cabal of women—led by a mystic who communicated with her dead husband—luring his wife to the pursuit of a rich husband. He concluded a rather bizarre letter to his wife by revealing just how threatened he was by her new-found independence: "So you have secured the pound of flesh and . . . now as I assume the role of a mind reader for the time being, I can see you as you fly away on the wings of fancy to some drawing room, yourself the central figure reposing as a boudoir flower, all troubles at an end."[68] Certainly his wife's association with these women, whatever the merits of their beliefs, gave her a degree of support and independence that left her husband angry, threatened, and slightly dumbfounded.

If women drew strength and support from other women, they drew them as well from friends and relatives. Disputes on moving to California offer evidence that wives were not powerless when husbands made unilateral decisions to head West and that family and friends stood behind women who would not migrate with their husbands. Women, it appears, were often reluctant migrants. A study of families on the overland trail found that whereas men invariably initiated the decision to go West, less than one-fourth of the women recorded agreement with their husband's decision and almost one-third noted their opposition to the decision.[69] In examining frontier women, Julie Jeffrey described the active struggle that sometimes occurred between husbands and wives over the decision to move West, a struggle in which women—in light of their indispensable contributions to the success of the trek—possessed considerable power.[70] But if a husband insisted on going despite his wife's objections, she could either sadly acquiesce or refuse to go. The latter decision was made by several women in this study, and although this evidence does not explicitly mention sororal ties, the desire of wives to stay behind likely reflected the intensity of their emotional ties to (female) friends and/or family (mothers). In the following cases, the women either refused to leave or returned to the state in which they were married. If we assume that marriage occurred at the bride's home, then these women chose their families of birth over their families of marriage. While this choice may seem like no great show of independence, it does suggest that women were not without options and that families were flexible and forgiving when daughters made choices that contravened the female role.

Jennie Denson, for example, refused to accompany her new husband to Galveston, Texas, soon after her marriage in 1876, but she did agree to move to New Orleans because it was closer to her home in Tennessee. To the detriment of his business, Richard Denson moved to Louisiana, where his wife joined him, but in a few days she announced her refusal to live "in any other city or place in the world except at her home among her folks at or in the immediate neighborhood of Moscow, Tennessee." Denson refused to "sacrifice all his business affairs," and she refused to budge from Tennessee. The marriage ended with Jennie at home and Richard in California.[71]

Parental security also provided Zilpha Plumb with the confidence to remain apart from her husband when, after going bankrupt, he decided to recoup his fortunes in the West. She refused to follow him. "We had been living in Boston, Massachusetts and I failed in business," he explained to the divorce court. "My wife left and went to her mother's home in Orleans County, New York since which time we have never lived together." His wife's stubbornness—coupled with economic support from her mother—enabled her to defy her husband's intentions: "She refused to return then, and repeatedly since that time. . . . She has refused all and every offer I have made to her for reconciliation."[72] Addie Gray was another who refused to leave her relatives behind. Her stepdaughter overheard Addie tell her husband that she would not leave Illinois, and Addie personally informed her stepdaughter "that she would not under any consideration reside in the state of California."[73]

The experiences of other wives reveal that unilateral decisions by husbands to move were often fraught with danger when women had alternatives at their disposal. Park Henshaw convinced his wife to leave Missouri, but he failed to keep her in California after they reached Chico in 1877. Soon after arriving, she told a friend that she "did not like California," "regretted that she had come," "would not live in California and wanted to return to Missouri." When her two childred died, Ella returned to her home in Missouri, later came back to California for one month, then returned again to Missouri, this time permanently, even though "Mr. Henshaw had gone to considerable expense in fitting up a house for them to live in."[74]

The love of kin and community also persuaded Emma Waterbury, Mary King, Jane Keith, and Emily Merrill to remain in their home state rather than make the trip to California. Like others, William Waterbury came to California in 1869 to "better my condition." A year later he sent for his wife because he "was anxious to have her with me." The feeling was far from reciprocated; she would neither leave her home in Virginia nor respond to his letters, and in 1883 William received a divorce on grounds of desertion.[75] Mary King and her husband married in Wisconsin and lived there for eight years before her husband was transferred to California. She refused to accompany him, an act of independence that resulted in a successful desertion suit against her.[76] For ten years, Jane Keith adamantly refused to leave Illinois to join her husband in California. Twice he sent his brother to Illinois to get her, and both times she refused to leave. Joseph Keith finally sued for divorce in 1865.[77] Brave words accompanied Emily Merrill's decision to stay in Maine when, five months after marriage, her husband announced they were moving to California. He could go where he pleased, she told him, but "she was capable of taking care of herself and intended to do so."[78]

Another important area of female independence is virtually inaccessible to historical inquiry. Much to the dismay of their husbands, some wives refused to suppress their extramarital sexual desires, a refusal suggesting that the Victorian woman's alleged lack of interest in sex stemmed more from the fervent hopes of moralists than from reality. Women were not sexless, passionless creatures hopelessly locked in a suffocating domestic world. Nineteenth-century moralists might insist on sexual fidelity in marriage, they might insist that all women, regardless of social class, subscribe to the tenets of Victorian sexual morality, but dissatisfied women could establish a new sexual relationship if the opportunity arose and their sense of independence overcame the pull of contemporary morality.[79] Ann Stevens was such a woman.

Five years after marriage, Lew Stevens suspected that his wife had committed adultery, and in late 1883 he brought a divorce suit against her. As part of the evidence, he included two letters his wife had written her lover, and though it was unclear how the letters made their way into court, they left no doubt that Ann was an independent woman enthusiastic about sexual activity. She was also quite clever. Ann wrote parts of the letters, specifically some of the sections dealing with sex, in an ingenious code composed of number substitutes for letters—the strange mix of "f38d th2 wly 5p y457 t94ws29s" became "find the way up your trowsers" when decoded. Moreover, she was not one to be put off by community pressure. When a friend disparagingly remarked that Ann apparently thought "a good deal" of Walter Knight, her lover, Ann defended her sentiments: "I told him I certainly did. I never should deny that at all. I told him I had a perfect right to think a good deal of you." Never mind that she was a married woman living in a small California town. Ann also described to Walter how she planned to increase the friction within her marriage: "There is going to be a picnic here in Woodside next Sunday and I am going just to plague Lew. I am going everywhere I can [and] nothing will make him mad so quick as that." She hoped by such behavior to drive her husband away so that she and Walter could get together. "He thinks I do not care anything for him. That is just what I want—I hope I can act so that he will go to Colorado and if he once goes I will take good care he never comes back."[80]

Until Lew left, Ann could only fantasize about the future, but her letters gave her lover a vivid sense of the sexual enjoyments to come. Ann Stevens—and certainly many other Victorian women as well—bore little resemblance to the "typical" Victorian woman described by William Acton as "not very much troubled with sexual feelings of any kind."[81] After lamenting her loneliness, Ann excitedly wrote that she might soon visit Chico, Walter's town: "Then there would be some tall diddling done and a little hugging thrown in. . . . And when I see you again, perhaps I might find the way up your trowsers leg. At the same time, if I could see you a few minutes, I should sit down on you a few times."[82] In a letter written several weeks later, Ann even more directly stated her sexual desires: "I wish you was here tonight. I am upstairs in my room where you slept—and if you was here, I suppose we should do some tall fucking." Ann ended this second letter on a bittersweet note as she reaffirmed her sexual desires yet bemoaned her separation from Walter: "Oh how I wish you was round so I could get hold of you now and then. I just feel like having a racket with you once in awhile and there *you* are and *here* I am. I hope we won't always be so far apart. I can be near enough to them I care nothing for."[83]

The behavior of Julia Grosjean, like that of Ann Stevens, exhibited a lusty independence not generally associated with Victorian womanhood. Camille Grosjean, a successful grocer, described the disgrace he incurred due to his wife's behavior. "Whenever I took her into society she would act like a woman of loose character, and finally she was shunned by the best people in town." Her impropriety consisted of "flirting with everyone she met, and making love to married men with whom she was thrown into contact, until her name had become a byword for extreme levity of character if nothing worse." Camille worried that she would "ruin and disgrace me," a fear that suggests the close relationship between female sexual propriety and social standing among the middle class.[84] He then offered an explanation for her behavior that was restrained but firmly anchored in Victorian morality:

> I can only say this. She could have no other reason than she could not be satisfied with the restraint of a virtuous life. She loved and coveted the admiration of other men, and in that respect she was unfit for the duties and responsibilities of wifehood and motherhood. I do not desire to speak stronger than this in regard to one that bears the station of wife to me.

Grosjean had offered a classic Victorian indictment of his wife. She lacked restraint and virtue, her dedication to her husband was grossly suspect, and her general character meant that she was ill equipped for that most womanly of tasks—motherhood. Camille concluded by sadly noting the strength of the public's association of a husband with his wife, an association that gave Julia a negative but powerful influence over her husband: "After she left, I remained some time intending to brave it out, but the disgrace of her conduct made it impossible for me to continue business [any] longer in Houston."[85] The moral weight of polite society was too great to bear; like others, Camille went West to get a fresh start.

While Lew Stevens and Camille Grosjean could not control their wives' extramarital affairs, Cornelius Paddock had a problem of a different sort. In 1877, the teamster complained that his wife repeat edly embarrassed him despite his patient efforts to curb her indelicacies. She sang lewd songs in front of friends and, on one occasion, had allegedly exposed herself to others at their home in Woodside by "lifting up her clothes and undergarments to her waist, having no drawers on and exposing her person." He also stated that she caused him great anguish when she would tip back in her chair, "open her limbs, and indecently expose her person."[86] To prove his wife's intractableness, Cornelius obtained the testimony of a former lodger, Charles Peterson, who at one time had shared the same bedroom with Cornelius and his wife. "She sat down in a chair," recalled Peterson, "and told Ida, her daughter, to wash her feet and [then] she pulled her clothes up over her knees. She had drawers on as far as I noticed. She pulled her clothes up above her knees. . . . She lay back in the chair and screamed something. I went outside." The court asked if Peterson considered her exposure indecent: "Yes, if a man had a good view of her." On other occasions, the lodger "saw her sit down in chairs and pull her clothes up and put her feet upon the stove." He also remembered a lewd song that the irrepressible Ann Paddock had insisted on singing. "She sung a song in 1876. The song was beef steak, mutton chop and a little old hat. Mr. Paddock told her if she wanted to sing such a song to go outside and sing it." Peterson was slightly uncertain about the lyrics but quite sure that a true lady had no business singing them: "The meaning so far as I understand must be a fast house song. It means if you get hold of a woman, you want a little from her."[87] Peterson, it should be noted, was no sensitive shrinking violet. At the time he testified, the laborer was a prisoner at San Quentin penitentiary.

The disposition of the Paddock case revealed a judge less concerned with household propriety than with a rising divorce rate. After Cornelius had presented his evidence, the judge dismissed the case: "The acts proven are only a little peevishness and some little jealousy," he declared, "but in my opinion are not such acts as are by the statutes considered good grounds for a divorce." They "do not endanger life or render matrimonial intercourse unsafe, and ought not even to render it unpleasant to a man of philosophic turn of mind."[88] Apparently Cornelius lacked—and the judge possessed—that turn of mind that might find something oddly refreshing in Ann's eccentric independence. Moreover, the judge believed that divorces "are becoming too common in this country and courts should in all cases require *full* statutory proof before dissolving so sacred a relation as that which should exist between husband and wife."[89] In light of the rising divorce rate, the judge reasoned that nineteenth-century marriage had ample room for female independence even if the wife's actions directly annoyed the husband's sensibilities.

As the importance ascribed to the domestic role expanded during and after the Revolution, the real options and power available to married women likewise increased. Once women were considered the moral guarantors of the Revolution and then of society in general, it followed that they deserved the utmost respect and consideration. The result was to temper male authority, to render relations in the home less hierarchical, to increase women's self-esteem, and to provide legal leverage against wayward husbands. An equally far-reaching result was to increase marital instability: domesticity, chastity, and invalidism were all turned in positive directions that increased the legitimacy of women's claims in court; likewise, husbands could use the absence of these virtues as the basis of their own claims. In addition, despite men's preponderance of economic power, women could rely on friends and relatives or their own abilities for support, thereby further limiting their dependence. Finally, the court, reflecting contemporary morality, recognized the legitimacy of women's complaints and the right of women to considerate and respectful treatment. While this positive assessment should be tempered with a reminder of the discrimination women encountered, nevertheless, the experience of these California divorce seekers suggests that domesticity—if only a transitional stage on the way toward full equality—redounded to the benefit of women.

# 5

# *Ideal Manhood in California*

In 1867, George Elliot testified in a divorce case on behalf of John Henning, a carpenter. Elliot, a painter, informed the court that Henning's character was above reproach and more specifically that the carpenter was "industrious and never I knew him to drink strong drink."[1] A year earlier, in a different case, Daniel Wilson defended his own character by asserting that he was "a good, kind, and affectionate husband."[2] These two examples capture the dual nature of nineteenth-century manhood: men commuted between life in the working world and life at home, and in each sphere proper manhood embraced a distinct set of values. In the working world, a secularized version of the Protestant work ethic comprised correct character; at home, kindness, affection, emotion, and even deference to wives constituted the ideal. In this chapter and the next, we will examine nineteenth-century manhood, a subject that has received surprisingly little attention despite history's traditional focus on male politicians, statesmen, warriors, workers, and reformers. Men's role as producers will be examined first, followed by an analysis of how the companionate ideal reshaped male behavior and how men's failure to meet the standards of companionship precipitated divorce. After all, the companionate ideal, as Kirk Jeffrey has recognized, "was addressed to the man of the family." To him were directed the demand to stay at home as much as possible, to defer to his wife's finer moral sensibilities, and to consult with her on important family matters.[3] How men performed their dual role as providers and companions determined their fate in divorce court, and a failure in either sphere could result in a successful suit against them.

## *Men and Work*

Most of these California husbands worked, but the emphasis they placed on their work—the fact that proper work habits were a central feature of male moral character—was a distinctive feature of preindustrial capitalism. The ennobling of work, the infusion of toil with high purpose, and the insistence that work rightly performed was a moral act were ideas that had taken root in the soil of rural and artisan society and belonged, as Daniel Rodgers has argued, "to a setting of artisans' shops, farms, and countinghouses."[4] In this preindustrial world, the dignity of labor and the independence that it brought were central components of proper manhood, and so long as men retained some control over their work, some ability to direct its rhythms and processes, the work ethic retained its coherence and functioned as a central component of male character. Only later, with the advent of large-scale industrialization, did the work ethic begin to unravel as the preindustrial world gave way to mechanized, routinized, wage-dominated labor.[5]

Until that time, in areas like San Mateo and Santa Clara counties, the rural and small-town residential pattern and the absence of large factories provided a milieu in which face-to-face relationships prevailed, in which men and women felt competent to judge their neighbors' work habits against well-accepted community standards. As the following evidence makes clear, how closely a man conformed to the basic tenets of the work ethic helped predict how his friends and neighbors judged his worthiness as a husband. Moreover, adherence to the work ethic was the sole measure of men's work attitudes and habits; no other competing models of behavior were put forward; no one registered a protest against the prevailing ideology; no one suggested that a man's failure might stem from anything other than individual character deficiencies. Like most rural America, these two counties provided a perfect setting for equating individual character traits with economic success or failure.

The reaffirmation of community values about work, male character, and the economy appeared regularly in newspaper stories, editorials, and epigrammatic advice columns. A Gilroy, California farmer perusing his favorite newspaper encountered a steady stream of advice that urged him to be diligent, temperate, frugal, and industrious. He also read that the economy was open, expanding, and meritocratic—boundless opportunities were available if men infused their lives with correct values. Success was anchored in individual morality, in an ethos that attritubed success to the presence and failure to the absence of proper personal values. The *Weekly Argus* noted the lessons to be learned from thrift and saving: "The direct consequence to him is steady, continuous, and solid discipline in the habits of industry—in patient, persistent, forecasting and self-denying effort, breaking up all the tendencies to indolence and frivolity, and making an earnest and watchful economist of time."[6] The same newspaper instructed young men: "Be a man. Show the world you are

7. Miners at the New Almaden mercury mine in Santa Clara County, 1885. This operation was one of the most heavily capitalized businesses in the county. Courtesy of the San Jose Historical Museum.

able to earn an honest living by patient and persistent industry. Quit loafing." Other advice was equally succinct: "Drink no intoxicating liquors." "Small and steady gains give competency with tranquility of mind." "Earn your money before you spend it." "Never play at any kind of game."[7]

The roots of failure, like those of success, were individual. An editorial in The *San Jose Daily Mercury* attributed bankruptcy to conspicuous consumption, particularly among men who "are coaxed into expenditures beyond their income by vain, showy, silly and ambitious wives." The same article counseled: "There is and can be but one moral: Live within your means! Make no expenditures for mere show!"[8] The *Weekly Argus* more bluntly ascribed failure to personal shortcomings: "The fact is, the miseries, poverty, beggary and want that prevail among men, especially in this country, spring very largely from their own prodigality."[9]

Such advice made sense only if achievement took precedence over privilege, and moralists responded by emphasizing the meritocratic nature of the nineteenth-century social system. The *Santa Clara Argus* inveighed against drunkenness not only for the personal havoc it wreaked but for the opportunity it thwarted: "The road to honor and fame is within the reach of all, and requires only courage and faith to grasp it. Our own will is all that is requisite; and if we have not the will to avoid contempt, disgrace, and misery, we deserve neither relief nor compassion."[10] Starting on the road to success was quite simple: "When I see a lad plunking his nickles down at the desk of a savings bank I know that he is one of the future men who is going to build our railroads and do our wholesale business."[11] Rags-to-riches sociology appeared regularly. The *San Jose Daily Mercury* confidently, if erroneously, asserted:

> It is probably well within the figures to say that 75 percent of the prosperous capitalists of today began life without a dollar; and where would most of them have been had they been led into undue agitation, into strikes, boycotts, or futile political attempts as so many of the alleged labor movements have been?[12]

The same article offered a stirring reaffirmation of the values of self-control, sacrifice, and determination; the lives of successful businessmen "prove with unanswerable logic that the making of every man's career in this country is in his own hands" and that "it isn't law nor politics nor agitation, but it is the close and UNFLAGGING EFFORT at self-improvement, the seizing and the making of opportunities, that avail to make men independent, comfortable, and very often rich."[13]

The assumptions of such advice are clear: the social system is open and just and no artificial barriers, no walls of tradition and privilege block the path of the determined and the deserving; competitive individuals define the community, and success and failure are dependent upon personal character traits. Whether people accepted this ethos, whether they spoke in such terms when judging a man's fitness as a husband, remains to be seen. Did rural Californians, for example, believe in the moralists' conception of society as an arena of open competition? Was economic failure viewed in individual rather than social terms?[14] The implications of these questions are important. If Americans accepted the competitive model of society and if they viewed success and failure as individually determined, then they likely understood and accepted their place in the social order, held themselves responsible for their wealth or poverty, and rejected challenges to the status quo.

*8.* Threshing machine and agricultural workers, Santa Clara County, 1887. In the 1890 census, Santa Clara County reported over 2,000 farms comprised of some 445,000 acres (281,000 improved). The estimated value of farm products from the county in 1889 was $3,562,290. Courtesy of the San Jose Historical Museum.

Uncovering men's actual attitudes about work is no easy task, but the divorce evidence takes us a significant step beyond the heady exhortations of moralists. It is true that divorce proceedings tend to emphasize, by their very character as adversarial proceedings, the responsibility of individuals. But that fact does not account for the frequent references to the work habits of men, and it is the value attached to certain habits of work that is important. What does account for the frequent mention of male work habits is their centrality to male character and to the husband's role as provider. Regardless of class background, men and women expressed belief in similar ideas about work and judged the worthiness of men by their allegiance to the work ethic. When, for example, people praised a man's work performance, the accolades centered on the worker's personal diligence and sobriety. The brother of Cornelius Paddock praised the teamster for having led "a strictly sober and industrious life"; moreover, Paddock eschewed vices detrimental to the working man and was never known "to drink a drop of liquor or use tobacco in any form."[15] William Hendrickson also exhibited correct habits; in the opinion of a friend, Hendrickson "has been all the time I have known him an industrious man of sober habits."[16] Martin Daves received similar praise from his friend, Charles Parr: "I have known him a long time. [I] know that he is a man of good habits, industrious and sober, and is a good citizen."[17] When James Williams, a carpenter, was questioned about co-worker John Henning's "industry and sobriety," he answered that Henning's character was "good—he is moral, steady, and industrious."[18] Businessman William Waterbury embodied the full measure of Calvinist virtues, at least in the eyes of Ansel Robison: "I know him intimately. His habits are good; he is temperate and remarkably energetic and industrious and I should think would make a good husband for any woman."[19]

Husbands who defended their own character appealed to the same values. H. F. Thurston, a carpenter, answered his wife's cruelty allegations by asserting he "labored hard, worked early and late," and finally saved enough to buy property in Redwood City; furthermore, he assured the court that his wife "might have a good and pleasant home . . . the best he can afford" if "she will return to the family home he had provided for her."[20] Harvey Kincaid described his own climb to economic success in terms fit for a poor-boy-makes-good novel. In defending himself against charges of intemperance, Kincaid carefully noted his own allegiance to the work ethic. The Redwood City lawyer was born in poverty, helped support his parents as a young man, later paid for his own education, and "after years of struggle and at the age of twenty-seven years," finally set up his law practice in Redwood City. Thereafter, he endured several years of poverty, during which time his "law office, bedroom, and kitchen [were] for some years . . . one and the same apartment"; finally, thanks to his "ambitious desire to succeed," Kincaid gained a fair degree of economic success.[21]

Men like Kincaid emphasized their work habits and their ability to support their families, but the divorce records suggest that more was involved than simple support; correct character enabled the good provider to indulge his family, to offer something beyond a decent but humble existence. Frugality, industriousness, and temperance would bring not only virtue but material success as well. People judged character not just in terms of values but in terms of buying power. Although Elaine May's recent study of divorce in post-Victorian America argues that people in 1880 agreed on what comprised the necessities of life (and that only years later did disputes about levels of consumption become common) nevertheless, people in nineteenth-century America regularly noted husbands' abilities to provide the finer things in life.[22] Particularly among the middle class, consuming power was important well before the great expansion of consumerism and advertising of the early twentieth century. A businessman like Joseph Garner, for instance, impressed a friend by the fashion in which he supported his wife: "She had everything that one could wish. He provided well for her. They owned their own home and kept their own horse and carriage."[23] Another businessman, Camille Grosjean, received accolades for the same reason: "He was a good businessman and doing a good business and lived in good style and had many friends"; nevertheless, his wife disgraced him, and in shame he left Texas for California.[24] A sense of style also graced the table of farmer Joseph Tuers who, according to his brother, "was in the habit of having a great deal of company and he entertained them with the best the market afforded, including champagne."[25] Other people also noted the level of a husband's support. D. S. McLelland praised rancher William Bennett for his generosity. Asked to comment on Bennett's support for his family, McLelland answered that Bennett's "family seemed to be enjoying themselves. They had a good team for his family to ride."[26] An old friend of Park Henshaw's applauded Henshaw's kindness and noted the support he gave his wife and children: "He took great pride in gratifying every wish they might have." Another friend also underscored Henshaw's devotion to his wife and children by claiming that Henshaw "left no desire of either of them ungratified."[27]

All of the foregoing comments came from friends, relatives, or neighbors, but husbands, in their own defense, repeated similar themes. Rural and small-town men in California evaluated their own character by their ability to provide more than just necessities. William Waterbury, a businessman, testified that he left Virginia in 1869 "to better my condition in a new country as my own state had been run down since the war." He intended to send for his wife but not until "I had got settled and in a condition to make her comfortable and

9. Harvest Scene. Agricultural workers in Santa Clara County, 1890. Courtesy of the San Jose Historical Museum.

furnish her a home." After meeting "with the ups and downs usual in California life," Waterbury decided, in 1882, to send for her because he was in "comfortable and easy circumstances and able to care for my wife *elegantly*." Sadly, for him, she refused to come. Waterbury's brother-in-law also praised William's virtues: "I know of no man more capable of supporting a wife in a comfortable manner than the plaintiff."[28] In another case, Camille Grosjean applauded his own kindness and affection and then drew attention to the good life his deserted wife had left behind: "I was in good circumstances and had a good and growing business and would have been wealthy if she had behaved herself."[29] Aaron Van Valkenburg likewise lamented that his wife left behind an "expensively" furnished house attended by five servants.[30]

The centrality of proper work values to good character emerges clearly in descriptions of men's failures—what men failed to do sheds light on what they were expected to do. Hapless, lazy, and intemperate husbands received rebuke, confirmed the assumption that individual effort brought economic success or failure, and, perhaps most significantly, illuminated, by the dim light of their own adherence to contemporary morality, the nature of deviance in rural and small town nineteenth-century society. And these men were deviants: because economic self-mastery and moral autonomy were central to proper manhood, and because the importance of domestic life rose during the century, drunken, shiftless husbands directly assaulted the whole moral structure of society.[31] Only community vigilance could turn back this threat, and women, wives especially, played a particularly key role in this regard. As society's moral keepers, they were responsible for setting the proper moral tone and for insisting that men, both inside and outside the home, adhere to recognized standards of morality.[32] This meant in practice that some marriages were fraught with tension as wives, trying to maintain standards, clashed with husbands who paid them little heed. Surely eighteenth-century marriages would have suffered under the strain of such husbandly behavior, but by the nineteenth-century increasing numbers of women turned to the courts for redress and the reaffirmation of correct marital morality.

Among the men of San Mateo and Santa Clara Counties, 133 husbands were sued for non-support (48 percent of male defendants) and 59 for intemperance (21 percent of male defendants); among these men, 39 were sued for both non-support and intemperance (14 percent). Though they came from all social classes, men at the lower levels of society were more likely to be sued on such grounds than were wealthier men. The following table shows the skewing toward the bottom of the social order of men sued for non-support or intemperance.

*Table 23.* Social Class of Men Sued for Non-Support or Intemperance

| Occupation of Husband | Percent in Each Class Sued for Non-Support | | Percent in Each Class Sued for Intemperance | |
|---|---|---|---|---|
| | % | (N) | % | (N) |
| Upper Class | 31.6 | 6/19 | 15.8 | 3/19 |
| Middle Class | 32.0 | 8/25 | 8.0 | 2/25 |
| Farmers | 30.0 | 6/20 | 35.0 | 7/20 |
| High Trades | 44.4 | 12/27 | 18.5 | 5/27 |
| Low Trades | 61.5 | 8/13 | 30.8 | 4/13 |
| Laborers | 70.5 | 31/44 | 40.9 | 18/44 |

The bias at the lower end of the social scale is just as pronounced when divorce judgments on grounds of non-support are compared class by class; again we see the inverse relationship—as the social class goes down, the incidence goes up.

*Table 24.* Social Class and Judgments for Non-Support

| Occupation of Husband | Percent of Men in Each Class Found Guilty of Non-Support | (N) |
|---|---|---|
| Upper Class | 15.8 | 3/19 |
| Middle Class | 32.0 | 8/25 |
| Farmers | 15.0 | 3/20 |
| High Trades | 22.2 | 6/27 |
| Low Trades | 46.2 | 6/13 |
| Laborers | 61.4 | 27/44 |

The judgments on grounds of intemperance were less dramatic, but though 15.8 percent of upper-class men and 8 percent of middle-class men were found guilty of intemperance, the same figures for men in low trades and laborers were 23.1 percent and 31.8 percent, respectively. The figures in these tables reveal that men at the bottom of the social scale were highly vulnerable to accusations of non-support and, to a lesser extent, intemperance. Such allegations were class specific, and, as we shall see, nineteenth-century Californians saw economic failure as a problem of personal morality and character deficiencies. Work by the husband was a responsibility owed to the wife, and nothing more detrimental could be said about a man than that he did not support his wife and family.

The emphasis on personal limitations emerges most clearly in the divorce complaints, and here we see how the adversarial nature of divorce court directed attention to husbands' moral shortcomings.

*10.* Blacksmithing and horseshoeing shop in San Jose, California, ca. 1890. Courtesy of the San Jose Historical Museum.

These complaints drew on a similar vocabulary. Mary Ann Knowles and Emma Ramey attributed their husbands' lack of support to "idleness, profligacy, and dissipation," and Celeste Britton and Melissa Ray each accused her husband of "indolent and profligate habits."[3] The complaint against William Jordan described him as "profligate, idle, [and] dissolute," and Euclid Isbill allegedly spent "his time in idleness notwithstanding he could have found plenty of work and profitable employment if he had not been too indigant [sic] and lazy to work."[34]

Neighbors and relatives also criticized men's work habits, understood economic failure in terms of character deficiencies, and subscribed to an ethic that stressed self-control and self-discipline; if a man were lazy, he could force himself to work; if he were idle, he could find employment; if he were a drunkard, he could make himself stay sober. In coming to such conclusions, these witnesses expressed their contempt for deviant behavior, rallied behind accepted morality, and in the process not only helped the aggrieved woman but reaffirmed community standards as well. The testimony of A. R. Sansman, who was Egbert and Elizabeth Etts' neighborhood grocer, was typical. Sansman recognized the Etts' poverty but found Egbert's behavior inexcusable: "Any common laborer enjoying as good health as the Defendant did could provide ample means for her support for she is a woman that would get along with very little." Unfortunately, though work was available, "he did not want it. He was and is recognized as a lazy loafer." Another neighbor, Elizabeth McCoy, testified that Egbert, rather than work, "seldom done anything except sometimes to go out with his gun." Etts's wife even considered him a financial drain who consumed much more than he provided: "I could have lived alone much better and with much less expense."[35]

Like Etts, other men faced accusations of laziness in light of the ready availability of work. Friends and relatives repeatedly emphasized the husband's duty and responsibility to support his family, and this expectation of support lay at the heart of the male role. In 1868 a neighbor of laborer George Dale averred that Dale received good wages when he worked—he simply was not willing to work with any regularity. His niece, Elizabeth Ray, also said he squandered his days in idleness. She was sure if Dale made "proper use of his time and means," he could support his family.[36] The same went for Edwin Parker who defied two social conventions; he would not work and thereby forced his wife—against social expectations—to support them. When Annie Parker told a friend of her husband's disinclination to work, the friend investigated the situation and then reported that Parker's idleness stemmed from simple indolence; he could find work, "but he has no proper pride of character and would be willing to see his wife slave at anything so that he might lie around in idleness. I think he is incurable and no account." According to his wife, Parker's character faults appeared immediately, and so did his irresponsible approach to the support of his new bride: "About two weeks after our marriage, the defendant spent what little money he had in extravagance and wastefulness, but not for any wants of mine, or for me." She further testified that he could earn "a good living for himself and me if he was disposed to do so," but he preferred to "lie around and permit me to borrow from my friends the means to sustain life."[37] Sarah Isbill showed similar disgust and maintained that her husband "could get remunerative employment whenever he desired and had it provided for him without having to look for it, but he would not do it."[38]

Parents of women suing for divorce rebuked idle husbands, in part

*11.* Sheet metal shop, San Jose, ca. 1894. This shop exemplifies the small scale nature of Santa Clara County manufacturing in the late nineteenth century. Courtesy of the San Jose Historical Museum.

because of paternal protectiveness, but also because they sometimes found themselves forced to support their daughters if the husband did not do so. Of the women who sued for divorce on grounds of non-support, 12.4 percent (11 of 89) received some aid from their parents, and of those women who received a divorce on grounds of non-support, 14.5 percent received such aid. Isaac Wixam, for one, excoriated his son-in-law, Euclid Isbill, for failing to support his wife, a task that fell to Wixam: "He [Isbill] was indolent and lazy beyond the power of description. He could have remunerative employment whenever he desired. He would rather see his family starve or become objects of charity than work, even when work was provided for him."[39] Like Wixam, Alice Crane supported her daughter, and she had only contempt for her son-in-law, Thornton Sharp: "[He] seemed to think when she could work, she would provide for herself; and when sick that somebody would take care of her, and he was content."[40] In a similar vein, Clara Spaulding openly questioned her son-in-law's sense of manhood and berated him for failing to support his wife, for spending too much time at the local pub, and for forcing his wife to rely on her mother and brothers for assistance: "I told him I thought it was a shame and no one having the spark of a man about them would be guilty of such [neglect]." She also testified that Sayers did not refute her charges, but he did summon enough courage to say that "we could all go to (*same place*) using a bad word."[41]

The interesting point in all of this evidence is not simply that witnesses criticized men for non-support but that in doing so they characterized husbands as misfits, as "incurable" deviants with "no proper pride of character," as men who shamelessly let their wives suffer while they loafed and drank. Given the assumptions of the culture, these men deserved the harsh condemnation meted out by members of the community. Their offense was to turn their back both on the gospel of work and on the responsibilities they owed their wives, and in a society in which labor was the "vital center of living" and marriage a close reciprocal bond, such behavior put these men in a precarious position indeed.[42]

Witnesses found idleness particularly objectionable if the husband was in good health; to avoid work when blessed with good health contradicted the basic assumptions of San Mateo and Santa Clara families. The contrast between healthy males and unhealthy females is striking. Whereas 19 percent (75 of 401) of the wives were unhealthy, only a handful of males were so described. And whereas people described women's health negatively or not at all, witnesses often singled out men as being "strong," "robust," or "able-bodied." Ellen Diehl, a miner's wife, characterized her husband as "a straight and able-bodied man of good health" who could support her but refused to do so, and Emma Ramey depicted her idle husband as "a robust, able-bodied man" who, if he tried, could find work "without difficulty."[43] Similarly, Egbert Etts chose idleness over work despite being a "strong, healthy man [who] could have procured employment and earned sufficient [income] to have made her comfortable if he had been willing to work."[44] Another laborer, George Dale, was "a man of limited means, but generally enjoyed good health and could always command the best of wages," but he, too, avoided work; and the same went for laborer Michael Fay, described by a friend as "a healthy able-bodied man but indolent and will not work. He is idle nearly all of the time—don't know of his doing but a few days work in the last two years."[45] Such confidence in economic opportunity also placed husbands like Robert Lucas and Samuel Brisbine in jeopardy.

Lucas refused to work despite being "an able, stout, robust, and healthy man," and Brisbine, a blacksmith, allegedly opted for idleness despite being "a man of robust health and strength."[46]

Husbands who combined indolence with other moral shortcomings—especially intemperance—confirmed Californians' belief that economic failure was a function of personal character deficiencies. Drink was the great incapacitator, the poison that destroyed manly habits of hard work and frugality. People from all social classes deplored its debilitating impact upon men, particularly upon working men who were the group most often sued for drunkenness. Just 8 percent of middle-class men were sued for intemperance, but over 40 percent of the laborers were so accused. The testimony against these working men, however, involved more than criticisms of intemperance; often men's general social habits were challenged, particularly their penchant for spending time in the all-male environment of the saloon rather than in the protective confines of the home. This criticism of male conviviality suggested to Julie Jeffrey that men and women had different conceptions of order: men wanted outward order but also the freedom to pursue their pleasures; women desired real order, "a place without disruptive threats to family unity and purity."[47] Frequent references in divorce cases to men's drinking, gambling, and loafing at local saloons support Jeffrey's claim and point to the presence of a counter-institution to that of domesticity, an alternative culture that tugged at men's loyalties. Characterized by an all-male ambience, saloons provided relief from work and an escape from the home, challenging both the work ethic and the claims of domestic life.[48] This threat to domesticity, it is worth noting, also accounted for the large number of women who worked in the temperance movement in order to protect domestic values. Drink and the man's world of the saloon, these reformers agreed, undermined domesticity and its high moral standards.[49] Surely many couples maintained a viable compromise between the claims of domesticity and those of male conviviality, but when the pleasures became vices and threatened the domestic sphere, morally upright citizens, as Steven Purdy and others found out, reasserted the primacy of domestic morality. Here, again, we also see how the heightened status of women's sphere precipitated divorce.

Purdy's case was representative of the ravages wreaked by insobriety. He occasionally worked in a paper mill, but more often he was, in the eyes of a friend, "an idle, profligate, intemperate man." The friend added that Purdy spent most of his time drinking and gambling and concluded that he defied all notions of manhood by refusing to work even when offered a job: "I have known him to be

*12.* Lumbermen working in San Mateo County. Although this photo dates from shortly after the turn of the century, it illustrates an important part of the late nineteenth-century San Mateo County economy. In 1870, the county had eleven sawmills employing 182 men; in 1890, there were still eight mills and 83 employees. These mills were the major manufacturing firms in the county. Courtesy of the San Mateo County Historical Association.

idling about Saratoga, and at the same time he was offered work that he could do and wages at the rate of three dollars and a half per day for feeding a threshing machine and he refused to work."[50] A long-time acquaintance of James Haun pictured Haun's habits in a succinct but even more disparaging way: "He is foul of liquor and is of an idle, lazy, and worthless disposition."[51] Other working-class men also allegedly lacked diligence and frugality and engaged in self-indulgent habits. Nicholas Dodge, a mechanic, gambled his money away, and Samual Brisbine, a blacksmith, devoted "at best" two-thirds of his time to work—he spent the other third in saloons.[52] Livery stable operator Edward Bliven lost his business because of intemperance, miner Marlin Mattson drank and caroused though "perfectly able to work," blacksmith Thomas Yates spent his wages on liquor, and Michael Ryan was "idle and dissolute and has failed to work and labor as an industrious man should."[53]

Though allegations of non-support and intemperance clustered among the lower classes, witnesses from all social backgrounds—as William Allen found out—linked moral failure with poverty. In fact, the entire class spectrum of San Mateo County voiced its disapproval of Allen's habits and reaffirmed contemporary morality with its emphasis on temperance, self-control, frugality, and industriousness. Michael Larkin, a laborer, lamented that Allen "would work awhile until he got some money, then go off and drink as long as he had money to buy liquor or could get it on credit." Farmer George Wyman noted similar deficiencies in Allen: "He was a man always able to work and could command good wages but would not work but little and spent everything he earned for liquor." And a merchant named Charles Kelly laid bare the nature and limitations of community censure when the court asked him how he and Allen got along: "I entertain no ill will toward him but can't say that I am friendly to him. [I] consider him a worthless loafer [but] have never had any disagreement with him." Apparently, Kelly found Allen amiable enough, but as a respectable businessman, the merchant simply could not respect Allen as a man.[54]

How do we explain this great emphasis on personal responsibility? Certainly part of the answer stems from the nature of the records; in divorce litigation, one party tries to prove the other party at fault. But the form of the criticism suggests that there is more to the issue than legal conventions. Men's failure to support their wives were invariably tied to allegations of moral turpitude, particularly among the twenty-four working-class men sued for both non-support and intemperance.[55] The drinking habits of these rural workers, as we have seen, represented a cultural challenge to domesticity, and by their actions they surrendered all claims to community respect and became "worthless," "shiftless loafers" of "no account." The equation of economic failure with moral shortcomings is also illustrated by the fact that although some husbands surely adhered to the work ethic yet failed to support their families—either through bad luck, hard times (California experienced a severe depression in the 1870s), or poor health—these men did not appear in divorce court. The virtuous poor escaped condemnation—evidently their wives were expected to stand by them.

Finally, the nature of nineteenth-century charity heightened the tendency to see economic failure as a function of individual character traits. When a husband failed to support his wife, friends and neighbors often did so, a situation unlikely to create an amicable relationship between the husband and his neighbors. In fact, friends and neighbors were the most common source of outside assistance, as the following table shows.

*Table 25.* Wife's Source of Outside Support

| Wife's Source of Outside Support | Women Receiving Such Support among Women Who Sued on Grounds of Non-support % | (N) |
|---|---|---|
| Friends and Neighbors | 58.4 | 52/89 |
| Relatives | 22.5 | 20/89 |
| Parents | 12.4 | 11/89 |
| Siblings | 10.1 | 9/89 |
| Children | 7.9 | 7/89 |

If neighbors found such assistance burdensome—as they most likely did—their tendency to see failure as a function of immorality was reinforced; to do otherwise would have cast doubt on the limited nature of nineteenth-century charity and on individualism generally.[56] At the local level, men's poverty could not be explained in social terms unless society was willing to take institutional steps to cushion the blows of poverty, but such welfare measures had to await a later day. When people looked at economic failures in their own towns—men whose wives were now receiving community charity—they could see only a husband's personal neglect of his wife.

## *Men: The Affective Demands*

Proper work habits comprised part of proper manhood, but men were also husbands and fathers, and although only limited research has been done on the nineteenth-century male role, two disparate conceptions vie for attention. On one hand is the Victorian patriarch—domineering, ascetic, aggressive, undemonstrative, repressed—whose power came at the expense of his wife's self-esteem. Nineteenth-century men, we are told, exaggerated the differences between male and female characteristics in order to boost their confidence and authority, which had sagged under the impact of industrialization, urbanization, high social mobility, and immigration. By emphasizing the distance between the spheres and underscoring the second-rate status of women's realm, desperate nineteenth-century men, in Barbara Berg's words, managed "to exercise some measure of control over their existences and environments. They finally found an outlet for these emotions through their domination of women."[57]

Urban men were not the only ones who exercised such power. Midwestern farmers and men on the overland trail were equally authoritative. Among the migrants, John Faragher found that men made the decision to move, determined the route and the speed of the trip, decided whether to turn back or push on, provided the leadership, and took credit for the success or shouldered the blame for the failure of the trip. Furthermore, along the trail, men were often suspicious and antagonistic to strangers and exhibited "rough, aggressive, and egotistic" character traits that led them to overlook their wives' contributions to the venture. This oversight stemmed, in Faragher's opinion, from men's basic competitiveness, worldliness, and lack of empathy.[58]

The other image of nineteenth-century manhood is considerably softer and describes a more expressive male role characterized by kindness, emotional commitment, attentiveness, and a willingness to share decision-making with wives. It is this image that more accurately captures the life experiences and self-conceptions of nineteenth-century Californians. As domesticity expanded women's moral influence, moralists insisted, as a logical corollary, that husbands respect their wives' judgment, that they defer to them in household matters, that they invest more time and emotion at home, and that they spend more time under the beneficent influence of their wives. Affection, emotional fulfillment, joint decision making, mutual respect and confidence—these ideals became the foundation for a new structure of marital unity.[59]

Such ideals entailed not merely a reevaluation of authority but a reconsideration of the nature of manhood proper. In 1874 the *San Jose Weekly Argus,* for example, carried a story describing the metamorphosis of James Thompson, "a man who looked upon his wife as upon his other possessions. If properly managed she might prove an advantage to him." Moreover, he thought she "should be strongly fenced within the bounds of her husband's law or she will become an enemy to his prosperity and happiness." But then the change! In the wake of her nervous breakdown, Thompson sadly realized: "I haven't used her as well as I have my horses for I've had some consideration for them when they were tired." After making his barnyard comparison, Thompson resolved to treat his wife with kindness and affection; soon regenerative love appeared and the story ended on the sweet note of domestic harmony.[60] Other articles and stories also reminded husbands of their wives' importance to the success and happiness of the family. The *Weekly Argus* offered the tale of one man's shameful ignorance of his wife's contributions: "He had always treated her as though she were dependent upon him, but had she not done as much for him as he had for her?"[61] Women's efforts deserved reward and recognition, but "too often these expressions of approbation are not forthcoming and with a mistaken silence, he shrinks from honoring his wife and represses those few words of praise which she so well deserves and would so greatly appreciate."[62]

This emphasis on respect for wives and the apotheosis of home life was reflected in the portrait of husbands drawn up by lawyers. These documents reflect the moral attitudes of the middle class, and if the ideal Victorian male was aloof, authoritative, calculating, and unemotional, then the lawyers' documents would likely reflect such characteristics.[63] Instead, the lawyers stressed affective, emotional attributes, qualities not generally associated with stern Victorian husbands. H. F. Thurston's answer claimed that he would give his wife "the best home he can afford and will treat plaintiff with the greatest of kindness as a husband should treat a wife if she will return to the family home he has provided for her."[64] Though druggist William Stewart admitted that he and his wife often quarreled, his answer to her complaint averred that he treated her "affectionately and with few exceptions with all the kindness and consideration due her as a wife."[65]

Other divorce documents also singled out male kindness and thoughtfulness. The complaint of Charles King, a fruit canner, pictured him as a "true, kind, faithful and indulgent husband and father," and Joseph Tuers, a farmer, was far from an emotional iceberg, at least according to one document that depicted him as a "loving, affectionate, and dutiful husband."[66] One could scarcely find two less patriarchal men than Stephen Burdick or Seward Jones; Stephen, a doctor, was something of a martyr who "has at all times been faithful and kind to her and sacrificed the earnings of a long and lucrative practice in endeavoring to secure happiness with her," and Seward, an unemployed clerk, had "at all times been kind and indulgent" to his wife and had repeatedly tried to reconcile their differences.[67]

As this evidence shows, lawyers' documents emphasized the affective, tender qualities of men. Perhaps, one might argue, this should come as no surprise, that the general decline of patriarchy and the emphasis on affection and companionship produced legal documents tailored to reflect these trends. Or, again, perhaps lawyers were more progressive than most people in their conception of proper male character; perhaps farmers, small-town merchants, laborers, and housewives conceived of proper male character in more patriarchal terms. Yet, everyday people evinced similar attitudes. If the California evidence is representative, Americans after 1850 viewed marriage as a complex, demanding relationship in which men and women ideally exhibited a similar range of emotions.

Husbands who found themselves forced, under oath, to describe their own character emphasized their kindness and affection, a self-conception that hardly squares with the image of the Victorian patriarch. In 1882, W. H. Russell sued for divorce on the grounds of desertion, and when asked if he had caused his wife's desertion, Russell replied: "I never did; on the contrary, I was always kind and indulgent in my intercourse with my wife and she had no cause to treat me in the manner she had."[68] Joseph Shepherd, a teamster, pictured himself in similar terms and linked his affective qualities to his abilities in the marketplace: "I had always been industrious and treated her with all the respect and affection due from husband to wife and always provided for her to the best of my ability."[69] Camille Grosjean, a grocer, testified, "I always treated my wife kindly and affectionately . . . and she could have been happy and made me so if she desired," and Aaron Van Valkenburg similarly gave himself high marks: "I treated her kindly and did all I could for her comfort."[70]

Aside from these personal testimonials, the divorce documents occasionally offer unexpected access to the private emotions of men. One extraordinary document revealed the sentiments of a husband, John Harris, who was a convicted felon in a Toronto prison; in prison letters to his wife, he apologized for his unkindness, pleaded for a second chance, and revealed that even to him, it was clear that a so-called Victorian patriarch was not an ideal husband. John Harris left his wife in California, headed East with another woman, and in May 1889 found himself convicted of robbery and sentenced to prison in Canada. In a prison letter to his wife, he told her he understood—though regretted—her divorce action, and he acknowledged the justification for his wife's decision: "If such be the case, I can hardly blame you after the way I have done to you." Then Harris revealed his own sense of guilt and his emotional attachment to his wife: "Edith, let me tell you the honest truth that I never will forget and always will regret that I treated you in the way I have done, but it is fate that has led me many a curious turn."[71] In a later letter, Harris again asked forgiveness and in an oblique way expressed affection for his wife: "Now you know that I admit that you have been wronged a great deal by me all for another one [woman], but if [you] will believe me when I honestly say that I am sorry that I done to you as [I] have done, and as you say that you may possibly forgive me for it—which I hope you will—and as to my coming back to Frisco all depends." In the same letter, Harris again asked forgiveness and pleaded for a second chance, evidence suggesting that at all levels of society, it was believed that sentiment, loyalty, and fidelity were expected in a marital relationship. Even criminal men understood that a woman had a right to expect such virtues in her husband: "Leaving gambling, drink, and bogus friends alone in the future, [I] think [I] can prove to those who know me that I am not quite so depraved as they think I am, and have a few good qualities left in me yet, and if I can get your pardon will be easy in mind always."[72]

Husbands were not alone in emphasizing their love, kindness, and affection. Friends and neighbors of both sexes also testified about male character, and they, too, highlighted male kindness, emotion, and patience. When Park Henshaw finally sued his wife for divorce in 1887, he called as a witness an old friend from Missouri who spoke glowingly of his character and suggested the kind of treatment wives might expect from their husbands. In a deposition, Mrs. E. R. Wayland effused: "I had good opportunities of knowing the treatment Mr. Henshaw gave his wife. He was always kind, considerate, and attentive, and very devoted to his children as well as his wife. He took great pride in gratifying every wish they might have."[73] Lodgers had special opportunities to view marital interaction. Hannah Marrs, who lived with her daughter and son-in-law for several months in 1860 and 1861, keenly observed the precipitous decline in her son-in-law's husbandly affection. At first, "he always seemed very loving and always kissed her when he went out and came in, but afterwards I noticed that there was a coolness on his part." As further evidence of his insensitivity, Marrs testified that "after the birth of the child he didn't seem to be pleased about it, seeming to regard it more as an encumberance."[74] On a more positive note, Eli and Helen Randell's marriage came under the scrutiny of H. D. Bartlett who lived with the Randells in the early 1860s. Bartlett, a San Jose barkeeper, linked Eli's kindness and generosity to his work habits: "He treated her well, and was kind and indulgent to her. . . . He is a sober, industrious, and kind man." Dr. A. W. Bell sustained Bartlett's opinion by testifying that Eli "treated her with kindness as far as I know. I never heard any complaint from her or from anyone of any unkind treatment from her husband."[75] Two lodgers of rancher Eli Hughes also praised Hughes for his kindness, and one even asserted that Eli's affection was excessive. Although Jonathan Smith testified, "I never heard any trouble—never heard plaintiff give her a cross word and thought he always treated her very kindly," fellow lodger Andrew Gordon believed Eli may have been too kind: "I never knew of plaintiff in any way ill-using defendant; on the contrary he treated her too well and that's what *spilt* [*sic*] her."[76]

Perhaps, one might argue, the true Victorian patriarch—the man who embodied the "qualities of coldness and manly reserve"—was found only among the middle class, among the businessmen and professionals who comprised the heart of the respectable social system.[77] But witnesses who testified on behalf of businessmen emphasized affective qualities, especially their attentiveness, kindness, and considerateness. Eugene Pasquard described the character of his friend, grocer and merchant Camille Grosjean, in confident and glowing terms: "I have known him many years and I can safely say that his disposition is kind and affectionate and he would make any woman a good husband."[78] Businessman William Gray received similar praise from his daughter, who applauded him for his work habits and said that her father "was a kind husband, considerate and thoughtful toward his wife."[79] Three business acquaintances of Augustus Belknap, a retail merchant, testified that far from being a stern, reserved man, Augustus was, in the words of William Smith, "a mild man, reasonable, peaceable, and kind in all the relations of life, especially so towards her and his family." A. M. White, a business partner, described Augustus as "a man of mild and good disposition and deportment," and George Sniffen depicted Belknap as a person of "mild disposition and kind, pleasant deportment—[I] believe him incapable of treating a woman unkindly."[80]

This litany of male qualities—the kindness, indulgence, respect, affection, consideration, and thoughtfulness these men exhibited—implies a mutual emotional dependency between husbands and wives. Other men's experiences more directly reveal the psychological currency men invested in their marriages, especially among those terribly hurt by marital problems; such emotional pain could come only if marriage (for men as well as for the allegedly more romantic women) was a highly charged emotional bond. For example, Charles Bowles ascribed Stephen Burdick's poor health to frayed emotions; his illness "is a case of a sympathetic nature overtaxed from house conflict and is not to be mistaken for anything else." For his part, Stephen admitted breaking down with grief when he realized he was starting life anew after parting from his wife.[81] Paul Reynaud, a fifteen-year-old field hand, witnessed the emotional despair of William Bennett during one dispute between Bennett and his wife. After one serious altercation, Paul noted that Abigail broke down, and when the court asked if William also started crying, Paul answered, "I can't say whether he was crying but [I am] sure he felt pretty bad."[82] Marital problems also shattered the emotions of James Megannon and Cornelius Paddock. William Cook, a friend of Megannon's, testified that when Megannon discovered his wife's adultery, he was "much grieved and has ever since appeared the same."[83] Paddock, in a neighbor's judgment, deteriorated physically and mentally under the corrosive effect of his wife's cruelty and shameless immodesty: "His health is failing and his spirits are dull. . . . He used to be gay and of a joyous disposition, now he is quiet and sad."[84]

The despair of these men, while perhaps more provocative than conclusive, does suggest that the image of the flinty, unexpressive Victorian male does not comport with the actual experiences of these Californians. In the next chapter we will explore some of the behavioral implications of the expressive, emotional male role—how men's failures in this regard led to divorce, how women insisted on emotional commitment from their husbands, how mutuality might even translate into shared housework—but before doing so, an examination of male sexual decorum is in order.

### *Male Sexual Decorum*

In addition to being kind and affectionate, the ideal man was also sexually restrained and chaste. The moral and social consequences for infidelity by women certainly outweighed those visited upon unfaithful men, but men, too, found themselves subject to community censure if their sexual behavior did not correspond to local standards. Central to male sexual decorum, in fact at the basis of Victorian manhood, stood the concept of self-control. The *Weekly Argus* advised in 1874, "Let a child be taught, let those in mature life sternly determine to teach themselves self-control . . . and they will find but little difficulty deciding correctly on the right course of action."[85] This control—or as historian Joseph Kett has described it, this "internal gyroscope, a self-activating, self-regulating, all purpose inner control"—pertained to all facets of behavior, including sexual habits.[86]

Controlling sexual desires, of course, was more than an expression of self-control: proper male sexual decorum was indissolubly linked to women's rising status in the family. More egalitarian marriages required not only that husbands recognize their wives' contributions and defer to their moral superiority; it also required (and in fact logically followed) that husbands respect their wives' sexual desires. Earlier it was noted how the concept of "passionlessness"—the belief that women lacked interest in sex—enhanced women's moral esteem in the community and offered escape from unwanted pregnancy. Juxtaposed to passionlessness was the corollary assumption that men indulged in sex too frequently and thus threatened their wives' more elevated sensibilities. This disjunction between female passionlessness and male indulgence provoked cries for reform, ranging from efforts to prevent the legal regulation (and hence recognition) of prostitution, to the demand for a single sexual standard for men and women, to the insistence that wives control the frequency of sexual intimacy.[87] As early as the 1840s and 1850s, some progressive marriages already reflected these demands: among feminists and abolitionists who married in the antebellum period, Blanche Hersh found that they operated on the assumption that women were vulnerable to sexual abuse, that men must control their lust, and that "spiritual union" was of a higher dimension than the carnal kind. The right of women to say no to their husbands, early feminists confided privately, was at the heart of female emancipation.[88]

To find true feminists among these Californians would be surprising, but wives did complain of husbands who indulged their sexual desires excessively and who exhibited a callous disregard for their wives' right to share in, if not control, decisions about the frequency and timing of sexual intercourse. Sexual relations were clearly a source of tension between couples, and some women, like Ellen Havely, pointedly insisted that they were not sexual objects, expendable and without say. In 1869, Ellen's discontent with her husband's sexual misconduct forced her to file a cruelty complaint, and she said in no uncertain terms that she felt exploited: "He was [unkind] regardless of my feelings or condition of illness or health—often insisting and compelling me to sexual intercourse with him when my nervous condition and ill health forbade it, and caused me repeatedly [severe] bodily and mental suffering thereby—and by such treatment my health which was robust before marriage became ruined and it became dangerous to my life to longer live with him."[89] Ellen's emphasis on her "feelings" and "mental suffering" revealed that more than physical suffering was involved in this sexual complaint; her husband's disregard for her emotional condition violated the mutual, companionate basis of nineteenth-century marriage.

Like Ellen Havely, Mary Coyl insisted that her health declined because of her husband's excessive sexual demands. Her formal complaint stated that she did not refuse "reasonable and proper sexual intercourse" but that her husband demanded sex "at all times of day and night" to such degree that it hurt her health.[90] Finally, in 1880 he drove her from their home when she refused to have sex in the middle of the day. His incontinence, lack of respect for his wife's desires, and assault on Victorian notions of proper male character brought legal rebuke—in 1880 his wife received a divorce. Caroline White's health also suffered because her husband would not control his sexual appetite. Despite a doctor's recommendation of abstinence, she complained that she "has been obliged by defendant to have intercourse with him to the great injury and outrage of her feelings," suggesting that her self-respect and personal autonomy were violated by her husband's behavior.[91]

Susan Gilbert similarly sought to establish a direct connection between her poor health and her husband's excessive sexual demands. She answered his adultery charges by revealing her husband's insensitivity. When her health failed, she said he sent her to a hotel for sexual rest and recuperation "so that she might be cured up and become able to have sexual intercourse with him, and that her said sickness was caused by the conduct of said plaintiff, and the unreasonable gratification of his desires."[92] Gilbert's actions were intolerable: the judge dismissed Frank's case and soon after his wife sued successfully for divorce.

In fact, Victorian sensitivity to sex provided women a powerful standard of appeal in cruelty complaints. The courts recognized that sexual relations were acts of mutual cooperation, and when sexual propriety dissolved in the acid of male lust, the court upheld the woman's complaint of cruelty. Grace Thomas enlisted the authority of a doctor to control her husband's sexual demands, but to no avail: "He would not," Grace testified, "obey the instructions of the Doctor but would force me to submit to him so at times when my husband insisted on having connection with me while I was so sick I thought I should die. I suffered greatly by such treatment on the part of my husband." Grace had no problem answering the court's question about the cause of her poor health: "I had severe womb troubles and my husband would insist upon having connection with me against my will many times so that often I could not get out of my bed." She concluded with a chilling description of her husband's cruelty: "I would beg him not to do it as I was so very sick. The only answer he gave me was 'you damned bitch, you no business to be a woman.' "[93] Her ordeal ended in January 1890, when the court granted her a divorce.

Such unbridled sexual desire placed these husbands among the sexually unrestrained, a distinct group who ignored all notions of proper self-control; in fact, evidence suggests that people divided male society into two groups, the restrained and the unrestrained. When Charles Seffens accused his wife of seeing another man, he described the "sexual character" of his wife's companion: "He is a furniture man and is known as a libertine [who] has broken up several families."[94] Eugene Pasquard testified that a friend's wife attracted the attention of similar men: "She was a very pretty woman and was much admired by the men, especially the fast men."[95] Even relatively minor indiscretions provoked harsh judgments about a man's sexual propriety. David Trayer, a laborer in a soda factory, sometimes stopped work and chatted with the young girls who stopped by, and once, according to a fellow worker, Trayer apparently gave one of the girls a kiss.[96] Jerome Hill's alleged indiscretions were even more trivial. An acquaintance, Sebastian Shaw, testified that on a trip to the coast, "it was the subject of remarks that [Jerome] neglected his wife for the attention of young ladies" and that he helped other women over difficulties on the trek but offered no such help to his wife. Jerome's lawyer challenged Shaw to give specifics, and because Shaw could not, the lawyer concluded with a rhetorical question affirming the sexual decorum of all the men on the trip to the sea: "Wasn't that a party of ladies and gentlemen where they were all gallant and agreeable to each other?"[97]

One additional indicator of the importance of male sexual decorum lies in husbands' sensitivity to accusations of adultery. Though women were far more likely to be so accused than men (nineteen women compared to six men included accusations of adultery as part of cruelty complaints), husbands defended themselves against such accusations no less vigorously than wives. In 1880 Christian Bollinger successfully parried his wife's cruelty allegations and then sued her for cruelty on the grounds that she accused him of sleeping with "respectable women" in the neighborhood. These false accusations, he claimed, caused him "mental torture."[98] John Ennor and William Stewart also stated that they had been falsely accused of infidelity, thereby ruining their good names, and Seward Jones complained that his wife referred to him as a "whoremaster" in the presence of children and neighbors.[99] In 1880 Peter Flynn maintained he had suffered false accusations of adultery for four years and could stand them no longer, and one year later, Charles King sought relief from his wife's charges that he had repeatedly had "improper conduct" with a "widow woman" in Oakland.[100]

Despite the indignation of these men, not all husbands were so righteous; the divorce records also illuminate the dark side of sexual relations, particularly in cases where a husband found himself accused of adultery with a prostitute. Two interesting points emerge: first, married men were not allowed "a certain amount of philandering with prostitutes," as one historian has recently claimed—to have permitted such adultery would violate the mutuality of the marriage bond and render meaningless the insistence that men and women adhere to the same sexual standard; second, although single men were also expected to exhibit self-control and sexual chastity, they described their contacts with prostitutes in a matter-of-fact, guilt-free manner.[101]

Orrin Dennis was one man who found that his nighttime companions proved to be daytime legal opponents. Dennis, dissatisfied with the restraints of marital fidelity, went with friends to San Francisco brothels, and an acquaintance by the name of Hoag testified that he and Dennis frequently discussed whoring and that Dennis never tried to keep his contacts with prostitutes a secret. Despite Dennis's denials that he committed adultery, Hoag stated that Dennis was incontinent: "He has told me that he could not get enough at home and had to go outside to get it." Dennis even commented, albeit tersely, on the quality of this sex experience. Hoag testified that after Dennis "remained away long enough to accomplish the object I suppose he went for," he asked Dennis how he liked the girl and Dennis replied, "Pretty good." Two other companions—who, like Hoag, were apparently single—helped to seal Dennis's fate by adding to the description of Dennis's infidelity. C. T. Fox boasted that on one occasion, "I think we ran all night," and R. S. Jenkins added that he and Dennis regularly discussed sex: "I have often talked with him and others about his sprees with the girls."[102] In the light of such testimony, the wife of Orrin Dennis received a divorce in 1869.

In a similar case, Seward Jones met his former confidants in court. Again, the testimony of these unmarried friends proved the husband's infidelity and led to his wife's securing a divorce. When Seward Jones alleged cruel treatment in 1882, his wife immediately responded with adultery allegations, and to prove her case, she called as witnesses men who had accompanied her husband to brothels. William Welles described how he, another man, and Jones stopped at a house in San Francisco and how Jones went into a back bedroom saying he was "going to have some fun with the girl." When he came out, Jones reported to P. M. Davenport, another witness, that "he had finished pounding her and she was a good pounder." "Pounding," Davenport explained to the court, was a common term for sexual intercourse.[103]

The significance of the Jones and Dennis cases is clarified by the experience of Douglas Woolley, who in 1882 found himself accused of adultery with a prostitute. J. B. Mikan, a witness for Woolley's wife, testified that he had seen Douglas at a brothel, adding that he disapproved of such behavior for married men. He then casually mentioned that he often went to whorehouses but excused his behavior because he was single. "I think his morals are bad," he told the court, referring to Woolley. "I am not a married man, and go around considerable myself."[104] Mikan did not feel it necessary to offer apologies for his behavior, seeing it as the typical indulgence of a single man. In the mind of Mikan, at least, there was a clear distinction between proper sexual behavior for single and married men. And apparently that was the point that underlay the willingness of the male friends of Jones and Dennis to testify against them. Notions of self-restraint may have been mocked by their own frequenting of brothels, but they well recognized that wives had a right to expect fidelity from their husbands.

Sexual attitudes and values for nineteenth-century men remain obscure, but the divorce records reveal that proper marital sexuality involved self-control and moderation, and these two values, the point is worth emphasizing, were grounded in respect for and recognition of the legitimate rights and desires of women. In short, such values reflected in the sexual realm the larger companionate image of marriage characteristic of the nineteenth-century family in general. The emphasis on male kindness, emotion, and respect for wives placed demands on husbands that assumed an egalitarian basis for husbands' and wives' relations in the home. When husbands fell short of the ideal and conflicts erupted over sexual relations or a lack of attentiveness and respect, wives in increasing numbers took their misery to the courts. The rising divorce rate, then, was a corollary of rising expectations in marriage. The marital tensions engendered by male work habits, temperance, affection, and sexuality may have been present in the previous century, but they lacked the social and legal standing to precipitate a divorce. That status came only after 1750 as marriage became less and less hierarchical.

# 6

## *Manhood and the Companionate Ideal*

When Annie Parker testified in 1882 that her husband "never treated me as a wife should be—that is with the respectful consideration a husband should show to his wife," she succinctly described the basic characteristic of the ideal nineteenth-century marriage. The task now is to explore more fully the relationship between ideology and behavior, especially how rising expectations in marriage and male failure to meet such expectations prompted divorce litigation. In the process, the sources of conflict between nineteenth-century husbands and wives become clear. The focus is primarily upon men because the onus of the companionate ideal fell most heavily upon them; women, as these records make clear, expected husbands to treat them as coequals in the home, to converse with them as more or less equals, to ask their opinions on domestic matters, to spend their leisure time at home, to respect their sexual desires, and to care for them when sick or pregnant. Failure in any one of these areas might appear as evidence in a divorce suit. Overall, these demands on husbands functioned to broaden women's claims to domestic happiness and provided a powerful standard of appeal for unhappy wives. If women deserved respect and admiration for their domestic contributions, it followed that cruel, insensitive husbands who were unmindful of their wives' needs and opinions would find little sympathy in court. In this negative sense, the companionate ideal had legal as well as behavioral consequences.

Husbands who treated wives autocratically defied the canon of mutual respect: they wronged the very soul of the family, insulted the guardian of morals, and degraded the redeemer of society. With one action, a husband might prejudice the respect he owed his wife and simultaneously defile the transcendent qualities ascribed to nineteenth-century womanhood. After all, how else to respond but with respect and affection to wives who "soothe the aching heart, soothe the wrinkled brow, alleviate the anguish of the mind, and pour the balm of consolation in the wounded breast. . . . She is the real companion of man, and does the work of an angel."[1] Domesticity, in short, honed the rough edge of patriarchy and infused marital tensions with new meaning, a development that left Minor Havely wifeless in 1869.

After seven years of marriage, Ellen Havely sued Minor Havely for divorce on grounds of adultery and cruelty. In her formal complaint, Ellen asserted that her husband, a farmer of eighty acres in Illinois, had driven her away from home by his "course of unkind, harsh and tyrannical conduct."[2] In testimony taken in Illinois, Washington Hopkins, a former neighbor, described the nature of this "tyranny." Hopkins underscored Minor's lack of sensitivity to his wife's desires: "He dictated to Defendant most everything she did and would have his own way whether it was right or wrong concerning the House Hold and other affairs."[3] At least in the domestic sphere, Minor's obliviousness to his wife's opinions was unjust. Ellen put her own case more strongly and emphasized her husband's domineering attitude: in her testimony she said Minor was "extremely selfish and tyrannical all during our married life. He treated me as a slave always speaking to me in the language of command . . . exacting the most rigid compliance and obedience to his wishes at all times."[4] Her misery ended in 1870, when the court recognized the illegitimacy of such behavior and granted her a divorce.

J. C. Koppell, a San Jose cigar seller, treated his wife in much the same way. He criticized and carped "until she was worn out and sick and crushed in mind and spirit."[5] William Steele, James Mitchell, and George Philbrick shared Koppell's patriarchal excesses. Steele's course of cruelty began when he harshly refused his wife's innocent request to go riding, and Mitchell either spoke to his wife dictatorially or not at all.[6] Philbrick, for his part, had no better sense of the limits of male authority in 1874 than he did when he married in 1858. His marriage had scarcely gotten beyond the reception line before the groom lost sight of his bride's feelings. The day after the wedding, congratulations to the bride from a male acquaintance sparked abuse from the groom: "D—n you, you shall not talk to other men now, you belong to me. I have got you and I will make you mind."[7] Sixteen years later neither Philbrick's behavior nor his language had improved, a point made by Esther Newton, the Philbricks' oldest daughter. She rushed to her parents' home in October 1874, upon hearing that her mother had been beaten, and when she arrived and found her mother nursing a swollen head, she asked her father why he did it: "He said the d—d bitch wouldn't milk when he told her too [*sic*] and he would teach her to mind him."[8] Philbrick's benighted lessons finally caught up with him, and Esther gained a divorce in August 1883.

Other women registered similar complaints and responded to a variety of provocations with assertions of dignity and self-respect. In 1888, Josephine Baldacci stated that her husband ordered her out unless she obeyed his wishes without question; moreover, "when he married her he intended that she occupy a position of a servant."[9] Christian Bollinger had the same charmless view of his wife and referred to her "as nothing but a menial," and Abigail Bennett also resisted being treated like hired help.[10] When her husband, William, pressed her to admit acts of adultery she did not commit, she replied with dignity: "I told him I had always told him the truth, that I was no servant and could say nothing else."[11] Under cross-examination, Abigail's sister-in-law deplored William's iron rule by noting his obliviousness to her time and labor: "If she happened to be at work she would have to drop it any time he wanted to go out and go with him."[12]

Even relatively trivial incidents might symbolize a pattern of male domination out of step with the assumptions of the companionate ideal. In 1869 Caroline Peters was hurt when husband John, a small farmer, "brought home a keg of beer and refused to allow the plaintiff to taste the same alleging that the plaintiff was poor when he married her—that he had bought the same with his own earnings, and that she was not worthy to partake of it."[13] As self-appointed patriarch, Peters extended his tyranny to creature comforts. His brother-in-law described the Peters' sparse seating arrangements: "He generally occupied the chair when he was in the house and the wife would sit on the bench."[14] John's petty despotism also included culinary matters. A hired hand and neighbor, William Nelson, noticed that John skimmed the milk and drank the cream himself, and if he felt charitable, he gave his wife and children the skimmed milk, but sometimes "out of pure meanness," he threw it out.[15] Such pathetic displays of male authority brought condemnation from his wife, his neighbors, his hired hands, and his in-laws. Women's contributions and labor merited approval and their physical limitations warranted respect: they were not to be considered powerless servants at their husband's beck and call.

More evidence of the limits of male authority comes in cases where husbands restricted their wives' contacts outside the home, evidence which suggests that wives desired a considerable measure of personal autonomy. These women demanded—and the court recognized—their right to establish outside contacts, a point contested by some husbands, who sought to control their wives' social freedom. That such conflicts surfaced in cruelty complaints meant that husbands' prerogatives were limited, that wives might include seemingly trivial incidents as indicative of a consistent pattern of excessive authority, and that women were willing to fight for control over their own lives, even if it meant dissolving their marriages. Vicenta Wilson, for instance, found serious fault with her husband Daniel, a poor laborer and mason until he married into Vicenta's money. His oppression lay in forbidding her "to leave her home and not permitting her to go to church or pay any visits outside of her house for her health when worn down by hard labor and the cares of her many children."[16] Such callousness to her needs and sacrifices helped her gain a divorce in 1867. Alice Kilday lodged the same type of complaint in 1886, averring that her husband, Edward, would not allow her to go out with him and that his jealously prevented her from extending "ordinary civility" to old friends.[17]

James Haun even meddled in his wife's correspondence, a transgression Polly Haun thought worthy to note in her complaint in late 1866: "defendant taking advantage of his authority as husband of plaintiff takes letters addressed to plaintiff from the Post Office, and which contain the money which her friends send her for her support, and converts the money to his own use, thereby depriving her of the support and assistance of her friends."[18] William Stewart was another who could not keep his nose out of his wife's mail. His wife, May, admitted demanding personal receipt of her mail, but these instructions went to the postmaster with good reason. She explained that her family often corresponded by postcard and that in the past her husband had read personal messages meant only for May's eyes; therefore, she "desired it to be delivered to herself as was and is her right."[19] Both of these women evidenced a strong desire for personal autonomy: one felt entitled to outside help independent of her husband's wishes and the other wanted a personal life free from her husband's intrusions.

Husbands could fail the requirements of companionship without being such tyrants. At a time when husbands were advised to "let her opinion be asked, her approval sought, and her judgment respected in matters of which she is cognizant," those who failed to converse with their wives or did so without affection might find their silence and ill-humor described in divorce complaints.[20] That fate befell Daniel Wilson, when Mrs. H. S. Hanson, a San Jose housewife, testified about Daniel's treatment of his wife. To Mrs. Hanson's mind, Daniel did not pay enough attention to his wife: "I thought he treated her very coldly." Asked to elaborate, she replied that while visiting the Wilsons in 1865, she noticed that Daniel rarely spoke to his wife: "As for the conversation he addressed but very few to her. I have answered the question the best I can; but allowing one to be the judge I shouldn't think his manner was such as a husband should observe toward his wife."[21]

Apparently, Thomas Warhurst was a veritable sphinx to his wife Ann. After many years of marriage, he reached the point where his silence became deafening. From January to September 1865, Thomas "maintained towards her during all that time a brutal silence for the purpose of intimidating and frightening her."[22] Ann Warhurst was not alone in being unsettled by silence. In 1882 Annie Parker testified that her husband "never treated me as a wife should be—that is with the respectful consideration a husband should show to his wife. His conduct was uniformly truculent and morose."[23] Similarly Sebastian Shaw, a thirty-one-year-old university student, noted that Jerome Hill's treatment of his wife was "not with what I considered common civility. His treatment was decidedly cool."[24]

"Arctic" would more accurately have described Joseph Tuers's treatment of his wife. Tuers's hired hand, William Spencer, commented on Joseph's iciness: "He never appeared to be very pleasant—seemed to be sulky and I have known him to go whole days without speaking to his wife or the people in the house."[25] Tuers's temperament was shared by Henry Simonds, at least according to lodger Abner Colburn, who condemned Henry for being "very cross nearly all of the time."[26] Both Tuers and Simonds found themselves losers in the divorce court, and their aloofness and inconsideration comprised part of the evidence against them.

These examples of daily discourse reveal what husbands failed to do. The divorce records afford still another angle of vision, this one coming from husbands who defended their own character in the course of the suit. In such instances, men emphasized their restraint and self-control, their ability to deal calmly with their wives, and their reluctance to resort to stern measures to force compliance with their wishes. Indeed, their behavior reveals that husbands ideally resolved marital tensions by compromise and conciliation, not by assertions of patriarchal power. Joseph Garner, for example, pictured himself as a model of Christian decorum and gentleness in describing his wife's cruelty to him: "I never gave her any cause. I would not quarrel with her but would leave the house rather than quarrel with her. Her disposition was such that I could not live with her."[27] John Planer, a baker, exhibited the same commendable qualities in discussions with his intemperate wife. According to Planer, he "used to remonstrate with her about her drinking—told her that she was destroying my business and tried all I could to induce her to desist—but never used any violence or harsh language to her."[28] Cornelius Paddock's problem came not from liquor but from his wife's lewdness, but he assured the court that he always tried to reason and speak calmly with her about her indecency. Paddock's roomer, Charles Peterson, supported Cornelius's testimony and recounted what happened when Mrs. Paddock insisted on singing a lewd song. Rather than getting upset or indignant, Cornelius simply told his wife that "if she wanted to sing such a song to go outside and sing it." Unfortunately, she usually met such moderation by insisted "that she will do as she pleases."[29]

James Quentin faced an even more intransigent wife. His bride, Maria, treated the wealthy rancher like an emotional punching bag, flailing away with epithets like "you mean old fool," "you dirty old bummer," and charging that "he was not fit to live with the hogs." The witness to this reckless abuse, a servant named Margaret Finisty, praised James for his patience and restraint, noting that when Maria began her attacks, James would simply "go off out of the way somewhere," saying before he left that Maria "was hurting herself more than she was him." His Christian deportment impressed the servant, who admitted that "I thought he put up with more than any man in the world could put up with."[30]

Though wives were not "servants" and "slaves," their place was in the home, and there true companionship and mutual respect would be fulfilled or ignored. If women's rising status meant more than empty paeans to the glories of womanhood, then important domestic issues required mutual resolution. The divorce evidence reveals women who transcended eighteenth-century injunctions "to use goods frugally and to obey," women who were angered by their exclusion from family financial decisions, and women who believed that if a wife's place was in the home, then that was the place where she would wield her influence.[31] The Peters case reveals one woman who turned her husband's excessive financial control against him.

Caroline Peters chafed under her husband's tight-fisted control of the family budget, and neighbors and relatives joined in condemning John Peters for his unilateral and misdirected use of the family money. In five years, Caroline claimed, her husband bought her "three dresses, two of which were calico, and two pair of shoes, and no underclothing whatever."[32] He also controlled the culinary side of family life. What food he bought was of poor quality, and when he did purchase meat, Caroline said that "her individual allowance of it was very short."[33] Neighbors, relatives, and even hired hands recognized that John failed to consider his wife's wants when making purchases.

John Coronett, who worked for Peters in 1870 as a field hand, outlined John's misplaced spending priorities and his lack of attention to his wife's needs and wants. He noted that their home "had one bed and bestead, one chair, two or three rough benches, and one or two rough tables" and that "there were cracks in some parts of the house that you could lay two fingers in." Despite such austere domestic furnishings, Coronett commented that the eighty-acre farm itself was prosperous, with one hundred horses, four to five cows, and "a lot of hogs."[34]

Others also noted Peters's misplaced consumptive emphasis, evidence that ultimately proved that John had steadfastly ignored his wife's desires. Mary Debernardi, a cousin of Caroline's, remarked that the Peters' food was limited to "a sack of flour, a sack of potatoes and a can of lard," and Joseph Fowler and Robert Evans, two hired hands, said that Caroline wore old boots and that the food consisted of stale bread and clabber cheese.[35] Amid this seeming poverty, Caroline's brother, Peter Monotti, described a farm of eighty acres of land with four to five cows, a small lot of hogs, seventy horses, one jackass worth $100 and one stallion worth $750.[36] Another, James Monotti, detailed still more evidence of John Peters's inattention to his wife's legitimate rights. James censured John's patriarchal pretensions and singled out one instance when John "would not allow the plaintiff to kill a chicken nor to eat an egg."[37] Clearly Peters's emphasis on land and livestock accumulation was misplaced, and the tyranny he exercised over family finances helped determine his fate in divorce court.

Other wives likewise objected to their husbands' unilateral decisions. Susan Battey defended her "desertion" of her husband by maintaining that he had made no effort to find out what she considered a proper home. When she arrived in California, she found that her husband expected her and her child to live in a run-down "bunk filled room with five or six Spanish men."[38] Mary Glover's complaint concerned not housing but food. She told the referee that her miserly husband portioned out money to her, and she clearly resented his domination: "And I only had my meals as he would take me to them and most of the time I only had one meal a day, except that sometimes he would give me 30¢ and tell me that I had to live on that for the day."[39]

Outright parsimony was not the only way husbands prevented wives from sharing in the use of the family finances. Other husbands kept economic control in more devious ways, and in their suits, wives and witnesses made it clear that husbands could not legitimately exercise monopoly control over family money. The conflicts over money also suggest that wives resented husbands who impeded women's legitimate involvement in the local market economy: in a partnership of equals, the authority of the husband did not extend that far. A San Jose dry goods dealer named Strauss testified that Herman Kottinger instructed local merchants to deny Mrs. Kottinger credit, a request Strauss honored but thought unjust.[40] Bridget Hanagan, a farmer's wife, complained that her husband did the same; moreover, he pocketed all the money they received from renting their farm.[41] Joseph Tuers found still another means to block his wife's rightful involvement in household finances. When she decided to sell the chickens she had been raising on their farm, he forbade her to do so, a fact she mentioned in her successful cruelty complaint in 1865.[42]

The lowly chicken engendered similar strife in the Nicholas Dodge family. In 1869 Mrs. Deborah McGowen, the mother of plaintiff Susan Dodge, registered disgust with her son-in-law's blatant disregard for his wife's economic prerogatives: "I know of his taking the last sack of flour and selling it; frequently also sold plaintiff's chickens and would and did spend the money for liquor and to gamble."[43] Dodge's lack of respect for his wife's economic contribution was matched by William Allen. Allen and his wife worked for neighbors immediately after their marriage, he as a field hand, she as a cook; and his wife complained that "he collected our wages and spent them in drinking and gambling, frequently coming home drunk."[44]

Not all men were such selfish rogues. In describing their virtues, some husbands mentioned turning their wages over to wives, and others stressed their willigness and desire to include a role for wives in the family's climb to economic success. W. H. Russell, for one, gave himself high marks in 1882: "I was kind and affectionate to her, gave her all the money I earned, was then and am now a temperate and industrious man and a good provider for my family."[45] Like Russell, Christian Schumann defended his own character by underlining his wife's economic responsibilities: "during all of said times when he received money for his labor or otherwise, he gave the same into the hands of his said wife which was expended by her in purchasing the common necessaries of life for his said family so far as said means would go."[46]

But wives were not merely partners in family expenditures and consumption: they were also expected to take an active interest in their husband's work by performing the role of psychological helpmate and cheerleader. Husbands complained about their wives' lack of interest in their careers, implying that upwardly mobile husbands considered their wives' role crucial in the family's economic fortunes. Mutual cooperation between husbands and wives was not, it appears, limited to household matters. The case of Harvey Kincaid, a Redwood City lawyer, illustrates the point. In 1881 Harvey's wife accused him of intemperance for over eighteen months, and Harvey responded eloquently if immodestly by describing his successful journey from poverty to success. Along the way, he revealed how his "law office, bedroom, and kitchen [were] for some years . . . one and the same apartment, and he himself . . . lawyer, cook, and general servant." He finally joined the ranks of self-made man, but no thanks to his wife, who "has never in fact assisted the defendant in his worldly acquisitions, either pecuniarily, socially or otherwise." She also failed in the role of psychological booster by never causing him "to feel encouraged in acquiring either property, reputation, or fame."[47] Frank Gilbert saddled his wife with similar shortcomings. The main portion of his complaint involved allegations of adultery and cruelty, but he also disparaged his wife's lack of interest in his work: she "would never talk to him about his business matters and would never take any interest in his affairs." Mixing indignation with personal pride, Frank complained that she "did not intend to help plaintiff save or make a cent" and that everything he possessed came from his own hard labor.[48]

Cooperation in domestic matters may have been more extensive than these examples suggest. Three tantalizing pieces of evidence, while perhaps not typical, illustrate the outer limits of companionship in the nineteenth century and prefigure twentieth-century extensions of domestic cooperation to the frontiers of shared housework. William Spencer, for example, worked on the Joseph Tuers farm in 1861, and later testified that Joseph had poor work habits around the house. In fact he "wasn't an early riser—he generally arose when breakfast was ready. I never used to see him trouble himself about the house or doing any chores and all. I never saw him do any cooking or assist in it." Joseph Winterbarn, a perennial hired hand of Tuers' corroborated Spencer's testimony: "He did nothing about the house, so far as I saw."[49] Both the hands clearly expected Tuers to help with domestic duties and found it noteworthy that he did not.

Elizabeth Hill aimed much the same kind of criticism at her husband Jerome. She charged him with cruelty and neglect throughout her marriage, and when asked under cross-examination to describe what she meant by neglect, she said: "By taking all the pleasures and comforts of life himself leaving me at home to work and care for the children alone."[50] Hill's shortcomings were Edwin Parker's self-described virtues. Parker defended his character in an 1882 letter to the Superior Court judge, a letter meant to answer his wife's allegations of cruelty. Though hardly unbiased in judging his own merits, his choice of virtues was surprising: "There has hardly a day passed during our housekeeping, we boarded a portion of the time, but that I have lightened her burdens of house work by washing dishes and cooking."[51]

Of course wives could get no help with housework if they could not get their husbands into the home. The following evidence reveals that not just urban women and moralists feared that husbands were being lost to outside temptations. Despite all the idealization of the fireside, some small-town California husbands found card tables more appealing than hearth sides. But this choice entailed risk: the carousing or unattentive husband could expect a divorce action, for it could be justified by the popular high esteem of the home.

Home life assumed a new significance in the nineteenth century, for it was there that marital companionship either blossomed or withered. But before the home could fulfill its important functions, before it could become an effective refuge and a repository of morality, husbands had to be convinced that home, not society, was where they should spend their leisure time. The injunctions urging men to spend time at home originated with the advent of rapid urbanization and industrialization in the Northeast in the early nineteenth century. In the city, many middle-class American men worked far from home, and moralists, who located virtue in the home and vice in the city, hoped that men might spend their leisure hours amidst the goodness, safety, and security of the home. Moralist William Alcott went so far as to call any place where men might congregate—a store, shop, barroom, etc.—an "anti-domestic life club."[52]

By mid-century even the *Santa Clara Argus* carried the theme of home as refuge: "Let him learn that, however bad the outside world may be, he is always sure of sympathy and consideration in one place."[53] And the salutary effects of domestic life knew no class lines: "Woe betide the man, whatever his lot or position, who has in his heart of hearts no memory of a home where the sunshine never faded out and the voices were always sweet."[54] Another article fairly quivered with sentiment: "Where will our sorrows receive the same solace, as in the bosom of our family? Whose hand wipes the tear from our cheek, or the chill of death from our brow, with the same fondness as that of the wife?" The coda was dramatic: "If the raging elements are contending without, here is a shelter. If war is desolating the country, here is peace and tranquility. Blissful and happy hours, that unite us together in sweet and holy companionship, I bid you a joyful welcome."[55]

Wayward husbands had only lame excuses in the face of local declarations like this one from the *San Jose Daily Mercury:* "The family and the home form the basis of a nation's civilization, and in their preservation should be enlisted every agency of custom and law and religion at the service of the race."[56] The *Santa Clara Argus* had less Olympian sentiments, but the sociological importance of the home could not be overestimated: "The idea of looking beyond the sphere of home for enjoyment is at the root of many of our modern ills. Home should be the very centre and sanctuary of happiness; and when it is not there is some screw loose in the domestic machinery."[57]

Some of the loose screws turned up in divorce court, and the celebration of home life reverberated in divorce complaints when husbands found their cronies more appealing than their families. Most of the following evidence appeared in intemperance and non-support complaints, and though the legal focus was on defendant husbands' inability to support their wives, the complaints also emphasized the husbands' continued absence from home: the caveats against absence from home did have actual consequences. Take, for example, Fred Sayers's problem with his mother-in-law, Clara Spaulding, who minced no words in describing his shortcomings. After mentioning his good health and ability to work, Clara criticized his character; he "might have provided her and the children with a comfortable living if he had chose [*sic*] to but he would spend his money about saloons playing cards and other places to his shame and disgrace." Mrs. Spaulding was not one to suffer in silence: "I told him I thought it was a shame and no one having the spark of a man about them would be guilty of such."[58]

The mother-in-law of Thornton Sharp had similar regard for her son-in-law's behavior, especially the wanderlust that kept the carpenter away from home. Alice Crane stated that Thornton "did not provide [his wife] with a home or any home comforts. He seemed to be entirely shiftless and indolent. He would work and get a little money and then spend it all tramping around from place to place and perfectly content that other people should take care of his wife and give her a shelter."[59] Hiram Ray, a laborer, shared Sharp's lack of interest in domestic joys, at least in the eyes of his wife, who described him as "indolent and profligate in his habits and would spend his earnings in visious [*sic*] habits and leave me to take care of myself as best I could."[60] A neighbor, H. C. Talbot, criticized Hiram for his flight from home life and claimed that Hiram could have supported his family "if he had been industrious and attentive to his business. But he was roving and . . . continually moving from place to place."[61] Edward Kilday had a penchant for nocturnal wanderings, and in August 1886 he left his wife and children alone for three nights.[62] Jerome Hill apparently did not rove far, but his absence from home angered his wife, who complained that he indulged in life's pleasures while "leaving me at home to work and care for the children alone."[63] John Kennedy matched Hill in his pursuit of pleasure at the expense of his family. His wife charged that the unemployed laborer slept by day, then—sufficiently rested—went to the saloons at night.[64]

Other fathers and husbands followed in Kennedy's weaving footsteps. Apparently Mary Allen's husband was an inebriated phantom who "would remain from home day and night—and as late as one o'clock [a].m. and when he did come would be drunk."[65] A neighbor, Mary Hull, testified that this phantom materialized one night in her bedroom when she found him "drunk in my house lying in bed with his clothes on. I was compelled to put him out of the house."[66] Katharina Wahl complained that her husband left her alone for days on end, and Lizzie Barnett criticized husband Robert for being gone all day on business, returning home for supper, and then heading for the bar and game tables in the evening.[67] Egbert Etts divided his time between hunting and drinking, neither of which involved much sustained contact with work or with his wife.[68]

Husbands could do far worse than the above ragbag of drunks and gamblers. The idealization of women in the nineteenth century meant that these "angels of consolation," frail by their very nature, needed and merited a husband's care and attention. Those who ignored their sick wives contravened both the cult of true womanhood and the injunctions to spend time at home. If nineteenth-century marriage formed a partnership of kindred souls, and if the family's key values were nurture, self-development, and privacy, then husbands had special obligations to attend to ill wives. Here we see how the cult of true womanhood coupled with the emphasis on companionship and collaboration could be turned to women's advantage; men who ignored their wives' frailty might find themselves facing stern criticism in divorce suits.

James Chesley and John Peters were two such men. The judge's findings stated that when Eleanor Chesley was "desperately sick and her life was despaired of," her husband, "instead of ministering to the wants of the Plaintiff," left her alone for the night, without so much as telling her where he went.[69] Peters behaved even more reprehensibly though he remained at home. Once when sick, his wife, Caroline, asked him to summon a doctor, a request he met by telling her "to lay still and behave herself."[70] Katharina Wahl accused her husband of leaving their home for days on end when she was sick, and Amilla Kelly fared no better at the hands of her husband, who left her sick in bed and headed for the saloons.[71] Herman Kottinger refused to contact a doctor or nurse despite his wife's extended illness; Egbert Etts found saloons more to his liking than sickrooms; and Scott Sabine refused his wife's request for money to buy medicine.[72] Stillman Moulton went a step further and not only ignored his ill wife, but added that he did not want to be bothered by her.[73] All of these men (in cases where the judgment is included in the record) lost the divorce suits, certainly in part because they failed their wives in their time of need.

Relatives, too, stood up for ignored wives. Mrs. Deborah McGowan, the mother of Susan Dodge, cared for her daughter when she was sick for three months and bemoaned the fact that Susan's husband visited her just once a week and refused to get a stove for the room despite doctor's orders.[74] Peter Monotti, in a different case, found his sister's husband equally callous. When his sister had a miscarriage in September 1870, Monotti cared for her because of her husband's neglect: "I remained with plaintiff seven or eight days after the miscarriage, taking care of her." During that time, Monotti said his sister's husband seldom came into the room "and never asked how she was getting along."[75]

Neighbors also noticed husbands' shortcomings. Like relatives, they involved themselves in other families' private affairs but simultaneously criticized husbands who failed to nurse their wives. Peter Monotti did not care for his sister alone but was assisted by a neighbor, Mary Evans, who scarcely suppressed her indignation: "I found nothing in the house fit for a well person let alone a sick woman. I prevailed on him after a good deal of talking to kill a chicken for me, to make some broth with."[76] Mrs. May Herd found the insensitivity of Nicholas Dodge equally repugnant: "Whilst plaintiff was very sick last winter in San Jose, I waited on her. Sometimes sat up with her. Was her neighbor. Defendant refused to get her anything either to eat or to make her comfortable. During her illness [he] went off and left her alone whilst she was unable to sit up in bed and her friends were compelled to come in and take care of her and provide her family with something to eat."[77] Timeteo Sierras, an old farmer who lived within one hundred yards of the Thomas home, described Manuel's coldness toward his wife: "The defendant is a man of harsh temper and was abusive to his wife. Much of the time she was sick—so sick that she actually needed the care of a nurse but none was provided. I never saw a doctor there."[78]

Husbands who not only ignored their sick wives but provoked or sustained their illnesses drew particularly sharp criticism. Women were far more than cogs in the family economy; their limitations deserved respect, and their central role was affective, not economic. Common women might be poor, but they were not pack mules, and husbands unmindful of this basic point received no sympathy in court. For example, a neighbor of Ellen and Minor Havely excoriated Minor's disregard for his wife's health: "I know that he compelled her to work in the fields in carrying on the farm habitually and beyond [her] strength to such an extent as to injure her health."[79] Twenty-three-year-old Ellen portrayed her husband as a true Simon Legree: "He habitually compelled me to work on the farm far beyond my strength or what my health would permit and this he well knew and rendered my existence miserable."[80]

Louisa Koppel suffered in the same way. Her husband's demands clashed with her health, and his callousness became unbearable by 1889. According to her complaint, he insisted she *"keep boarders and cook for them* and work in the kitchen and house beyond her strength."[81] Another woman, Susan McMahill, also accused her husband of forcing her to work as a cook despite her poor health; furthermore, he also forbade Susan's employers to pay her her wages.[82] Steven Purdy was even more hardhearted in brazenly ignoring the advice of Dr. Alexander Luse. Luse examined Purdy's wife and told her she would not recover from a liver ailment unless she stopped working at a hotel, but Harriet insisted she must work to support herself and her child. Luse then called on Stephen Purdy: "I went to him and told him his wife would never get better unless she has better care taken of her. His reply was—I remember his exact words—'By God! she can work and pay her own board. I have to pay mine.' "[83] Purdy ultimately had to pay her costs and counsel fees; they were divorced in 1871.

A husband's maltreatment of his sick wife was doubly shameful if her weakness came from pregnancy and childbirth. Nineteenth-century "American culture," according to historian Ann Douglas, "seemed bent on establishing a perpetual Mother's Day," and husbands needed to be extra solicitous of their wives' welfare when true womanhood took on the added dimension of motherhood.[84] Once the doctor or midwife was gone, the husband was expected to attend to the needs of the new mother. If he performed this role successfully, the emotional ties between husband and wife tightened and the psychological bonds central to the companionate ideal increased; but if the husband ignored his wife or even abused her during her pregnancy, then he defied all notions of companionship and blemished the beauty of motherhood.

William Allen was one husband who failed his wife when she became a mother. His behavior during the birth of their first and only child in 1870 formed the core of the testimony against him. Allen, a laborer, faced his new fatherly responsibilities by adjourning to local Spanishtown saloons, and he provided his wife with "neither medicine nor food." Fortunately for his wife's sake, neighbors were not so heartless: "The neighbors brought me medicine and food and attended me. I don't know what I would have done but for their assistence [*sic*]."[85] One Samaritan, Mary Hull, cared for Mrs. Allen and criticized William for failing to obtain medicine needed by his wife; and Charles Kelly, a local merchant and friend of the new parents, noted that community knowledge of William's failings extended beyond the sickroom doors: "His neglect of her at that time was a matter of public notoriety."[86]

David Savage started his cruelty before the baby arrived by remarking when his pregnant wife asked for food, "I never knew a cow or mare in your condition to eat so much."[87] When the child finally arrived, David disappeared for a week and left his wife with no provisions for a doctor, nurse, or any other help. Mary bore the child with no assistance. Compared to Mrs. Savage, Vicenta Wilson gave birth to her last child in a veritable commune, but she, too, felt neglected by her husband. David Hildebrand, a farm laborer, described the situation when Vicenta gave birth: "She had a female attendant but no doctor at the birth of her child: nor did she receive any medical attendance at any time during her confinement. On the day the child was born there was a Spanish woman there and an Irish woman."[88] Hildebrand noted that the Spanish woman left the day after the birth and the Irish woman left the day after that; thereafter, Vicenta had no female attendant. Daniel matched his failure in the medical department by his collapse in providing emotional support for his wife. Hildebrand remembered that Daniel "went away on the same day the child was born and remained away all day and night. He returned the second day and staid [*sic*] home that night. From that time he was away all day and would only return [at] night."[89] James Stevens, another hired hand, also witnessed Daniel's singular lack of interest in his wife's recovery. Stevens arrived just two days after the birth and was shocked that Daniel was absent all day long and failed to look after at least some of the household chores; instead, hired hands cooked and waited on the new mother.[90]

Mattie Hoehner received much the same treatment from her husband. Just ten days after Mattie gave birth to her first child, her husband, a bookkeeper, left her bedside and went away for the night, an action that comprised part of her cruelty complaint in 1887.[91] Jerome Hill stayed with his wife, but he might as well have left, at least according to Mrs. E. J. Thompson who recounted how Jerome refused to build a fire or summon a doctor on the night his child was born.[92] Enoch Ellis's impatience appeared in his wife's cruelty complaint of 1885. Within one week of her giving birth, he forced her to feed the horses and pigs, thereby delaying her recovery and causing her much physical suffering.[93]

If emotion and companionship characterized the nineteenth-century family, surely repercussions were felt in the domains of sex and love. But sexual relations and love comprise the two most inscrutable areas of nineteenth-century family life among common Americans. The divorce seekers provided only slight clues to sexual attitudes, but it would appear that an ideal of sexual companionship existed among nineteenth-century Californians: women were entitled—in their own eyes and in those of the court—to control over their own sexuality. Husbands who refused to check their sexual desires exhibited a lack of proper self-control, but they also violated the mutual regard so central to the companionate ideal. As we saw in the previous chapter, such blatant disregard for female prerogatives appeared in cruelty allegations. Thus, Ellen Havely testified that her husband was grossly insensitive, "often insisting and compelling me to sexual intercourse with him when my nervous condition and ill health forbade it," and Mary Coyl criticized her husband for demanding sex "at all times of day and night."[94] Caroline White denounced her husband for forcing her to have sex "to the great injury and outrage of her feelings," and Susan Gilbert attributed her poor health to "the unreasonable gratifications of his desires.[95] Grace Thomas also attributed her poor health to her husband's incontinence, particularly his insistence "upon having connection with me against my will many times so that often I could not get out of my bed."[96]

One other aspect of sex, companionship, and cooperation involved the decision whether or not to have children, and if so, how many. Historian Daniel Scott Smith speculated on the basis of fertility rates that the nineteenth-century decline in the birth rate evidenced a rise in female power within the family. Terming this development "domestic feminism," he argued that wives controlled family planning in the nineteenth century by gaining power over sex and reproduction, undoubtedly through *coitus interruptus* or abstinence.[97] Both required cooperation on the part of the husband, cooperation suggested by the comment of William Duncombe in an 1883 divorce case.

Duncombe, who had no real complaint with his wife but simply found his three-year marriage "uncongenial," explained his dilemma to his lawyer, emphasizing that his wife would oppose a divorce because "she had had a good time of it as my wife." Apparently the marriage was harmonious but boring, and the harmony even extended to matters of reproduction. Writing to his lawyer, the unemployed Duncombe volunteered information on his and his wife's efforts at birth control: "We have never had any children, through careful management on our parts however."[98] Duncombe's remark was tantalizingly brief, but obviously the two of them successfully cooperated in limiting family size.

More detailed evidence comes from the case of Frank and Susan Gilbert, whose experience provides an unexpected look at birth control and marital cooperation. Frank, a laborer, alleged that one month after their wedding in 1868, his wife went to Sacramento for six months in order to have an abortion, an action that sparked a vehement conflict between them. He lamented that his objections did not deter her, that she almost aborted her second pregnancy as well, and that thereafter, she had several more abortions, all the time claiming she would never have another child. He claimed that when she returned from Sacramento, she refused to have sex for eighteen months; and thereafter "for as long as one, two and three months at a time refusted [*sic*] to have intercourse with plaintiff."[99]

Not so, said Susan, who in response provided a glimpse at one aspect of birth control in the nineteenth century. She first described the uterine troubles that had plagued her since the age of twelve, and after establishing her physical frailty, she explained that her trip to Sacramento was an effort to escape her husband's unrestrained sexual passion. More important, Susan claimed that they had *both* agreed on the trip after realizing that because of her weakness, she "was unable to satisfy the sexual desires and demands of plaintiff and he was unable or unwilling to control them." Sacramento was, in short, a mutually agreed-upon haven from lust. While in Sacramento, she miscarried, and returned to San Mateo County on the condition "that in the future he would be more careful of her, and in his sexual intercourse, have a due regard to her health and physical condition." After their first child's birth and the health problems that ensued, they also decided that she would have no more children. Thereafter, when Frank and Susan found she was pregnant, they worked together—in what must represent the most private of husband-and-wife agreements—to abort the fetus. As she described it, "before there was any quickening or life in the fetus whatever, with the approval, consent, and assistance of plaintiff, she used injections of pure water, and by that means alone produced a miscarriage." She claimed she induced four abortions in this way, all necessary "as plaintiff could not, or would not restrain himself so as to prevent her from becoming with child." In conclusion, she reiterated the cooperative aspect of their efforts at family limitation. She had not acted alone; rather, her husband had "consented to and assisted in producing miscarriages in manner and form herein before stated."[100]

Like sex, evidence of affection and love among common Americans remains hidden behind a veil of historical privacy. But other studies have shown that in the middle to late eighteenth century, affection and romance became increasingly evident in prescriptive literature and in private correspondence; moreover, parental power in mate selection declined as the prerogative of choosing a spouse shifted from parents to children.[101] The result was to infuse marriage with romance, in the process making marriage more fulfilling emotionally but, equally important, more volatile as well. In fact, divorce petitions after the Revolution placed more emphasis on affective tensions than those preceding the Revolution, and this development continued into the nineteenth century and helps account for the rise in the divorce rate in the second half of the nineteenth century.[102] By that time, more and more Americans from all levels of society expected emotional satisfaction from their marriages, and there is some evidence that the need for love and affection in marriage even outdistanced legal conceptions of proper marital relationships. Nineteenth-century Californians placed greater emphasis on love and affection than the law thought was necessary; for example, Stephen and Alice Burdick expected love in their relationship even if the law did not. After two years of hearing acrimonious charges and counter-charges, Judge Edward Head dismissed their respective complaints by concluding that "although the parties have lost all affection for each other, still no such extreme cruelty is proved upon either side as would under the law justify a divorce."[103] The law may have been unromantic in its conception of marriage, but the absence of affection brought grief and sorrow to couples who expected emotional support and fulfillment in their marriages. And these romantic expectations transcended class lines.

John Cardinell, a common laborer in San Mateo County, endured his wife's abuse for several years, but he lamented that despite his patience, she always "met me with a frown and was cross; she would snap and snarl and when I asked her to get a meal of victuals would order me to get it myself." Cardinell finally asked her "why in the name of God she acted so toward me—she answered that she did not love. I asked her why she did not love me—and she replied that there was another man she loved better than she did me."[104] Finally, in 1863, she deserted John, presumably to attend to her new romance.

Like Sarah Cardinell, William Steele, owner of a stationery store, left no doubt in his wife's mind that his love had vanished. In October 1879 she finally learned the source of the past months of poor treatment: "'Damn you, I have lost my love for you and I want you to understand that.'"[105] The loss became brutally clear in the following year, when he sought to seduce his wife's sister and a friend of his wife. Archibald White, on the contrary, turned his frustration inward when love departed. His wife vividly recalled how Archibald approached her bed late one night in 1878 with razor in hand, leaned over her, and threatened to "cut his throat from ear to ear if plaintiff would not love and kiss him."[106]

If Sarah Cardinell and Archibald White represented the extreme response to love's absence, Mary Laine stood for the genteel reaction. She deserted her husband, a doctor, in 1876, but not before telling a family friend of her reasons for doing so. The friend, George Thummel, testified that Mrs. Laine bemoaned the lack of love in her marriage: "She wanted something besides bread and butter. She could not live on that. She said she had left him once before and wished she had never gone back, that they did not love one another and there was no use trying any longer." He added that Mrs. Laine also told him that Joseph "did not love her as much as he should." In a summary remark, Thummel offered his own surprisingly modern interpretation of the Laines' dilemma: "I consider that their tempers were incompatible for them to live together—the Defendent [Mary] never complaining of anything but always saying they could not love one another and it was useless to try to live together in that way."[107] Thummel's testimony foreshadowed the course of divorce litigation in the twentieth century. Already by 1877 some Americans like Thummel recognized that the marital knot could legitimately unravel due to irreconcilable differences; though as yet such personality conflicts had no formal legal standing in divorce court, Thummel's testimony suggests that the law was already being pressed by a remarkably modern conception of marriage.

This same modern conception underlay the bizarre case of Eugenia and William Duncombe in 1883, bizarre because the case was a fraud perpetrated by William against his wife. William desired a divorce, but lacking grounds against his wife, he filed a specious complaint in his wife's name against himself. His legal partner in deception was lawyer

J. K. Finley, a barrister with the scruples of a riverboat gambler. In a letter to Finley, Duncombe outlined his legal dilemma succinctly: "I am confident she would bitterly oppose me in a trial and never allow a separation for she had had a good time of it as my wife." The unemployed Duncombe even mentioned his wife's affection for him: "I think she thinks considerable of me and I have no reason to doubt her virtues." Still, William wanted out, even if he had to commit fraud: "We have been married three years and I have no particular fault to find with her but the marriage is uncongenial to me and I am going to be free. We never had any serious quarrels, only such petty disputes as everyone has daily."[108] A harmonious home life and an affectionate wife were not enough, and the missing something—love, romance, excitement—drove Duncombe to deceit. The ruse, however, failed; the judge dismissed the fraudulent complaint, and Duncombe was again faced with an "uncongenial" marriage.

If Duncombe only hinted at the missing element in his marriage, Edwin Parker could not have been more graphic. Two personal letters in the divorce evidence—one to the judge and one to Parker's wife—provide a glimpse of his private sentiments. The first letter, written to the judge soon after his wife filed her complaint, consisted of a lament, an appeal, and a response to her accusations of cruelty. The unemployed schoolteacher first defended himself: "Very early in our married life she soured on me because I was not perfect. She has threatened to leave me because of differences with her in opinion on some trivial matter. While she possesses many excellent qualities, she is vindictive in disposition and cynical in nature." Elaborating on her disposition, Edwin wrote: "She has treated me with great coldness during the last few months we were together. She has had pleasant words for other men and cross words for me. It has been a source of great unhappiness to me." Parker described himself as the reconciler: "Oh: How many times I have asked her to make new resolutions with me that we would do all we could do to make each other happy." Warming to the task, Parker outlined why he could never treat her cruelly: "The first [reason] is; that my whole heart is bound up in her. My life is blighted without her." Then, "I do love her dearly and my daily prayer to God is that she may see things in their true light, and that through these blinding tears we may see our way ere long." He concluded with a melancholy appeal to the judge's sense of pathos: "I will not bore you farther [*sic*]. If you as judge will use your high office to cement instead of sunder the sacred ties which bind us together, you would confer a lasting favor upon a wronged and almost heart broken man."[109]

But the judge was unmoved, and several months later Edwin

revealed the measure of his affection when he recognized that his wife's allegations of cruelty and non-support would stand. In a December 1882 letter to his wife, he lamented that both he and her first husband, who now lies in "a headless grave," both "enjoyed the rich blessings of unrequited love." Then, in a bittersweet passage, he reaffirmed his devotion and love while trying to salvage his honor and self-respect: "I could love you to day [*sic*] as much as ever, but despise the dishonorable course you have taken. Gladly would I become your helper and long after sharing my last dollar with you if necessary should you display penitence for your cruelty and ask forgiveness, but until then I am only too glad to be rid of you."[110] Parker's brave words surely belied his true feelings. As he surveyed the wreckage of his marriage, he sadly realized that the emotionally charged companionate family had its sorrows as well as its joys.

# 7

## *Parents and Children in Nineteenth-Century California*

If any one aspect of nineteenth-century family life signaled the arrival of the modern family, it was the heightened emphasis placed on parenthood and childhood. The change had begun in the previous century, but the nineteenth century was decisive, for it was then that a fundamental rethinking of the relationship between parents and children occurred. Nineteenth-century moralists underscored not the child's innate depravity but his malleability; character was not inborn but rather molded and shaped by parents; bringing the child to God became less important than bringing him to a proper maturity. These ideological recastings were reflected in the increasingly important role children played in divorce suits. Whereas eighteenth-century divorce petitions scarcely mentioned children, petitioners from the nineteenth century exhibited a high degree of self-consciousness about children, especially about establishing a proper moral environment for children. Husbands and wives fought bitter custody battles as each tried to show why he or she was more capable of providing the love, affection, and moral guidance so necessary to a proper modern childhood. Moreover, the law recognized the special status of children and tried to award custody to the parent most likely to provide the child with needed loving care.

The rising emotional significance of children began sometime in the mid-eighteenth century and was a part of the emergence of the companionate family discussed earlier. But prior to the mid-eighteenth century, children were not the objects of such affection. With perhaps the exception of the children of the wealthy—who were, according to Philip Greven, reared in an atmosphere of genteel indulgence—most children received little special love, affection, or attention.[1] This is not to say that children were "miniature adults" and that seventeenth-century colonists recognized no differences between adults and children. As David Stannard and Ross Beales have demonstrated, Puritan journals, autobiographies, and histories clearly differentiated children from adults. Seventeenth-century writers often spoke of the "ages of man," noting that humans passed through stages from infancy and childhood, to youth, to middle age, and finally to old age. Religious practices reflected cognizance of such age divisions. In seventeenth-century Massachusetts, children were forbidden to take communion due to their lack of knowledge of scripture, and churches examined the children of the newly saved to see whether they were to be baptized on the strength of their own faith or that of their parents. Political and legal rights also exhibited awareness of the difference between adults and children: in Plymouth, Massachusetts, the revised laws of 1671 made twenty-one the earliest age for freemanship, and in seventeenth-century Massachusetts, the age of discretion in slander suits was fourteen.[2]

The political, religious, and legal prerogatives extended to seventeenth-century children reveal a recognition of childhood as a distinct stage of life, but they shed little light on the nature of affective relations between parents and children. The best evidence that does exist in this regard is concentrated among literate middle- and upper-class New England colonists who either saw their children as depraved vipers or, if their religious temperament was more moderate, as innocents in need of careful nurture. In short, there was no universally accepted view of children: some saw them as innocents, some as corrupt; some believed they should be repressed, some were more lax.[3] Among the more rigid, curbing willfulness engendered by innate depravity lay at the core of child rearing, and to this end, evangelical families were authoritarian and repressive in their child rearing. Obedience and submission were the only acceptable responses by children to parental authority—authority that was unlimited and incontrovertible—and parents used this authority to wage war on their children's will, a war which could end, in Philip Greven's words, "only with total victory by the parents and unconditional surrender by the child."[4] This battle against the will, to follow Greven, appeared again in later life, as evangelicals, hoping for spiritual rebirth, waged war on their own wills in an effort to reject their very selves. Such debasement of the self, in the minds of evangelicals, necessarily preceded salvation.[5]

Yet such repressive and authoritarian child rearing did not preclude love and affection between evangelicals and their children. If the belief in infant depravity was incompatible with the sentimental and romantic image of children that developed in the nineteenth century, Puritan journals, nonetheless, were filled with deep-seated affection for children.[6] This affection, to be sure, was mixed with fear and distrust, and it is just this ambivalence, this uncertainty whether the infant was an "embryo-angel" or an "infant fiend" that separated the seventeenth-century Puritan from the nineteenth-century child nurturer.[7] Evangelicals, although preoccupied with infant depravity and ultimate salvation, still responded to their infants with pleasure and appreciation. Cotton Mather, for example, believed in the sinfulness of infants and small children, yet filled his journal with loving references to his "comely infant," his "lovely Son," and assumed that his unbaptized deceased child was heaven-bound.[8]

Although evangelicals dominated the intellectual life of the seventeenth century, there were others of more moderate religious views who exhibited none of the fierce ambivalance toward children that characterized the evangelical perspective. For these colonists, human nature was sinful but not totally corrupt, and hence children, though in need of guidance and vulnerable to sin, were not the depraved, fearful creatures that gripped the evangelical mind. Instead of focusing on the depravity of the self and the evil of human nature, these religious moderates "felt confident that human nature contained much good and promise as well. Their emphasis," wrote Greven, "was upon the frailties and contrarities of human nature, rather than upon total depravity."[9] This more generous view of human nature accorded individuals a degree of influence over their own salvation, for in the view of moderates, conversion was not a dramatic crisis but a gradual process guided by reason and free will.[10]

The responsibility of these moderate parents—who welcomed their infants with love and affection and assumed they were born innocent—lay in properly shaping the child's will in an environment suffused with love and piety. More sanguine than their evangelical counterparts, colonial moderates saw the child's will as malleable and pliable, in need of shaping and bending but not breaking. Child rearing was a process of nurture and growth, not a battle between unlimited parental power and the corrupted willfulness of children. Obedience to parents was important, even crucial, but it was to be voluntary rather than forced. Overall, moderates tried to strike a balance between their intense love for their children and the necessary authority over and distance from their children required to produce the desired sense of duty and respect so central to proper family relations.[11]

Taken together, the evidence on seventeenth-century children is sketchy, concentrated among the literate and the upper class, and somewhat ambiguous. Greven's findings—the most thorough study of parent–child relations—suggest that the evangelical temperament predominated. While he ably documented the evangelical approach to child rearing in the seventeenth century, his vein of evidence documenting the moderate perspective was considerably less rich. In fact, the moderate approach appears to be far more characteristic of the eighteenth century, a finding in keeping with other evidence that will be discussed later in this chapter.

Certainly demographic data on seventeenth-century parental authority suggests that paternal domination of children was central to early American family relations. Greven's earlier important study of Andover, Massachusetts, demonstrated how fathers used their land to keep even their adult sons in a state of semidependence. Long after their sons reached adulthood, seventeenth-century fathers still refused to grant them the property necessary to establish an independent household, thus making it impossible for these sons to marry until their middle to late twenties. Fathers went even further than this: the majority refused to relinquish formal title even after their sons married and settled on family lands. In so doing, they maintained considerable control until death finally released the patriarchal grip from their sons' futures.[12] Not until the mid-eighteenth century did Greven find a generalized reduction of paternal control and a willingness by fathers to recognize the autonomy and independence of sons, a change in keeping with Daniel Scott Smith's data on New England marriage patterns. Smith found that seventeenth-century (and early- to middle-eighteenth century) parents exercised considerable power over their children's mate selection and age of marriage but that this power waned in the late eighteenth and nineteenth centuries. He concluded that traditional parental authority collapsed in the middle and late eighteenth century and that the kind of control exercised by seventeenth-century parents was no longer viable as marriage shifted from a parental-run system to a participant-run system. What this meant, in short, was the recognition of the happiness and autonomy of the children at the expense of the power of the parents.[13]

By the mid-eighteenth century, the status of children was less ambiguous, and while evangelicals still talked of crushing wills, more and more people—at least among the literate and genteel—believed in the innocence of children, indulged them, and expressed the profoundest grief at their deaths. Who cannot but feel, for example, the grief of James Kent, who lost his eighteen-month-old daughter in 1793? Writing six years after her death, Kent lamented, "[N]o Event in my Life had ever taught me the genuine agonies of Grief. My whole Soul seemed to be buried in my child."[14] But if eighteenth-century parents grieved for their lost children, they celebrated their living ones. Mary Beth Norton found late-eighteenth-century mothers intently committed to breast-feeding and indulgent in their weaning practices; moreover, both parents delighted in their children's antics and freely expressed intense affection for their offspring. A measure of paternal affection is found in the letters of fathers, absent on business, who hungered for information on the doings of their sons and daughters. And although moralists still directed most child rearing literature at fathers, late-eighteenth-century mothers from middling and upper-class backgrounds, Norton concluded, "devoted a great deal of thought to the problems and pleasures of raising children."[15] After the Revolution, child rearing increasingly became the province of mothers, who, entrusted with instructing their children in the virtues appropriate to a republic, tried to follow moralists' advice to reason with children, to teach by example, and to avoid acting tyrannically.[16]

Other evidence supports Norton's contention that at least among the literate upper class, eighteenth-century parent–child relations exhibited a level of affection and closeness largely absent from seventeenth-century bonds. Among the northern eighteenth-century gentry, especially in the years after 1750, some families indulged their children to a degree that would have shocked seventeenth-century parents. Characterized by intimacy and domesticity, these genteel families were "intensely affectionate. . . . The family circle," Greven explained, "was felt to be the most secure place in the entire world—happy, embracing, forgiving, reliable, and free from selfishness." In these upper-class homes, children were loved and adored, "a source of constant delight and pleasure to parents, whose affection for their offspring knew no bounds."[17] The family bonds within wealthy planter homes in the Chesapeake shared the intimacy characteristic of upper-class homes in New England and the Middle Colonies. Daniel Blake Smith found planter families in the years after 1750 delighting in the innocence and playfulness of their children. Whether charmed by their offsprings' prattle or the liveliness of their "little Monkies," these parents exhibited none of the anxiety and ambivalence so common to parents of the previous century. Instead, they wrote and spoke affectionately of their children, bemoaned separation from them, applauded their motor and verbal accomplishments, even participated with gusto in their children's play, and tried to increase their children's sense of personal autonomy. Nor were parents alone in expressing affection for children or in fostering a relatively permissive environment: aunts, uncles, and grandparents wrote affectionately and with pride of their young kin.[18]

As this evidence makes clear, some eighteenth century parents began to exhibit attitudes and behavior that appear remarkably modern. In many homes, parents cherished, at times even indulged, their children and accorded them a degree of autonomy completely at odds with the sentiments of seventeenth-century will smashers. Yet, too much should not be made of this evidence: it comes predominately from upper-class, highly literate families, and represents—as the California data will demonstrate—not generalized eighteenth-century attitudes but rather the shape of things to come. For it is the nineteenth century that witnesses the widespread emergence of modern conceptions of childhood and child rearing. Whereas the evidence of such attitudes was substantial but hardly overwhelming in the eighteenth century, the following century offers an avalanche of data revealing the essential modernity of nineteenth-century attitudes toward children. These modern attitudes, in turn, give children a centrality to nineteenth-century divorce suits wholly lacking in suits from the previous century, suggesting that if upper-class eighteenth-century families evinced great concern for their children, neither the average family involved in eighteenth-century divorce suits (as later evidence will demonstrate) nor the law as yet gave recognition to children's special needs. Such attention would come only in the nineteenth century.

By the 1830s and 1840s, the essential features of the modern child-centered family had emerged: the belief in children's innate depravity had been replaced by one emphasizing childhood innocence and malleability; coercion, strict parental authority, and corporal punishment had given way to permissiveness, appeals to conscience, and a sparing of the rod; parental coolness had yielded to affectionate devotion and a commitment by fathers and mothers to provide a loving, supportive atmosphere for their offspring.[19] These changes, we should note, were not isolated phenomena but an essential part of the emergence of the modern family. Just as husband–wife relations became more equal and affectionate in the years following the Revolution, so, too, did those of parents and children. It is the simultaneous development of these two processes that created what we call the modern or companionate family.

Nothing more clearly reveals the new status of the child than the rejection of the doctrine of innate depravity. In the eighteenth-century, the more liberally inclined already voiced optimism about the innate qualities of children, but in the nineteenth century the belief became far more widespread. Influential clergy and lay moralists now assumed that children were born innocent but might gradually become corrupt; therefore, the task of parents was to prevent this declension by creating a protective atmosphere in which innocence and right values could survive.[20] Although the belief in the innate depravity of children did not disappear overnight, its acceptance steadily eroded until by the 1850s some popular writers rejected the idea that any such inborn depravity limited the child's potential. By the 1870s, explains Bernard Wishy, "the victory of the more optimistic nurture ideas of the two previous generations was almost completely assured," and by 1900, infant depravity was virtually abandoned as a theory.[21]

Rejecting the belief in innate sinfulness placed new demands on parents, for if children were not naturally sinful but might become so, and if children's character was malleable rather than fixed, then parents needed to shape carefully their children's development; moreover, the acceptance of Enlightenment psychology underscored the crucial importance of the early years in character formation. How parents performed in these years, how they sculpted their child's early personality, would be decisive.[22] And the method of this task also changed. No longer were parents to rely on formal precepts and psychological coercion, much less corporal punishment, to guide their children and exact obedience; instead, "affectionate persuasion addressed to the understanding, the conscience, and the heart," instructed Heman Humphrey in *Domestic Education* in 1840, "is the grand instrument to be employed in family government." Love and gentleness, mixed with shaming and guilt manipulation, replaced physical punishment. If reared properly, the child—having internalized proper standards—would in essence be self-guided: conscience, not any fear of physical punishment, would be the moral gyroscope.[23]

These assumptions meant that parenthood itself, especially motherhood, received increasing attention from moralists. The responsibility for rearing children, for instilling in them a "self-activating, self-regulating, all purpose inner control" could no longer be left to chance or to the hands of uniformed parents. Consequently, after 1820 a spate of tracts and pamphlets appeared advising parents on child rearing, in particular on the ways and means of proper motherhood.[24] Mid-eighteenth-century advisers had addressed child-rearing literature to fathers, but in the next century the duties of motherhood increasingly preoccupied moralists. While some writers in the immediate post-Revolutionary-War period underscored mothers' responsibilities to the republic—for it was they who would nurture the next generation of citizens—in the next century the primacy of mothers' role in child rearing was established.[25] This new focus on motherhood went hand in hand with the rise of domesticity and the elevation of women's status generally. It was also linked to the new status of children, a point made by Carl Degler, who noted why mothers benefited from this development: "Exalting the child went hand in hand with exalting the domestic role of women; each reinforced the other while together they raised domesticity within the family to a new and higher level of respectability."[26]

Although less optimistic than Degler about the consequences of this elevation of domesticity and motherhood to women's lives, Nancy Cott also noted the heightened significance of motherhood, the increasing attention paid to children, and the special function of the home in an increasingly unstable society. Given the perception of disorder outside the home, nineteenth-century writers called on mothers to establish a sanctuary within its walls, a place where children would be nurtured and instructed in proper moral values, a task whose ultimate purpose was the stabilizing of society through the regeneration of moral character. The function of the home, Cott concluded, was ultimately in society: "It was to fit men to pursue their worldly aims in a regulated way."[27]

The increasing concern with children, the home, and motherhood meant that no part of child rearing was unworthy of attention: proper clothing, diet, play, and exercise all promoted virtue and sound character. Clothes were to be simple and promote freedom of movement, thereby fostering a straightness of character unobtainable by children overdressed in gaudy frills and showy caps and bonnets. Child nurturers also recommended a republican simplicity in diet: cakes, candies, and spices were to yield to milk, bread, and vegetables, foods that would promote active exercise and vigorous play. Thus, the malleability of children's character—in fact, the very process of character building—invested mundane tasks with new meaning. Bernard Wishy concluded his analysis of these trends by noting that all of "these new notions about food, clothing, and play meant that the mother could let no detail of general household management escape her eyes."[28]

Mid- to late-nineteenth-century child nurturers continued these antebellum trends. After the Civil War, the notion of innate depravity was in full retreat, replaced by an even stronger faith in the rationality and tractability of children. Support for corporal punishment continued to wane as moralists urged parents to use reason, affection, and persuasion instead. By the 1870s and 1880s, child-study clubs formed, and by the 1890s such clubs tried to make sense of a growing body of scientific expertise purporting to explain the relations among evolution, heredity, environment, and child development. Other child rearing literature was less intellectually weighty but simply offered advice on avoiding excessive restraint, providing children adequate freedom to roam, experiment, and play, recognizing youngsters' limitations, and building character by example, not by formal precept.[29]

Other data confirm the child-centered nature of the nineteenth-century family. If the genteel indulged their children in the eighteenth century, many common nineteenth-century parents apparently did so, at least in the eyes of European travelers, who expressed surprise at the permissiveness of American parents. While Tocqueville kept his observations on a high theoretical plane—noting that democratic governments brought less authoritarian, more intimate, tender, and affectionate relations between fathers and sons—other foreign observers were not so charitable and expressed shock and dismay at the lack of authority exercised by American parents.[30] British travelers repeatedly deplored Americans' unwillingness to discipline their children, their lamentable tendency to indulge and spoil their offspring, and worst of all, their incomprehensible lack of guilt over the way their children turned out. Many were of the opinion that Americans were rearing a nation of brats. Even those who praised the children and approved of the intimacy, equality, and companionship of the American family, described the children in terms familiar to those used by critics: saucy, self-reliant, arrogant, wild, independent, and irreverent.[31]

This indulgent and permissive approach to child rearing led David Rothman to an intriguing thesis on the origins of child-care institutions that blossomed in the 1830s and 1840s. Concerned about the general instability of American life—its excessive commercial activity, extreme democracy, social libertarianism, and general lack of cohesion—child reformers sought to rehabilitate youthful orphans, vagrants, and incorrigibles, and at the same time promote social stability and establish a model of proper family government; furthermore, although the reformers spoke of creating a family environment within the asylums, what they in fact created were prison-like institutions that placed a premium on order, silence, obedience, control, and discipline. Rather than a reflection of the antebellum family, Rothman speculated that the asylums were a rebuke to the permissive family and the disorder such permissiveness helped to produce. In the minds of those who established these military-like institutions, "the family," explained Rothman, "had to emulate the asylum as constituted—that is, put a greater premium on order, discipline, and obedience, not on domestic affections, pampering the child, or indulging his every whim." Only in this manner would social stability be encouraged.[32]

This institutional response to permissive and indulgent child rearing suggests the child-centered quality of the antebellum home. Actual expressions of affection offer more direct evidence on the high status of the nineteenth-century child. Julie Roy Jeffrey found that women settlers in the West filled their letters to Eastern friends with details about their children: no accomplishment was too small to warrant recognition.[33] Fathers, too, freely expressed affection for their children. Charles Jones, a Georgia planter, wrote his thirty-year-old son a birthday greeting in 1861 and described his feelings thirty years earlier: "I was as conscious of the flowing of a new affection through my soul . . . as I would have been of a warm stream flowing over the most sensitive part of my person."[34] Mother–daughter relations, as Carroll Smith-Rosenberg found, were particularly close. At the center of the sororal world of nineteenth-century women lay the intimacy, concern, and mutual dependence of mothers and daughters. This intimacy, fostered by the shared world of domesticity, continued throughout the lives of mothers and daughters and produced intense sadness when marriage pulled a daughter from her mother's home.[35] Lydia Maria Child, although childless herself, commiserated with a female friend whose daughter was marrying: "My sympathetic thoughts have been with you. I know people are accustomed to congratulate mothers when their daughters are married, but to me it has always seemed the severest trial that a woman can meet, except the death of her loved ones."[36] And we have already seen how some wives refused to leave their home communities when their husbands decided to head West, a hard decision that reflected the affection and intimacy at the core of the nineteenth-century family.

As all of this evidence suggests, modern attitudes about children became widespread in the nineteenth century, especially in the child-guidance literature that flourished after 1830. Changing assumptions about the nature of children and heightened respect for the role of mothers brought new attention to child rearing and increased consideration for the autonomy of each child.[37] For whatever reasons—Enlightenment psychology, the decline in family production, the separation of the work place from the home, the perception by the middle class of social chaos, or the decline in Calvinist conceptions of innate depravity—moralists conceived of childhood and parenthood in a new way that ultimately percolated down to the California hinterland and affected the lives of people from all class backgrounds. As we shall see, mid-nineteenth-century divorce court often bore sad but dramatic testament to the high status of the child in these California families.

The farmers, tradesmen, and housewives of San Mateo and Santa

Clara counties certainly did not lack for expressions of the new sentiments about childhood and the new obligations for parents. The small-town newspapers were full of advice that presupposed a conception of childhood innocence. Nothing produced a greater outpouring of overwrought prose than the death of an infant: "Few things," wrote the *Santa Clara Argus,* "appear so beautiful as a young child in its shroud. The little innocent face looks sublimely simple and confiding amidst the terrors of death."[38] In a memorial service, Reverend T. S. Dunn of San Jose eulogized a child's untimely death with a celestial simile: "She had disappeared like a star behind the mountains that hide the invisible from the visible world, to shine more resplendently in another hemisphere."[39]

But innocence, paradoxically, permitted corruption, and while the Puritan child was born corrupt, the nineteenth-century child might become so. Once started on the downward path, the descent was swift and irreversible: "So there is in youth a beauty and purity of character which, when once touched and defiled, can never be restored."[40] Only parents could provide the protective shell against corruption, and the *San Jose Daily Mercury* warned parents to combat the defilers of innocence: "Every incentive to virtue, every safeguard against temptation should daily, by the skill of parental affection, be laid, like a network, round the life of the child."[41] Part of the protective cocoon came, according to the *Weekly Argus,* from the creation of a proper domestic environment: "Fathers and Mothers look out for your boys when the shadows of evening have gathered around you. Where are they then? Are they at home, at the pleasant, social fireside, or are they running in the streets?" The article then challenged parents to save their sons from temptation: "If you would save them from vulgarity, save them from ruin; see to it that night finds them at home. Let parents solemnly ponder this matter, and do all they can to make home attractive to the children, so attractive that boys will prefer it to roaming in the streets."[42]

Proper home life required the proper ambience—enough discipline but none too severe. County newspapers instructed parents to treat their children with respect and love, to avoid callousness and severity, and to recognize their children as sensitive innocents in need of affectionate guidance. An article in the *Weekly Argus* fairly swelled with romantic sentiment: "Never speak angrily or harshly, but mildly, kindly, and, when needed, firmly—no more. By all means arrange it so that the last words between you and your children at bed-time, especially the younger ones, shall be words of unmixed affection."[43] Bedtime tranquility concerned other moralists as well, in part because the image of the sleeping child protected by loving parents captured the perfect combination of childhood innocence and parental solicitude: "Let parents make every possible effort to get their children to go to sleep in a pleasant humor. Never scold or give lectures, or in any way wound a child's feelings as it goes to bed."[44]

The key to exemplary parenthood lay not in suppressing the child's will, not in choking off signs of personal autonomy, but in shaping the child's character, in recognizing that the child, born innocent, needed parental love and advice. The *San Jose Daily Mercury* hoped for a new parental resolution: "To the fathers and mothers of California, the sacred duty of training up their children in the way they should go, by example, precept and patient love, should be considered and resolved upon anew."[45] A measure of permissiveness replaced suppression of the will, as in this advice from the *Weekly Argus* that recognized the legitimacy of a child's pursuit of pleasure: "Never compel a child to sit still, nor interfere with its enjoyments, so long as it is not injurious to person or property, nor against good morals."[46] And generations of Calvinist fathers received a rebuke for their severity: "Never threaten a child: it is cruel, unjust, and dangerous."[47] The *San Jose Daily Mercury* contrasted the apparent latitude of the 1880s with the discipline of an earlier period by noting former restrictions on children's freedoms: "The rule in most houses was for the children to stand up to eat. The biggest pieces of pie went to father and mother, and the children were not allowed to sit up until 10 o'clock at night, or to argue a question after the head of the family had decided it."[48]

The question remains whether Californians took this advice to heart, whether they threw a blanket of domestic warmth and affection around their children, thought of them as innocents, and had a high degree of self-consciousness about the relationship between parents and children. The answer from the divorce records in each case is affirmative. Child-rearing abilities and custody disputes figured in many cases and help to document the degree of change that had occurred since the eighteenth century. Although some upper-class families in the previous century were affectionate and attentive toward their children, eighteenth-century divorce documents suggest that such child-centeredness was the exception. In a study of eighteenth-century Massachusetts divorce cases, Nancy Cott found little mention of children: only one-third of 229 divorce petitions even mentioned children, and, more important, only "two petitioners explicitly requested to keep their children."[49] Moreover, the documents did not routinely give the number of children in the family and their sex was never mentioned. To Cott, the eighteenth-century divorce records "suggested that parents did not consider their children's well-being of overriding importance."[50] This general inattention to children supported Ariès' theory that premodern conceptions of children lacked the sentiment, affection, emotion, and innocence characteristic of modern attitudes. Cott concluded her analysis by noting that "together with the minimal concern for children in the divorce records, and the tendency of even the righteous petitioners to view children as economic quantities, they suggest that an unsentimental, instrumental approach to children prevailed within families."[51]

The nineteenth-century California data differed dramatically from the earlier Massachusetts evidence. Among all cases, 51.6 percent mentioned children, 25.5 percent specifically stated that there were no children, and only 22.7 percent made no mention of them whatsoever. In marked contrast to the eighteenth-century data, cases with children not only always mentioned the number of children but gave their names and ages as well. But figures on custody requests provide more telling evidence of the importance of children. Table 26 compares custody requests and custody grants for male and female plaintiffs. In addition, 19 male defendants requested custody of their children and 24 female defendants did so. These 43 requests by defendants plus the 162 requests by male and female plaintiffs totaled 205 petitions for custody, a figure that stands in dramatic contrast to the 2 requests found in eighteenth-century Massachusetts records.

*Table 26.* Custody Requests and Grants by Male and Female Plaintiffs

| | Custody Requested | | Custody Granted | |
|---|---|---|---|---|
| | % | (N) | % | (N) |
| Male Plaintiffs | 70 | (30/43) | 37 | (10/27) |
| Female Plaintiffs | 95 | (132/137) | 91 | (83/91) |

The other point of interest of Table 26 is the significant difference between male and female success rates; female petitioners received custody in 91 percent of their suits, men in just 37 percent. The disparity stemmed from the comparative success of defendants in gaining custody. Only one male defendant but ten female defendants received custody of the children, a difference surely attributable to the nineteenth century's apotheosis of motherhood.[52] The judge who in the morning paper read the lines,

> I know not what the Angels hear,
> In Mansions's in the skies
> But there is not a sound on earth
> Like mother's gentle voice,[53]

was very likely to give wives the benefit of the doubt in custody disputes.

Moreover, legal interpretations bolstered women's claims to custody and simultaneously codified the new status of the child. An 1860 appellate case in the California Supreme Court was especially important. After a lengthy discussion on the father's ultimate control over the children, the court argued that this "natural right" ended when divorce occurred; the mother's right to custody then equalled that of the father's, and custody depended on the fault of the parties involved. Even more significantly, the court (quoting from Joel Prentiss Bishop's mid-nineteenth-century law commentaries) contended that the overriding factor in custody disputes was the well-being of the child:

> Therefore, the good of the child should be the leading consideration; and this, it may be observed, will rarely require that he be placed beyond the control of both parents; for care that is prompted by the paternal instinct, and responded to by filial affection, is the most valuable of all.

Using the "best interests" argument as its guide, the court overturned the lower court's custody decision, granted custody to the mother, and noted the need for regular parental care and guidance: "That a child of the tender age of this could be better cared for by the mother, with whom she could be almost constantly, than the father, whose necessary avocations would withdraw him, in a great measure, from personal superintendence and care of her, is plain enough."[54] By 1892, the court still claimed discretion over custody grants, but now mothers were defined as the natural guardians because they best suited the special needs of the child: "Although a mother is naturally and presumptively entitled to the custody of minor children, especially girls of tender age, it is for the trial court to say upon all the evidence, in divorce, whether she is in fact more worthy of their custody than the father."[55]

In addition to custody requests and legal interpretations, evidence from individual divorce cases supports the argument that the nineteenth-century child gained new status. This fact is no more evident than in statements attesting to the success or failure of mothers and fathers. Through examining both the praise and condemnation of parents, we gain a sense of the importance of parenthood and childhood in nineteenth-century America. By way of emphasizing the significance of this evidence, it will be recalled that the divorce records from eighteenth-century Massachusetts contained almost nothing on children or child rearing, certainly nothing like the material that follows.

*Mothers and Children*

Women's natural delicacy and sympathy, so argued moralists, made them ideally suited for child rearing, and women in rural California made the same claim. In asking the court for custody, lawyers drafted complaints averring that wives provided the necessary guidance for children. The complaints also revealed allegiance to an idealized vision of childhood innocence; for example, in 1869 Frances Springett, the wife of a San Jose harness maker, requested custody of her three children, all under the age of six. Her complaint claimed that if the children remained with her husband, they would "sustain great injury in the formation of their character, habits, manners, and especially their temper"; moreover, given their "tender age," they "absolutely required the attention and nursing care of a mother."[56] Nellie Rathburn's answer to her husband's complaint made much the same claim; it, too, stated that the special needs of her child—needs usually unrecognized a century before—required motherly solicitude. Not only did her husband threaten to place their eight-year-old son with another family, he also forced his wife to work as a cook "at the houses of strangers without the comfort and enjoyment of the society of her child and without the opportunity of bestowing upon her said child the care and attention which his delicate health and tender years required." The document also maintained that the boy's feeble health and life-threatening back spasms "required that care and tender watching which a mother can best bestow."[57] Likewise, Ellen King, a fruit canner's wife, claimed that the inability to see her children caused her "much mental anguish from the separation" and that they were "all young and required the watchful care of a mother."[58]

Other evidence also highlighted mothers' natural abilities in child rearing. While fathers' complaints never argued that men were uniquely suited to raise children—on the contrary, male requests for custody usually focused on wives' failures as nurturers—women's custody requests often did so. Hannah Obberson, the wife of a day laborer, contended that her children were of "tender years and required the constant care of the plaintiff"; the custody request of Susan Gilbert claimed that her son Lorenzo "needs and ought to have the care and attention of a mother"; and Mary Flynn, a blacksmith's wife, argued that she "always cared for and tenderly nursed and protected all of said children."[59] Given these special abilities, the court occasionally granted custody to the wife even if she were the guilty party. Although Albert Hammond successfully charged his wife with adultery, the court rejected his custody request and awarded the child to his wife, apparently because the child was just ten months old. Hence, the needs of the child could even outweigh the moral turpitude of the mother.[60]

The praise of motherhood included more than recognizing innate aptitudes for nurture and nursing. The duties of motherhood also comprised part of the purposeful, instrumental conception of womanhood discussed earlier. Rearing children—molding their character for future service to the republic—required abilities that neighbors and friends recognized as admirable. When the referee asked Mrs. E. E. Staples if Lorenzo Milliken left his wife with good reason, she quickly came to Mrs. Milliken's defense: "He did not. She was a good, kind, affectionate, and industrious wife; worked hard and took care of her children."[61] Friends of Polly Haun gave Mrs. Haun similar praise in her 1866 suit, particularly her organization of the family's finances after her husband left her. A friend described how she managed to support her seven children: "She has provided the children who were old enough to work with places to work and she has kept the younger children with her and worked for their and her own support ever since defendant left her in December, 1863." He added that Polly, a domestic, raised a mutually supportive family: "Mrs. Haun has worked to support the small children and the older children have worked to support themselves and the smaller children."[62]

Mothers defended themselves in similar terms and described how they met the needs of their children; in so doing, they revealed both their self-consciousness about the duties of motherhood and their recognition of children's new status in the family. While Lovina Taft simply praised her own general resourcefulness—"I raised and supported my children to manhood and womanhood without any aid from him"—a woman named Apphia Milliken emphasized that her three children "have been raised and educated through and by my labor and the help of my friends."[63] Similarly, Susan Battey, a laundress, claimed that she taught her five-year-old son English and sent him to Sunday School, and Nellie Jones, a seamstress, testified that she worked ten to fourteen hours per day in order to support her family and educate her two children.[64] Annie Zander, upset that her daughter was in a Catholic school, even assured the court that she would educate her daughter in prestigious company. If the court would grant her custody, she would have the child tutored under a "private lady teacher, with the grandchildren of the late Professor John LeConte, and the child of Professor Perry."[65]

Evidence of affection between mothers and children supports the argument that children contributed significantly to the high emotional level of the nineteenth-century family. The sentiments of Abigail Bennett, a farmer's wife, indicate the depth of this attachment. When her husband tried to make her admit committing adultery—an admission she steadfastly refused to make—Abigail insisted on her claim to the children: "William, if it is property you want, take it, but my children I must have." Her refusal came not just because the charges were false, but also because such an admission would destroy her family: "I told him that was something I wouldn't do. I wouldn't have my little family broken up."[66] Nor was affection expected to be a one-way path; people recognized and tried to consider the feelings of children for parents, a measure of the new concern for children. Witnesses for Ellen King claimed that a loving, reciprocal bond existed between mother and children. When Dr. T. C. Coxhead gave an affidavit on behalf of Ellen, he underscored the mutuality of the love between Mrs. King and her children: "I have no hesitancy in saying that she is a devoted, careful, affectionate mother, very warmly attached to her children and that the affection of the children for her is equally great." He added that her devotion had been especially strong "when the three younger children all had severe attacks of diptheria."[67] Other people supported Coxhead and highlighted both Ellen's qualities as a mother and the strong bond between the children and their mother. John Swenarton's affidavit described Mrs. King as "a kind, affectionate, and good mother" who was "devoted to her children who in turn manifest great affection for her." Swenarton's wife added similar sentiments: "From all I have seen and know about Mrs. King, she is an affectionate, dutiful mother, fit and proper in every way to have the custody of her children who are devotedly attached to her." And W. M. Searby, a druggist, praised Ellen for her attachment to her children and believed that the children felt the same about her: "as far as I can judge, the children are very much attached to her."[68]

The affection between parents and children and the malleable character of children in general needed a special place to develop properly, a place pervaded by wholesomeness and right-minded values. Newspaper advisers spoke of "the dear sanctuary of home," of "a calm house," and of a place where one might "keep pure and make sacred" the country's traditions and values.[69] In contrast to the tumult of premodern domestic life, home now meant quiet, calm, order, and privacy. No longer would children socialize with people of all ages and classes; instead, parents sought to isolate children from the hubbub—and occasional ribaldry—of daily life. If the home environment was not proper, parents tried to protect the newly recognized sensibilities of their children, a step taken by Mary Rohrer in 1874.

When Fred and Mary Rohrer temporarily separated in 1871, he and his twelve-year-old daughter, Nellie, moved to Summit Springs, a town in the coastal mountains of the San Francisco peninsula. Soon after, Mrs. Rohrer decided to join her husband and daughter, but she quickly found the rough lumbering town offensive and left within a couple of weeks. She also tried to remove her daughter from what she considered the town's debauchery. In Mary's eyes, what Summit Springs lacked most was a moral environment appropriate for the innocence of girlhood. The carousing lumbermen made the town "totally unfit" for a child of Nellie's sex and tender years, and she would likely become morally stunted if she continued to witness the crudeness and vulgarity of woodchoppers and lumbermen. Nellie's mother also saw sexual dangers on all fronts—the young girl had already gone "from Summit Springs to Petaluma under the sole charge of a boy of sixteen and a man not related to her"; and if this were not enough, her father, a store and tavern keeper, "dresses her up in boys' clothes and has her dance for his drunken guests in his barroom—for money."[70]

Mary Rohrer acted to save the virtue of her daughter by seeking help from people who shared her views about the proper moral environment for children. George Webb, a longtime resident of Summit Springs, pictured his hometown as no place for an innocent young girl. Webb claimed he had seen Nellie dancing in the bar, the only girl amidst lumbermen and laborers, and he believed Nellie's father neglected his daughter's moral development.[71] A relative of Nellie's felt the same way. Annie Wood had visited the child in Summit Springs, and the town's lack of "schools and society" troubled her; moreover, Nellie's father did not instill in his daughter a proper sense of discipline. According to Wood, Nellie "runs wild around there and does pretty much as she pleases."[72] Another opinion came from one Minnie Hogan, Summit Spring's former schoolteacher, who added her professional opinion by bemoaning the town's lack of civility and decorum. Offended by the obscenities "that filled the night air," she had left after a couple of months; moreover, she thought it imperative that Nellie leave Summit Springs before she was totally corrupted. Like Mrs. Rohrer, the potential sexual perils and the general raucousness of the town troubled Hogan's mind; she noted that Nellie

> was allowed by her father to go off in the company of men—that on one occasion she went with one Charley Brackett to Formeret's Mill, a distance of five or six miles through the redwoods, with no houses on the road—and Brackett was noisy and boisterous and fired pistols from the buggy.[73]

The court's decision on Nellie's future illustrated the law's concern for the girl's moral development. Although the judge rejected Mary Rohrer's custody request—the court found her guilty of desertion in 1875—he did rule that the child could not remain in Summit Springs. Apparently convinced that the rough, predominately male community destroyed childhood innocence, Judge Sharpstein ordered Nellie placed in San Francisco's Notre Dame Academy, where she would find sufficient examples of exemplary womanhood. He also granted both parents visiting privileges and ruled that the girl was not to be removed from the school unless so ordered by the court.[74]

The rowdy, uncivilized quality of Summit Springs contrasted dramatically with cosmopolitan San Francisco, but urban life had its own dangers, at least to Annie Zander, who tried to remove her daughter from that city. Again, a proper moral environment for the child became the central issue, and again the mother claimed that her child's corruptible innocence demanded removal to a more appropriate atmosphere. This time the problem was not woodchoppers but hotel life. When William and Annie Zander separated in 1889, they agreed that he would take the daughter and she the son, but soon after, her son died, and in 1893, Annie tried to gain custody of her daughter Mattie. What the child needed, claimed Mrs. Zander, was a real home, not the succession of hotels her husband had managed since their separation: "He has resided at such hotels and has never been able to surround said minor child with the comforts or moral influences or advantages of a home." The child also lacked motherly protection: "Hotel life, without the kind and protecting care of a mother, is not conducive to the wellfare [*sic*] of said child, said child being of tender years."[75] Furthermore, Mattie's religious training demanded attention because the girl was in a Catholic school, a situation that would "not conduce towards bringing up said child in accordance with the religion of its parents."[76]

The child, claimed Mrs. Zander, also lacked the personal attention best bestowed by a mother. When Annie went to see her child in San Francisco, she found the seven-year-old "walking on the street during the cold afternoon, without anything warm to protect her neck, and after she had just recovered from a severe illness." Due to her husband's oversight, Mrs. Zander found her daughter one week later sick in bed, "the result of that afternoon's walk without sufficient wraps."[77] Mrs. Theodore Grady supported Annie's account of finding the child on the streets, added that the young girl looked pale and thin, and "believes that hotel life will not promote the welfare of said child."[78] Warring Wilkinson, a school superintendent, also supported Mrs. Zander and claimed she was "a woman of good moral character," perfectly capable of supplying the child a good home.[79]

In defending his right to the child, William Zander claimed he supplied what his wife said he negelcted—a correct moral environment suitable for the sensibilities of a young child; more important, he revealed that care for the child was the central concern of both parents. No disagreement occurred over what the child needed; the dispute, instead, concerned who could fulfill those needs better. To support his case, William asked his own mother (the child's grandmother) to give evidence. In an affidavit, the woman stated that the child was "happy and contented" and "greatly attached" to her father; in addition, the girl received "the principles of morality and rectitude and has been under none but the best of moral influences." Mattie's grandmother also pledged her own abiding love for the child and stated she "would sacrifice everything for said child's welfare."[80] Though the ultimate disposition of the case was unclear, the evidence revealed both parents' strong concern for the moral development of their child and their conviction that proper moral training required parental solicitude and a wholesome domestic environment.

Mothers tried to be models of propriety by setting the right moral tone in the home, but when husbands slandered their wives in front of the children—particularly when they questioned their wives' sexual fidelity—they undermined women's role as moral guardians and destroyed the mutual respect between parents and children at the heart of the companionate family. This evidence also suggests that people assumed children were aware of sex, a fact in contrast to eighteenth-century evidence that revealed a cavalier disregard for children's sexual awareness.[81] By the mid-nineteenth century, the concept of childhood innocence and the glorification of motherhood could not tolerate the abuse of a man like storekeeper J. C. Koppell, who told his children that when he married their mother "she was nothing but a street walker." Mrs. Koppell complained that he made such accusations repeatedly and that they caused her great suffering.[82] In a similar vein, Antoinette Johnson claimed that while her children were present, her husband accused her of adultery with a local shopkeeper, and Mary Ann Evans stated that her husband told the three children that he had caught a venereal disease from their mother and that these charges "degraded [her] in the estimation of her children."[83]

Many other wives complained about sexual insults in front of the children. How could a mother guide her children's moral development amidst such accusations? How could she protect their innocence and maintain a "dear sanctuary" if her sexual reputation were under attack? Caroline Planer, the wife of a baker, thought she could not, so long as her husband, John, continued abusing her "by vulgar language [which] lower[ed] her in the opinion of his children by a former wife."[84] Sarah White and Mary Ann O'Connell suffered similar abuse in the presence of their children; Sarah's husband called her a "damned whoring bitch," and Thomas O'Connell let his children know that his wife was a "bitch" and a "whore."[85] The "nervous temperament" of Esther Philbrick suffered when her children heard her accused of adultery and when her husband forced one of the daughters to spy on Mrs. Philbrick while she allegedly made her "adulterous rounds."[86] Polly Haun, a poor farmer's wife, also endured the imprecations of her husband, but she finally brought her children into court to testify on her behalf. Her son Jacob drew particular attention to his father's false allegations of adultery: "He often flew into a passion and when excited is revengeful. He is of a jealous disposition and was always charging mother with allowing other men to come to the house when she should not alow [sic] them." The referee then asked the boy whether his mother had ever received male visitors improperly, and Jacob attested to his own vigilance and his awareness of sex by asserting, "No, I certainly should have known it." Jacob's fifteen-year-old sister added that her mother "always treated him [James Haun] kindly. She always tried to do the best she could for him and his family."[87]

The veneration of motherhood and children in the nineteenth century provided powerful leverage for husbands seeking a divorce. If a man could prove that his wife neglected her duties as a mother, if he could show that she failed to meet her children's needs and desires, then he could most assuredly obtain a divorce. Thus, criticisms of a mother's nurturing abilities both attest to the importance of children in the nineteenth century—no such criticisms appeared in divorce evidence from the previous century—and help define the nature of acceptable motherly behavior.[88] In 1883, for example, Carrie Gray linked her stepmother's failure as a housewife to her failure as a mother: "She was disorderly in her household, neglected her family, was quarrelsome with her neighbors, and she was heartless and irritable in her conduct toward children." Gray added details about her stepmother's child-rearing habits, especially her regrettable lack of consistency: "One day she would be very indulgent allowing them to do what they pleased, and the next day [she] would be needlessly severe and cruel." Finally, the stepdaughter excoriated Addie Gray's insensitivity to children's need for nurture, guidance, and education: "I have heard her say that children should learn to take care of themselves, and should leave school as early as ten years of age and should be put in the mills or factories to earn their own living."[89]

Other people also drew attention to a mother's insensivity or outright cruelty, and all, regardless of social class, agreed that children deserved and needed careful treatment. Frank Gilbert, a laborer, noted his wife's failure to comfort her sick son. When their young son became suddenly ill—so ill that he "required all the care and attention of a mother"—she did not remain with him but instead left for a Fourth of July celebration. In an affidavit filed after his complaint, Frank again claimed that she neglected the child's health. He added that "she was either scolding or whipping the child and was in the constant habit of saying she wished to God she had no young one." He concluded by charging that his wife "has no love or affection for said child," a statement supported by a neighbor, who accused Mrs. Gilbert of "an unmotherly manner" of child care.[90] In a different case, Eleanor Miles and William Tuers testified that their stepmother treated them in the same way, and Eleanor specifically mentioned the disrespect she incurred: "She always treated me as if I was a menial in the family." William lodged a similar grievance by noting his stepmother's impatience—"she was very quick tempered"—and the iron rule she maintained by physical intimidation: "I always had to do as she said"; otherwise, she hit him.[91]

Husbands sometimes linked their wives' failures as mothers to general moral dissipation, particularly the dissipation brought on by drink. Just as alcohol destroyed men's capacity to work, it also eradicated the refinement, nurture, and sensitivity necessary for proper mothering. In 1880, Will Frisbie criticized his wife's homemaking, especially her care of the children; excessive drink, claimed Frisbie, kept Angelina from "properly attending to her household business and duties, and particularly for the care of her children and the discharge of her duties as a wife and Mother."[92] Thomas Howard, a cook, complained that his wife sometimes went on all-night drinking binges that left their four children to "care for themselves as best they can alone," and Wesley Schuyler condemned his wife's drunkenness for the same reason: throughout 1877, Schuyler claimed his children were "repeatedly cared for by relatives and neighbors, the defendant being at such times in such a state of intoxication as to have become oblivious of her duties as a mother." Specifically, she "neglected to wash and dress her children or to provide them with suitable food when both fuel and provisions had been provided."[93] Two other women, although not charged specifically with intemperance, found themselves accused of child neglect. In 1867, carpenter John Henning claimed that his wife had run off with another man, and "regardless of the natural instincts and affections of a Mother," left behind her infant daughter, and John Kennedy alleged that his wife left him with a "young suckling baby" for an entire night.[94]

All of this evidence leaves no doubt that Americans accorded nineteenth-century childhood and motherhood a status and a spectrum of obligations not recognized in the previous century. But the apotheosis of motherhood clearly was not an unmixed blessing: while exalting women's status in the home and society, it also both relegated women to a sex-specific work role and heightened the possibilities for marital failure.[95] Children's new needs translated into mothers' (and fathers') new vulnerability in divorce court. But what about the obligations of fathers? Where did they fit into this emerging child-centered family?

### *Fathers and Children*

The rising status of children and the declining authority of fathers brought a reevaluation of the paternal role in the nineteenth century. Although some writers attributed the decline in authority to fathers' frequent absences from home in an increasingly urban, industrialized society—and this factor was undoubtedly at work in some city homes—the trend to reduced paternal authority, as the research of Greven, Daniel Scott Smith, Daniel Blake Smith, Norton, and Kerber has already demonstrated, was under way well before urban living or industrialization became widely established.[96] Rather, the decline in paternal power dates from the late eighteenth century and appears to be the result of the more general emergence of the companionate family, with its emphasis on affection and intimacy. The result was to soften the patriarchal role and to insist that mothers and fathers both take an active role in rearing the children. Although most eighteenth-century child rearing literature was addressed to the fathers, authors were careful to specify, as Mary Beth Norton explains, "that parents should agree on both the means and the ends of child-rearing and that neither parent should undercut the other in any way."[97] And although late-eighteenth century nurture literature ascribed a paternalistic and didactic stance to fathers and underlined the children's duty to parents, Norton also found that "men quickly came to rival their wives in their interest in, and attachment to, their youngsters."[98] By the nineteenth century, these earlier trends had become the dominant pattern, and child advisers, although now directing their advice to mothers, assumed that mothers and fathers were equally involved in and responsible for the upbringing of their children.[99] Nineteenth-century child-rearing literature underscored the collaboration of mothers and fathers in child care, and, as Kirk Jeffrey found in his analysis of this material, expected both parents to be supportive, affectionate, and even companionate with their children. Jeffrey argued that a convergence of the cultural definitions of mother and father was under way, as each was expected to act in more complex ways toward the young.[100] The divorce evidence supports Jeffrey's theory: witnesses praised or condemned fathers to the degree that they did or did not establish close, loving bonds with their children.

Nowhere is the affection and concern of a father for his child clearer than in an 1884 case involving Nancy and Harrison Moore. In proving her husband's desertion, Nancy introduced as evidence a letter from Harrison proving his intention to remain separated; fortunately, the letter also included Harrison's request for custody of their young daughter and some revealing comments on how the laborer felt about his child. He first promised that all he wanted was custody of Angie, age six: "If you will [kindly] give her up to me, I will not trouble you aney morr [sic]." Harrison then expressed concern about the child's health and promised to give the girl the attention she needed: "You say that little Angie is feeble. If you will pray give her up to me, I will give her a good education and keep her in good health. I will not let any one abuse her." He also promised to contact a doctor, and he even recognized his wife's love for the child, but Harrison insisted that only he could support Angie adequately: "I am afraid she will die if she stays in Missouri all summer. You know that you cannot give her aliveing [sic] that I can. I know that you love her as well as I [do], but you know that she must [have] something more than love." He also asked his wife to think beyond her own interests. "You know that the poore [sic] little thing's life depends on good care and enough to eate [sic]. Now do not think unjustly but think what is best for your little Angie." Moore concluded by promising his wife that he would always be attentive and responsive to the child's needs: "I will always live with Angie and when she is old enough I will send her to schoole [sic] and make her as happy as I can and then you will be able to make a goode liveing [sic] for yourself."[101]

The Moore case was particularly rich in detail, but other fathers showed great concern for their children as well. William Bennett, a farmer, expressed to a neighbor his abiding affection for his wife and children, and the neighbor in turn assured Bennett's wife that William would mend his ways: "I told Mrs. Bennett that her husband would go away, sell out, and do anything she said, if she would come back with the children. [He would] do anything sooner than be separated from her and his children."[102] Businessman Joseph Gardner likewise assured the court that he tried for a reconciliation with his wife, not because of duty or community pressure but because of their children. Gardner recalled that when she left in 1884, he tried "to reconcile her and have her live with me on account of our children but she refused. Up to the time I came to California about February, 1885, I endeavored to have her live with me but she would not."[103] A century earlier, Gardner might have tried to save his marriage for God, or for the sake of relatives, or for continued respect in the eyes of the community, but hardly for the sake of his children; they usually did not count for that much.

The importance of children also appeared from evidence among those fathers who raised their children alone, and these men assured the court that they quite capably met the special needs of their children. Most relied on outside help, but that point should not obscure the fact that they felt obliged to convince the court of the propriety of their children's care. When John Henning's wife left him in Portland in 1865, he returned to Santa Clara County, resumed his trade as a carpenter, and immediately found a good home for his daughter. According to carpenter Samuel Gummer, Henning "placed the child with Mrs. Oldham at first, and afterwards with Mrs. Elliot, with whom the child still remains." John Williams, another co-worker, added that "the child is always well dressed and apparently well cared for"; and George Elliot testified that Henning gave Elliot and his wife ample money for the child's support and often visited his daughter. Elliot concluded that Henning was a "kind and good" father.[104] Samuel Brisbine, a blacksmith, also assured the court that his two-year-old son would be in a proper home environment surrounded by "female friends who are also friends of the said plaintiff [his wife] who will undertake on the part of Defendant the care of said infant during its tender minority." He, like other fathers, also promised to give his child a "substantial and liberal" education.[105] One last example reveals the extreme sense of attachment one father felt for his child. Camille Grosjean, a merchant, had the misfortune of marrying a free-spirited young woman who ran off with another man. At the time she deserted, she was pregnant, and though the records suggest Grosjean never saw his child—if indeed it was his child—he nevertheless "provided for the child ever since and . . made provisions for the child in my will."[106]

Because women brought two-thirds of the complaints in this study, the divorce records contain more negative than positive information about fathers. But husbands were at a disadvantage for a second reason; though ideal fatherhood included love, kindness, and affection for children, it lacked the basic naturalness—born in biology—of a mother's tie to her children; thus, we find no mention of "fatherly instincts" in the records but several references to motherly ones. In short, husbands were more vulnerable than wives to accusations of child neglect or abuse because, though the behavioral expectations for mothers and fathers were much the same, the source of such behavior was different. Mother's love and affection was instinctual, father's was learned.[107]

Judging from complaints lodged against them, husbands were not as conscious as their wives about the boundaries between home and society and childhood and adulthood. For example, child care suffered when either parent was drunk, but women were not accused of taking their children along on their binges. By contrast, the wife of Jean Portier, a poor San Jose hauler, charged him in 1854 with giving "intoxicating drink to said child Frank until he was inebriated."[108] The sight of the drunken seven-year-old boy on the streets of San Jose troubled John O'Neil, and he recalled his intervention on the child's behalf: "I took the boy away to the police officer and shut him up in a room there for several hours [where] he became sober and I permitted him to depart." The boy's inebriated father came to the station, admitted he had given his son "a little wine," and asked to be allowed to take his son home, a request the police denied.[109] J. P. Noyes had an equally poor regard for his son's sensibilities. As part of her cruelty complaint, Eliza Noyes claimed that in June 1878 her husband took their three-year-old child to "a low boarding house and bar in said town of Redwood City in charge of persons unfit to have the charge and care of said child."[110] Clearly, the boundaries between home and society were not as permeable as J. P. Noyes would have liked them to be.

Husbands did not have to take their children to saloons to offend their youthful innocence; they could easily do so right at home. The nineteenth-century's sentimental view of home life placed husbands who defiled the domestic refuge in a vulnerable position. The significance of the following evidence is not simply the criticism of fathers for child abuse and drunkenness—though that point is important—

but the fact that the status of children had increased to the point where lawyers, litigants, and witnesses mentioned the fact in divorce suit; such was not the case in the previous century.[111] Samuel and Louisa Cook, for example, feuded for two years over the custody of their children, and though the ultimate custody disposition remained unclear, Louisa left no doubt as to her own opinion; in her view, Samuel was "not a fit or proper person to have the care and charge of female children of tender age for the reason that he is hasty, and of a violent temper, and in the habit of using the most vulgar and obscene language in the presence of his children."[112] Nicholas Dodge, a ship's carpenter, apparently behaved no better, and witness William Hughes thought the intemperate seaman "should not be among children either male or female."[113]

Intemperance, in fact, repeatedly appeared as the destroyer of domestic virtues. Both male and female plaintiffs added power to their intemperance complaints by linking their spouse's drunkenness to abuse of the children. Being a parent required attentiveness and consideration and the task presupposed sobriety, and men who failed, men like laborer William Allen, were excoriated by their neighbors. Mrs. Mary Hull emphasized that because of Allen's "continuous habit of drunkenness, I do not think he would provide for it properly and do not consider that the child would be safe in his keeping."[114] Adelle Kincaid's complaint made the same point about her husband by describing the Redwood City attorney as a man of "drunken, dissolute habits and wholly unfit to have the custody, control, or management of said children."[115] Ida Turner, a sixteen-year-old San Jose dressmaker, put livery stable operator Edward Bliven in the same category, primarily because of Bliven's penchant for drinking himself unconscious. On one occasion Turner saw Bliven topple out of a wagon headfirst—such drunken acrobatics convinced Turner that Bliven had no place among children.[116]

The final evidence on fathers and children involves child abuse, and though it perhaps seems odd to end a discussion of the companionate family with an analysis of family cruelty, this material nevertheless shows that courts recognized a child's right to a violence-free upbringing; true, seventeenth- and eighteenth-century Americans also condemned parental violence against children, but only in the nineteenth century does such behavior warrant mention in divorce cases.[117] The reason for this change was that the core of nineteenth-century family life was the emotional attachment among its members; once those bonds of affection were broken—and what clearer evidence of such a break than an attack on one's children—the family lost its right to exist.

Such was schoolteacher Jerome Hill's fate when his wife accused him of cruelty in 1875. Though Elizabeth Hill included herself among her husband's victims, she concentrated on proving his brutality to their own children and to children generally by successfully proving that Jerome had a callous disregard for his pupils at school as well as for his own son. In her testimony, Elizabeth linked his public and private behavior: "I know that he is not fit. He is cruel. Because he was a cruel father and he has had a great deal of trouble as a teacher for abusing little children." She went on to describe acts of cruelty in the classroom and his eventual dismissal from a Mayfield, California, teaching job, allegations that received support from other witnesses who knew of Hill's cruel treatment of his pupils.[118] The court agreed that Hill's acts were totally unacceptable, and in 1875, Elizabeth received a divroce.

Unlike Elizabeth Hill, Margaret Maloney concentrated on her husband's behavior in the home, particularly his failure to recognize the physical limitations of his two sons. When they faltered doing the work he assigned them—work "beyond their physical power and endurance"—he beat them; in fact, his general manner was so harsh that "they stand in terror, trembling in his presence." He also failed to provide his sons with proper moral guidance, and instead of counseling the boys kindly, he terrorized and humiliated them.[119] Other cases included similar accusations, but the significant point in all was the children's right to respect and an abuse-free life. David Savage had no more right to call his son a "long lop-eared son of a bitch" than had Edward Evans, Christian Schumann, or Oliver Boyer to abuse their children.[120]

Nor was the law particularly interested in rationalizations for parental abuse, a fact carpenter J. P. Noyes found out when he tried to defend his attack on his stepdaughter. Noyes provided a lengthy discussion of his teenaged stepdaughter's "unruly, insolent, and disobedient" behavior, objected to his wife's intervention on the child's behalf, and lamented that "his road has been a rough and rugged one for the past few years"; but his problems really did not become acute until his stepdaughter called him a vulgar name: he then tried to hit her; his wife protected the child; the girl filed a battery claim; and he found himself in the county jail "where he still languishes—contemplating the felicity of step-fathers in general."[121] That a child, with the help of her mother, could incarcerate her own stepfather suggests the high status of children in the nineteenth-century family.

Nineteenth-century Americans witnessed the widespread elevation of concern for children. Beneath the sentimentality about childhood innocence, beneath that which sounds to modern ears like patronizing attitudes toward children, there emerged the basis of the modern view of childhood: children were now neither sin-filled creatures at the mercy of an angry God nor submissive and cowed creatures dominated by parental authority; rather, as the divorce evidence makes clear, children were individuals who deserved the mutual respect, consideration, and affection due all members of the companionate family. The experience of these Californians also reveals another way companionate ideals increased family unity for some but undermined it for others. While many parents, perhaps the great majority, forged loving ties with their children and thereby heightened the emotional satisfactions of family life, for others the rising status of children brought new opportunities for parental failure: some parents, in demonstrating their inability to create a relationship that most eighteenth-century parents were never called upon to develop, saw their families dissolve. Herein lies another cause for the rise in divorce.

# *Afterword: The Family, Victorian Culture, and Twentieth-Century Developments*

The origins of the companionate family were related to two processes: first, women's rising sense of personal autonomy; second, the emergence of sexually segregated, sharply defined spheres. Together, these two factors decisively reshaped personal relations within the family, changed the meaning of manhood, womanhood, and childhood, and heightened the degree of consciousness about the family itself. Under their impact, family relations took on new meaning in rural as well as urban society, among working-class as well as middle- and upper-class people: both men and women were now expected to act in more complex ways, childhood and parenthood assumed new dimensions, and, ironically, family stability became more problematic. The divorce courts bore dramatic and, to contemporaries, alarming testimony to the reality of these changes, as husbands and wives struggled with the new meaning of the nineteenth-century family.

The emergence of the modern family, however, had ramifications beyond those involving personal relations or the redefinition of proper male and female roles. This new family also embodied, reflected, upheld, and tried to extend the influence of Victorian assumptions about human ability and self-improvement, the malleability of character, and the nature of proper character itself—in particular, the Victorian emphasis on social respectability, strict personal morality, duty, hard work, sobriety, and moral autonomy.[1] In a slightly less direct and ultimately paradoxical manner, the nineteenth-century family also became crucial to the Victorian search for order and to the restructuring of authority relationships in a democratic society.

The Victorians' belief in rationality, human ability, personal efficacy, and self-improvement, and their sense that America was a redeemer among nations, a civilizing force, and mankind's "last best hope," stemmed, in part, from their faith in the malleability of character. Harmonious, democratic social relations (and ultimately America's mission in the world) depended upon the character of the nation's citizens, and more particularly, upon the ability of various institutions to transform the unchristian, the ignorant, the immoral, and the youthful into virtuous republicans. Just as reformers underscored the ability of schools, churches, asylums, and prisons to shape and reconstruct character, so, too, did moralists ascribe such capacities to families: a proper environment and careful moral guidance would create self-guided, dutiful, responsible citizens.[2] This faith in self-improvement reflected the optimism of Victorian culture, and though Victorians simultaneously worried about the disintegrating effects of rapid social change, they believed in their ability to infuse individual character with values—punctuality, obedience, self-control, moral autonomy, and responsibility—appropriate to the needs of a well-ordered, prosperous, capitalist society.

Reformers in prisons, insane asylums, almshouses, and reformatories tried to rebuild character by constructing an artificial but morally sound environment; meanwhile, popular moralists, religious reformers, temperance advocates, and sexual purity crusaders harped on the theme of individual renewal. Yet, even more attention was directed to the family's role in character building.[3] After all, every citizen spent the early years in some sort of family, hence the intense concern about parental duties and responsibilities, the insistence that all aspects of child rearing—from diet, to dress, to play— be carefully regulated, the determination to establish a correct moral climate in the home. These factors could not be left to chance: they were decisive in establishing the internal moral compass so necessary for life in a changing society. We have already seen how Californians translated these concerns into everyday realities. Women complained of inebriated, loud, and abusive husbands, in part because such behavior sullied the moral climate of the home and made child rearing impossibly difficult. How could a boy grow up to be respectable, frugal, and hardworking if his father were a drunk, much less took the poor child along on his binges? Could a girl develop proper habits of sexual modesty if her father abused her mother with false allegations of infidelity? Fathers were not the only culprits who threatened the character-building potential of the upstanding home. Could a drunken or shiftless mother demonstrate by word and deed the necessary habits of moral righteousness and purposeful work? Was there any conceivable way an immodest mother could impart proper notions of sexual restraint to her children? With social order dependent upon the character of its citizens, no wonder the family, the chief agent of socialization, assumed such importance.

But the family molded more than the character of children: while churches, newspapers, lodges, and voluntary associations tirelessly promoted strict personal morality, social responsibility, and sexual decorum among adults, the family reaffirmed these basic themes and redefined and delineated the boundaries of correct moral behavior. This function, moreover, was not restricted to the middle class. In keeping with the hegemony of Victorian culture and its ability, as Daniel Walker Howe has written, to "reach out beyond the social group with which it originates and become a vital element in the consciousness of others," families translated the didactic moralism of the middle class into the moral code of common Americans.[4] Men and women from all class backgrounds evinced concern about women's chastity, social respectability, domestic tranquility, and moral rectitude and with men's diligence, industriousness, sobriety, sexual decorum, and kindness. With such strong roots in the family, these ideas provided one important source of social cohesion in a society deeply anxious about questions of order and disorder.

Troubled by the decline of deference, worried by large-scale immigration, anxious over the growth of cities, and apprehensive about the emergence of industrialization, the Victorians' search for order took a variety of forms. For some, religion was the answer, and the Benevolent Empire, with its religious tracts and missionary societies, tried to reach and redeem the unregenerate. This massive and sustained effort sought to revitalize the Christian faith among a population grown more interested in material acquisition than spiritual rebirth.[5] The revivals that swept America expressed the same doubts, especially among an emerging middle class who feared the growing distance between employers and workers brought on by commercial capitalism. With more and more workers no longer closely supervised by or coresiding with shop owners, the new shopkeeper capitalists sought, through religious conversion, to establish their own moral credibility, to extend conservative religious precepts to the working class, and to legitimate a new sense of order based not on human interdependence but on individual piety and self-restraint.[6]

Others, impressed by the malleability of human character and the need for a properly regulated moral environment, sought stability through new institutions such as almshouses, penitentiaries, orphanages, and school reformatories. Originally, each of these was to be less a custodial institution than a redemptive one, a place where character could be reshaped within a carefully designed, morally correct environment free from the evils of everyday life. In David Rothman's judgment, such institutions represented a direct response to the decline of colonial order, a "vigorous attempt to promote the stability of the society at a moment when traditional ideas and practices appeared outmoded, constrictive, and ineffective"; moreover, in the case of orphanages and children's asylums, the new institutions functioned as a rebuke to permissive families and as an example of the correctly ordered home.[7]

These public and institutional responses to disorder were paralleled by developments in the family. The new family that flowered in the nineteenth century should be seen, at least in part, as a response to disorder and as a basis of a new form of order appropriate to a democratic republic. Women in the home, as Catharine Beecher and others argued, were the moral ballast of society, the first defense against the "storms of democratic liberty." Old patterns of authority and deference might crumble and new uncertainties emerge, but regardless of the tumult outside the front door, women at the hearth would insure tranquility and the right moral tone for their families and for the rest of society as well.[8] In this sense, domesticity symbolized the general Victorian concern with sources of union and disunion and provided both an important source of social cohesion and an effective standard of social propriety and deviance that transcended class: thus the concern among Californians with order, sobriety, and decorum in the home and the corresponding vulnerability of both men and women (but especially men) to allegations of idleness, intemperance, rudeness, and ill-mannered behavior.

The cult of domesticity did more than function as a source of stability in a changing society; its impact on women's self-esteem helped create a new basis of order appropriate to a republic. In the nineteenth century and well into the twentieth century, domesticity provided the context within which the companionate family emerged. The celebration of womanhood, the apotheosis of motherhood, the insistence that women's work was indispensable, the belief in female moral superiority, all of these facets of domesticity increased women's claims to respect and consideration and checked the power of husbands. Although inequalities persisted, domesticity provided an important source of female identity and spurred the development of more equal, less patriarchal marriage relations. In the process, family relations more appropriate to a democratic republic began to emerge.

Although the linkage cannot be pushed too far, the shift to less hierarchical family relations reflects the general decline of deference and authority in the nineteenth century.[9] While Catharine Beecher may have emphasized womanly self-sacrifice to preserve order and stability, others—even Beecher in many respects—sought to increase woman's influence in the home and in society. As the companionate family developed, domestic relations became more egalitarian, cooperative, and respectful, values perfectly in line with the rational order of liberal democracy. Marriages that did not reflect these values increasingly broke up as the century progressed. For in truth, could a truly democratic society permit husbands to exercise excessive power over their wives? Could mothers be asked to rear republican-minded children in an atmosphere of domestic oppression? Clearly not, and thus the nineteenth-century family not only reflected but promoted the shift to more equal power relations within society.[10]

Despite this new order emerging in families, the family's overall impact on the Victorian search for stability was negligible if not negative; for whatever success families had in providing a refuge or in molding self-regulating, temperate, and industrious citizens was undermined by the rising number of broken marriages. This development, moreover, followed predictably from the assumptions of the modern family itself: the trail from the early stirrings of the companionate family in the mid-eighteenth century to "no-fault" divorce today is faint, but it can be traced. As marital expectations and demands steadily rose, so, too, did possibilities for failure; as men and women expected each other to act in more complex ways, more people fell short of such expectations. By the late nineteenth century, wives complained to the courts about cold, aloof husbands, of husbands who did not spend enough time at home, who failed to check their sexual desires, or who ignored women's emotional needs. Men countered with complaints of unloving, peevish, quarrelsome wives, of wives who were poor housekeepers or insensitive mothers. Tensions like these arose as a logical, even necessary consequence of the companionate family: marriages predicated on emotion required a safety valve when affection waned, hence the emergence of the "divorce crisis" that began in the 1880s.[11] But safety valve theories were (and are) scant consolation to those who consider the family the bedrock of civilization, who see social decay behind every addition to the divorce court docket. Thus it happened that domesticity and the companionate family—meant to promote order in keeping with a democratic republic—brought instead marital breakdown. The Victorian search for order through the family would remain elusive.

The impact of the companionate ideal did more than increase family instability; it helped change the very meaning of womanhood, manhood, and childhood, and profoundly affected twentieth-century personal life. Until well into this century (and perhaps in most families to the present day), companionate marriages developed in conjunction with the domestic ideal, and although this ideal angered feminists, for most women it provided worthy values and standards of behavior: women's status within the family increased, their claims on husbands' time and emotions rose, and the expected behavior of men became correspondingly more demanding and complex. Within the boundaries of domesticity, a new sense of womanhood evolved, a new sense of self-confidence and self-esteem became evident.

These developments, in turn, established the foundation for later changes. As women became more self-confident, more sure of their own importance and the legitimacy of their own desires, more women began to question the assumptions of domesticity itself: now their exclusion from the rewards of equal involvement in economic, political, and social life became increasingly unacceptable.[12] At this point, domesticity and the future development of the companionate family became, for many women, incompatible. A truly equal marriage, argued feminists, required full equality for women, a demand that domesticity could not accomodate: for this reason, feminists rejected the separation of the spheres because it functioned as a barrier to full equality and to the logic of the companionate family itself. For how could genuine equality develop and a true partnership of equals evolve so long as women were denied equal access to the political and economic world outside the home? Related to this question was another: What must occur within the family and within society—in the distribution of power, in childrearing, in sex roles in general—to insure that wives could lead a fulfilling life both inside and outside the family? Once an ideal that produced positive change, domesticity was now regarded by many as an obstacle to the development of marriages based on equality between men and women. Thus the crucial issue facing the family: how to build lasting, egalitarian marriages and simultaneously end social and economic discrimination against women.[13]

As women's roles changed, so, too, did men's, and while women struggled with discrimination and the implications of domesticity, men tried to reconcile the disparate demands of the marketplace and the home. In the commute between the calculating world of work and the emotional world of the home, men continually shifted psychological gears, one moment the industrious, frugal, and determined worker, the next the understanding, kind, affectionate companion. Whether at work or at home, the complexity of the male role brought new possibilities for failure. Profligate, dissolute, lazy, and intemperate husbands were sued for divorce, but so, too, were cold, unkind, and inconsiderate ones.

The expressive demands of the modern male role have not been easily achieved. As we have seen, the companionate ideal was in many ways directed at husbands: they were the ones asked to reduce their power, to soften their demeanor, to become more loving and understanding. That many succeeded is undeniable, that many failed, equally undeniable. But the problem for men has remained: how to reconcile their traditional role as providers—and the status and power that comes with that role—with women's insistence on emotional commitment and (later) social and economic equality. So long as domesticity flourished, disparities of power and some emotional distance could be condoned, but as patriarchy dissolved, such behavior became increasingly unacceptable. Since the revival of feminism in the 1960s, feminists have taken special aim at the last vestiges of patriarchy, in particular some men's unwillingness to commit themselves emotionally to their marriages. Some observers even suggest that men, threatened by the steady decline of male power, withhold emotional commitment from women "either because they cannot tolerate it," or as Barbara Easton adds, "because withdrawal itself can become a weapon in their struggles with women."[14]

Regardless of the reason, men today continue to wrestle with the implications of the companionate ideal, especially the loss of patriarchal control and the emotional and social challenges posed by placing marriage on a progressively more equal basis. The crucial issue now involves men's response to such demands. Will they carry out the logic of the companionate family and become equally involved in child rearing? Will they be willing to sacrifice their own careers for those of their wives? Can domestic tasks be distributed more equitably or will even working wives continue to assume most of the burdens of housework? Finally, will men provide the emotional support to their wives that women once received from each other within the "bonds of womanhood"? These questions are fundamental, follow directly from the previous two centuries of change, and remain unanswered.

While the emotional requirements of manhood exhibit continuity from the nineteenth to the twentieth century, the relationship between male identity and work lacks such coherence. Although vestiges of the work ethic have survived, the conditions of modern work have rendered it problematic. An ideology predicated upon moral autonomy and independence and appropriate to a world of farms and small shops may no longer hold in a society dominated by large corporations and hired labor.[15] For California men in the nineteenth century, work provided a sense of identity, a tie to values regarded by all as legitimate and commendable. Today that concensus no longer exists. The dignity of work still receives an occasional and obligatory nod, but the moral unity of manhood and work has been sundered. Study after study confirms the alienation of present-day workers, their sense that work is meaningless, repetitive, and unfulfilling.[16] Whatever the long-range solution to this problem, an important source of male esteem and self-respect has eroded; men, challenged to forge a new identity inside the family, have simultaneously lost an important sense of male identity outside it.

Finally, the impact of the modern family on children is not without ambiguities. The crucial point is the development after 1750 of intense bonds between parents and children, bonds predicated on the belief that children required and deserved all the respect and affection at the core of the companionate family. Young children in particular needed the kind and loving attention of parents, especially of mothers who, innately endowed for the task, saw to their children's emotional needs and provided an atmosphere conducive to proper moral and spiritual development. Certainly these attitudes redounded in many ways to children's benefit. Increased parental affection and care, a decline in corporal punishment, legal protection against abuse, child labor and abandonment laws, educational reforms, all these and more attest to children's high status.[17]

But the story is more complicated than this rather Whiggish view suggests. The apotheosis of motherhood and the tendency to sentimentalize children, for example, only heightened sex role stereotypes about child rearing. Divorce courts confirmed this situation by giving custody to women as a matter of course.[18] Despite pleas that men take an interest in child care, the romanticization of motherhood and children increased the identification of women with children, thereby creating severe psychological and social problems for women who chose not to have children. For men, the results were equally troubling: the assumption that children's "special needs" and "tender sensibilities" required a mother's care undercut the bonds that might have developed between fathers and children. Today, some fathers are fighting the legacy of these assumptions by demanding more equitable custody policies, paternity leaves, and an end to stereotypes about women's alleged superiority as child rearers.

Other unfortunate consequences developed as children's status rose. Some observers suggest that parental confidence diminished as self-styled experts and agents of the "therapeutic state" increasingly dictated child-rearing norms. With children so highly valued, parents desperately tried to follow the latest fad, all the time feeling guilty and incompetent as they sought to adhere to the program of one child expert or another. This loss of competency, linked to other family functions absorbed by the state, has rendered people increasingly powerless, dependent on the judgment of experts they do not know, on trends they cannot affect. The confidence and sense of efficacy of the eighteenth-century mother or father, so the argument goes, has been replaced by the nervous anxiety of the modern parent, now a compulsive reader of child-rearing literature.[19] Although the elevation of children within the family did not alone create this situation—it grew out of broader changes in late nineteenth and twentieth-century society—the high status of the young was a critical precondition of this phenomenon. For unless parents loved and cared deeply about their children's development, would they devour child-rearing literature with such interest? Would they turn to child-guidance experts, counselors, and psychologists with such frequency? Would they have been so willing, in general, to trust the advice of experts?[20] If this theory is correct and such a loss of confidence actually exists, then the rise of the modern family has, indirectly and unintentionally, helped heighten the sense of powerlessness so pervasive in modern society.

The high esteem for children also facilitated more formal state involvement in the affairs of the family. In his study of nineteenth-century family law, Michael Grossberg found that late-nineteenth-century courts—determined to protect children and defend the sanctity of the household—began to see parents as mere agents of the state, entrusted with a "revocable authority to rear their children."[21] Insisting that such assumptions were based on "the best interests of the child," judges used their discretionary power to set standards of parental fitness and child welfare, in the process undermining parental rights and increasing the power of the state. A judge might, for example, declare a parent unfit and remove the child from the home, decide that a surrogate parent was a better guardian than the child's natural parents, or define as unacceptable behavior for youths—drinking, gambling, carousing, fighting, dancing—what was in reality only lower-class behavior that offended middle-class sensibilities.[22] These attitudes culminated in the juvenile court movement, which in theory "exercises that tender solicitude and care over its neglected, dependent wards, that a wise and loving parent would exercise with reference to his own children under similar circumstances"—but which in reality denied children civil rights by basing such proceedings on a therapeutic rather than a legal model.[23]

The point is not that the companionate family directly caused this expansion of the state or the decline in parental efficacy and self-confidence; rather it functioned as a necessary prerequisite for such developments. Changes in personal relations ultimately affected, in logical but unforeseen ways, social relations outside the home, in this case the expansion of the state's power over individuals. This connection between private and public life deserves close attention, for in many instances—child saving being one of them—public actions depend upon earlier and more fundamental changes in the private realm. Thus, even if child saving arose in the late nineteenth century as part of an upper-class movement to "achieve order, stability, and control, while preserving the existing class system and distribution of wealth," the fact remains that this movement was inconceivable without the prior transformation in the status of children.[24]

The roles, values, and expectations that developed in nineteenth-century families established the contours for twentieth-century marriages. What emerged in the twentieth century was less a repudiation of Victorian marriage than an elaboration of its central assumptions; although some historians see the twentieth-century emphasis on marital romance, expression, excitement, personal fulfillment, and sexual gratification as a distinctive product of urban life, consumerism, and increased leisure time—and therefore as a break with the "duties and sacrifices" of Victorian family life—the continuities between the two eras appear more striking than the discontinuities.[25] It was the nineteenth-century emphasis on affection, companionship, and mutual respect and regard that built the foundation for the later developments: romance, expression, playfulness, sexual gratification, all these well-known desiderata of twentieth-century marriages depended upon and grew directly from the moral assumptions of the nineteenth-century family. Perhaps urban life, working wives, consumerism, and the cult of youth heightened and drew attention to the importance of marital romance and the like, but the basic values from which they emerged developed in the previous century. In speaking of sexual ethics, but applicable to other areas of family life as well, Christopher Lasch is surely correct in arguing that "the present age . . . greatly exaggerates the moral distance between its own practices and those of the Victorians."[26]

# *Appendix Composition of the Social Classes*

The occupations of slightly more than one-half the husbands were found, either directly in the divorce records or indirectly in census schedules, county directories, or contemporary histories. These occupations were then grouped to form the six social classes described in Chapter II. This appendix gives the names of the occupations comprising each class and the number of men working at each occupation. The occupations are listed just as they appeared in the documents. Thus we find some men describing themselves as "capitalists," whereas others preferred to be known as "businessmen."

| I. *Upper Class* | |
|---|---|
| businessman | 12 |
| capitalist | 2 |
| lawyer | 1 |
| merchant | 5 |
| physician | 6 |
| rancher | 9 |
| Total | 35 |

| II. *Middle Class* | |
|---|---|
| architect | 1 |
| bookkeeper | 2 |
| clerk | 5 |
| dentist | 2 |
| druggist | 3 |
| fruit grower | 1 |
| hotel keeper | 5 |
| livery stable operator | 1 |
| orchardist | 1 |
| real estate salesman | 1 |
| sea captain | 1 |
| cigar seller | 1 |
| storekeeper | 5 |
| teacher | 4 |
| veterinarian | 1 |
| Total | 34 |

| III. *Farmers* | 28 |
|---|---|

| IV. *Skilled Trades* | |
|---|---|
| baker | 1 |
| blacksmith | 7 |
| candy maker | 2 |
| carpenter | 6 |
| carriage maker | 2 |
| constable | 1 |
| cook | 2 |
| gas fitter | 1 |
| house painter | 3 |
| plumber | 1 |
| printer | 1 |
| pump maker | 2 |
| saddle maker | 2 |
| skilled workman | 1 |
| tailor | 1 |
| tanner | 1 |
| wagon maker | 3 |
| wheelwright | 1 |
| Total | 38 |

V. *Unskilled Trades*

| | |
|---|---|
| barber | 2 |
| factory worker | 2 |
| mill worker | 2 |
| mine worker | 5 |
| saloon keeper | 2 |
| teamster | 6 |
| Total | 19 |

VI. *Laborers*

| | |
|---|---|
| laborers | 28 |
| wage workers | 3 |
| unemployed | 18 |
| Total | 49 |

# Notes

## I.
## Introduction: From Patriarchy to Companionship

1. Emily v. Samuel Chandler, Case 1283, San Mateo County, 1878. This form of citation will be used throughout. The date refers to the year in which the plaintiff's divorce complaint was filed. The cases are without pagination.

2. Especially useful on the social importance of the nineteenth century family are the following. Carl Degler, *At Odds: Women and the Family in America from the Revolution to the Present* (New York: Oxford University Press, 1980); Nancy Cott, *The Bonds of Womanhood: "Women's Sphere" in New England, 1780-1835* (New Haven: Yale University Press, 1977); Joseph Kett, *The Rites of Passage: Adolescence in America, 1790 to the Present* (New York: Basic Books, 1977); Kathryn Sklar, *Catharine Beecher: A Study in American Domesticity* (New Haven: Yale University Press, 1973); Bernard Wishy, *The Child and the Republic: The Dawn of Modern American Child Nurture* (Philadelphia: University of Pennsylvania Press, 1968). Several fine articles on nineteenth-century family life are collected in Michael Gordon, ed., *The American Family in Social Historical Perspective,* 2d ed. (New York: St. Martin's Press, 1978).

3. United States Bureau of the Census, *Special Reports: Marriage and Divorce, 1867–1906,* vol. 1 (Washington, D.C.: Government Printing Office, 1908–1909), p. 12. From 1867 to 1929, the United States population rose 300 percent, the number of marriages 400 percent, and the divorce rate 2000 percent. See Elaine Tyler May, *Great Expectations: Marriage and Divorce in Post-Victorian America* (Chicago: University of Chicago Press, 1980), p. 2. On divorce statistics in general, see Alfred Cahen, *Statistical Analysis of American Divorce* (New York: Columbia University Press, 1932).

4. Carroll Wright, *A Report of Marriage and Divorce in the United States, 1867–1886* (Washington, D.C.: Government Printing Office, 1889), p. 144. This report and the report noted in the previous citation are indispensable to the study of late nineteenth-century family life. Both contain vast amounts of statistical data.

5. William O'Neill, "Divorce in the Progressive Era," *American Quarterly,* 17 (Summer 1965): 205–17. For a fuller treatment of the same subject, see O'Neill's *Divorce in the Progressive Era* (New Haven: Yale University Press, 1967).

6. On speculations as to why the divorce rate steadily climbed from the

nineteenth century on, see Walter F. Willcox, *The Divorce Problem* (New York: Columbia University Press, 1897), pp. 66–69; O'Neill, *Divorce in the Progressive Era,* chapters 1, 2, and 4; and May, *Great Expectations,* chapters 3–8. May provides a useful survey of theories on divorce, pp. 2–7. Useful, too, are Nelson Blake, *The Road to Reno: A History of Divorce in the United States* (New York: Macmillan Co., 1962), pp. 226–29, and Cahen, *Statistical Analysis of American Divorce,* pp. 45–62.

7. A detailed discussion of both the sample and the limitations of this data are found in Chapter II.

8. John Mack Faragher, *Women and Men on the Overland Trail* (New Haven: Yale University Press, 1979), p. 3. Mary Beth Norton notes problems with prescriptive literature as a source in "The Paradox of 'Women's Sphere' " in Carol Ruth Berkin and Mary Beth Norton, eds., *Women of America: A History* (Boston: Houghton Mifflin Co., 1979), pp. 140–41; also, on the need for caution when using such literature, see Jay Mechling, "Advice to Historians on Advice to Mothers," *Journal of Social History,* 9 (Fall 1975): 45–63. In discussing the question of prescription and behavior, Lois Banner noted that "the real question here is to what extent women, and men, too, had internalized within marriage the roles that their society expected." This study is an effort to answer that question. See Banner's "On Writing Women's History," *Journal of Interdisciplinary History,* 2 (Autumn 1971): 345–58.

9. The emergence of new family values after 1750 will be treated at length later in this chapter, but the point here is that divorce cases help explore the intersection between ideology and behavior.

10. Cott, *Bonds of Womanhood,* p. 200.

11. The most comprehensive treatment of the emergence of the companionate family in the nineteenth century is Degler's *At Odds,* a work organized around the theme of the emergence and elaboration of the companionate ideal. On men (and the companionate ideal in general) see Kirk Jeffrey, "Family History: The Middle-Class Family in the Urban Context, 1830–1870," Ph.D. diss., Stanford University, Stanford, Cal., 1972, especially chapter 5. Also see Daniel Scott Smith, "Family Limitation, Sexual Control, and Domestic Feminism in Victorian America," *Feminist Studies,* 1 (Winter/ Spring 1973): 40, 44, 47, 53. On children's place in the family, see Wishy, *Child and Republic,* and Robert E. McGlone, "Suffer the Children: The Emergence of Modern Middle-Class Family Life in America, 1820–1870," Ph.D. diss., University of California, Los Angeles, 1971, especially chapters 2 and 4. The eighteenth-century development of more affective family relations can be traced in Daniel Blake Smith, *Inside the Great House: Planter Family Life in Eighteenth-Century Chesapeake Society* (Ithaca: Cornell University Press, 1980), pp. 25–54, 126–74.

12. Edmund Morgan, *The Puritan Family: Religion and Domestic Relations in Seventeenth-Century New England,* rev. ed. (New York: Harper & Row, 1966) pp. 29–64. Daniel Blake Smith reviews the literature on the colonial family in "The Study of the Family in Early America: Trends, Problems, and Prospects," *William and Mary Quarterly,* 39 (1982): 3–28. In the same issue of the *William and Mary Quarterly,* Gerald F. Moran and Maris A. Vinovskis review

past work and future research possibilities on the relationship between the Puritan family and religion: see "The Puritan Family and Religion: A Critical Reappraisal," pp. 29–63.

13. Morgan, *The Puritan Family,* p. 43.

14. Barbara Harris makes this useful comparison in *Beyond Her Sphere: Women and the Professions in American History* (Westport, Conn.: Greenwood Press, 1978), p. 19.

15. The following include useful discussions of Puritan social theory: Morgan, *Puritan Family,* chapters 2 and 3; Richard L. Bushman, *From Puritan to Yankee: Character and Social Order in Connecticut, 1690–1765* (New York: Norton, 1970), pp. 3–21; T. H. Breen, *The Character of the Good Ruler: Puritan Political Ideas in New England, 1630–1730* (New York: Norton, 1970), chapters 1 and 2; Stephen Foster, *Their Solitary Way: The Puritan Social Ethic in the First Century of Settlement in New England* (New Haven: Yale University Press, 1971).

16. John Demos, *A Little Commonwealth: Family Life in Plymouth Colony* (New York: Oxford University Press, 1970), p. 82.

17. Ibid., p. 83.

18. Ibid., pp. 84–91. Lyle Koehler's recent study of seventeenth-century New England women exhaustively documents their subordinate role in early Puritan society. Faced with a rigid, conservative, male-dominated social structure, Puritan women suffered political, legal, educational, occupational, and religious discrimination that left them even worse off, in many respects, than their English counterparts; see *A Search for Power: The "Weaker Sex" in Seventeenth-Century New England* (Urbana: University of Illinois Press, 1980).

19. J. William Frost, *The Quaker Family in Colonial America: A Portrait of the Society of Friends* (New York: St. Martin's Press, 1973), pp. 175–76.

20. Philip J. Greven, Jr., *Four Generations: Population, Land, and Family in Colonial Andover, Massachusetts* (Ithaca: Cornell University Press, 1970), p. 99.

21. Lorena S. Walsh, " 'Till Death Us Do Part': Marriage and Family in Seventeenth-Century Maryland," in Thad W. Tate and David L. Ammerman, eds., *The Chesapeake in the Seventeenth Century: Essays on Anglo-American Society and Politics* (New York: Norton, 1979), pp. 126–52.

22. Ibid., pp. 128, 139–40.

23. Cott, *The Bonds of Womanhood,* pp. 20, 22. Two articles by Cott, both using Massachusetts divorce data, document women's secondary position within the eighteenth-century home. See "Divorce and the Changing Status of Women in Eighteenth-Century Massachusetts," *William and Mary Quarterly,* 33 (1976): 586–614; and "Eighteenth-Century Family and Social Life Revealed in Massachusetts Divorce Records," *Journal of Social History,* 10 (Fall 1976): pp. 20–43.

24. Smith, *Inside the Great House,* p. 21. Smith argues (pp. 140–41) that prior to the mid-eighteenth century, parents exercised great control over their children's marriage selections and that these marriages were largely bonds of property rather than affection.

25. Mary Beth Norton, *Liberty's Daughters: The Revolutionary Experience of American Women, 1750–1800* (Boston: Little, Brown & Co., 1980), pp. 61–62.

26. Mary Beth Norton, "Eighteenth-Century American Women in Peace

and War: The Case of the Loyalists," *William and Mary Quarterly,* 3rd Ser., 33 (1976): 386–409. On women's own sense of inferiority, see Norton, *Liberty's Daughters,* pp. 117–19. On women's second-class status in Enlightenment thought, Linda Kerber's recent book is most helpful: *Women of the Republic: Intellect and Ideology in Revolutionary America* (Chapel Hill: University of North Carolina Press, 1980), pp. 15–27. Not all historians agree with Norton's contention; some, like Barbara Berg, argue that women had higher status in the eighteenth than in the nineteenth century, mostly because of their economic indispensability; see Berg, *The Remembered Gate: The Origins of American Feminism* (New York: Oxford University Press, 1978), pp. 12–16. Gerda Lerner argues that professional opportunities and women's status in general declined in the early nineteenth century in "The Lady and the Mill Girl: Changes in the Status of Women in the Age of Jackson, 1800–1840," *Midcontinent American Studies Journal,* 10 (Spring 1969): 5–14. The better claim, however, is with those who see women's status rising in the nineteenth century. Norton dismisses the high status of eighteenth-century women as a myth in her short essay, "The Myth of the Golden Age," in Berkin and Norton, eds., *Women of America,* pp. 37–47. Her view of eighteenth-century women is succinctly summarized in the following sentence: "If any quality was antithetical to the colonial notion of femininity, it was autonomy." See her *Liberty's Daughters,* p. 125.

27. On women and law, see ibid., p. 45. Richard B. Morris, *Studies in the History of American Law* (New York: Columbia University Press, 1930), in chapter 3, "Women's Rights in Early American Law," points out the favorable legal position of colonial women vis-à-vis women in England. A useful study of women's legal status in colonial Pennsylvania is Marylynn Salmon's "Equality or Submersion? Feme Covert Status in Early Pennsylvania," in Berkin and Norton, eds., *Women of America,* pp. 92–111. In *Women of the Republic,* Kerber includes (pp. 120–36) a long discussion of coverture, especially the Revolution's impact on the concept.

28. Salmon, "Equality or Submersion," p. 105.

29. Kerber, *Women of the Republic,* p. 136. Joan R. Gundersen and Gwen Victor Gampel have recently suggested that coverture did not prevent eighteenth-century New York and Virginia wives from participating in a broad range of legal and economic activities including disposing of property, filing joint suits and deeds, administering their deceased husbands' estates, and acting in the economic sphere "as representatives for absent husbands, as managers of family businesses when husbands were present, and as operators of their own businesses." (p. 129) However, the authors concede that new obstacles arose by the mid-eighteenth century as a more strict interpretation of coverture eroded women's participation in legal and economic affairs; see "Married Women's Legal Status in Eighteenth-Century New York and Virginia," *William and Mary Quarterly,* 39 (1982): 114–134.

30. On women's educational liabilities, see Norton, *Liberty's Daughters,* pp. 256–63, and Kerber, *Women of the Republic,* pp. 185–99. On colonial literacy in general and male–female disparities in particular, see Kenneth Lockridge, *Literacy in Colonial New England: An Enquiry into the Social Context of Literacy in*

*the Early Modern West* (New York: 1974), 38–44. Kerber and Norton both discuss the impact of the Revolution in improving women's education, as does Ann D. Gordon, "The Young Ladies Academy of Philadelphia," in Berkin and Norton, eds., *Women of America,* pp. 69–87.

31. Norton, *Liberty's Daughters,* p. 110.

32. Michelle Rosaldo explores several interesting theoretical points regarding the impact of gender on cultural status and personal identity in "Woman, Culture, and Society: A Theoretical Overview," in Michelle Rosaldo and Louise Lamphere, eds., *Woman, Culture, and Society* (Stanford: Stanford University Press, 1974), pp. 17–42.

33. The following are helpful regarding the decline in fertility in the late eighteenth and nineteenth centuries: Degler, *At Odds,* pp. 178–226; Robert V. Wells, "Family Size and Fertility Control in Eighteenth-Century America: A Study of Quaker Families," *Population Studies,* 25 (1971): 73–82; Richard A. Easterlin, "Factors in the Decline of Farm Fertility in the United States: Some Preliminary Research Results," *Journal of American History,* 63 (1976): 600–612; Robert V. Wells, "Family History and Demographic Transition," *Journal of Social History,* 9 (Fall 1975): 1–19; Daniel Scott Smith, "Domestic Feminism," pp. 40–57; Warren C. Sanderson, "Quantitative Aspects of Marriage Fertility and Family Limitation in Nineteenth-Century America: Another Application of the Coale Specification," *Demography,* 16 (1979): 339–58. Both Degler and Smith tie falling birth rates to the emergence of the companionate family, and both, too, see the decline in fertility as an effort by women to gain control over their own lives.

34. Smith, "Domestic Feminism," pp. 43–44.

35. On demography and the life cycle, see Robert V. Wells, "Demographic Change and the Life Cycle of American Families," *Journal of Interdisciplinary History,* 2 (1971): 273–82.

36. Greven, *Four Generations,* pp. 222–29 ff., and chapters 7 and 8.

37. Daniel Scott Smith, "Parental Power and Marriage Patterns: An Analysis of Historical Trends in Hingham, Massachusetts," *Journal of Marriage and the Family,* 35 (1973): 419–28.

38. Smith, *Inside the Great House,* pp. 126–34.

39. Ibid., p. 142. The role of children in the companionate family will be treated at length in Chapter 7.

40. Quoted in Smith, *Inside the Great House,* p. 138. In a recent study of the Virginia gentry, Jan Lewis concluded that these Virginians sought affectionate but not intimate family relations and that their chief desires were order, peace, and tranquility, not deep personal affection and self-expression: managing the emotions—keeping family relations warm but not hot—was their goal. From this perspective, gentry family life in eighteenth-century Virginia represents a transitional phase between the coolness of the seventeenth century and the intimacy of the nineteenth century; see "Domestic Tranquillity and the Management of Emotion among the Gentry of Pre-Revolutionary Virginia," *William and Mary Quarterly,* 39 (1982): 135–49.

41. Kerber, *Women of the Republic,* p. 175.

42. Quoted in Degler, *At Odds,* pp. 34, 40.

43. Quoted in Julie Roy Jeffrey, *Frontier Women: The Trans-Mississippi West, 1840–1880* (New York: Hill & Wang, 1979), pp. 66–67.

44. Herman Lantz et al., "Pre-industrial Patterns in the Colonial Family: A Content Analysis of Colonial Magazines," *American Sociological Review,* 33 (1968): 413–26; Lantz et al., "The Changing American Family from the Pre-industrial to the Industrial Period: A Final Report," *American Sociological Review,* 42 (June 1977), pp. 406–21. Lawrence Stone sees a similar development occurring in England, noting that romantic love and the romantic novel grew together after 1780: *The Family, Sex and Marriage in England, 1500–1800* (New York: Harper & Row, 1977), p. 284. Especially useful on the rise of love and affection in English marriages are chapters 6, 7, and 8.

45. Smith, *Inside the Great House,* p. 160. This trend of women's rising status dates from the Revolutionary years, according to Nancy Cott, Linda Kerber, and Mary Beth Norton. See Cott, "Divorce and the Changing Status of Women," pp. 592–94, 605–6, 612–14; Kerber, *Women of the Republic,* chapter 9; Norton, *Liberty's Daughters,* pp. 228–99.

46. Jeffrey, "Family History," pp. 155–86, 194. Jeffrey argues that a decline of kin ties in cities also helped produce closer emotional ties between husbands and wives (pp. 199–201); Lantz et al. noted that moralists as early as the 1790s emphasized the desirability of "mutual cooperation" between husbands and wives; thereafter, women's power within the home continued to rise as it became increasingly their domain. The authors added that the development of the "contemporary democratic–companionship family" accelerated in the years 1850–1865: "The Changing American Family," pp. 411–12. Julie Jeffrey found that among frontier settlers, men made the major decisions but women had the right of consultation. Women were copartners in the move West, and as such, expected husbands to discuss and consult with them regarding details of the move. Jeffrey, *Frontier Women,* pp. 63–64. Most historians assume that the shift to companionate marriages was most pronounced in urban homes and is in some ways related to urbanization and the rise of industrialization. Perhaps, but too little evidence exists on rural marriages to argue the point convincingly.

47. Jeffrey, "Family History," p. 185.

48. Quoted in Faragher, *Women and Men on the Overland Trail,* p. 61.

49. The implications for women of domesticity and the separation of the spheres has produced divergent views, ranging from those who see domesticity as a prison to those who see it as a source of sororal strength, as a way station on the road to liberation. Nancy Cott, who provides a useful analysis of this debate, notes insightfully "that the more historians have relied on women's personal documents the more positively they have evaluated woman's sphere." Cott, *The Bonds of Womanhood,* pp. 197–206.

50. On republican motherhood, see Norton, *Liberty's Daughters,* pp. 197–98, 243, and Kerber, *Women of the Republic,* pp. 47, 204–10, 227–29, 283–87.

51. On the education of republican mothers, see Kerber, *Women of the Republic,* chapters 7 and 8, and Norton, *Liberty's Daughters,* pp. 256–65, 276.

52. Norton, *Liberty's Daughters,* p. 250.

53. Catharine Beecher described women and the home as a shelter from "the storms of democratic liberty." See Sklar, *Catharine Beecher,* p. 135. Many scholars have noted the perception of social breakdown in the antebellum years. For a sampling of this literature, see the following: Paul E. Johnson, *A Shopkeeper's Millennium: Society and Revivals in Rochester, New York, 1815–1837* (New York: Hill & Wang, 1978), chapters 5 and 6; Stephan Thernstrom, *Poverty and Progress: Social Mobility in a Nineteenth Century City* (New York: Atheneum, 1971), chapters 1, 2, and 3; David Rothman, *The Discovery of the Asylum: Social Order and Disorder in the New Republic* (Boston: Little, Brown & Co., 1971); Ronald G. Walters, *American Reformers,* 1815–1860 (New York: Hill & Wang, 1978); Berg, *The Remembered Gate,* pp. 33 ff.

54. Nancy Cott, "Passionlessness: An Interpretation of Victorian Sexual Ideology, 1790–1850," *Signs: A Journal of Women in Culture and Society,* 4 (1978): 219–36.

55. Sklar, *Catharine Beecher,* pp. 135–36, 158–59, 211. Other scholars, too, see domesticity as a response to the disorder of antebellum life; for example, see Julie Jeffrey, *Frontier Women,* p. 7, and Nancy Cott, *Bonds of Womanhood,* pp. 62–74.

56. Carroll Smith–Rosenberg, "Beauty, The Beast, and the Militant Woman: A Case Study in Sex Roles and Social Stress in Jacksonian America," *American Quarterly,* 23 (1971): 562–84.

57. Julie Jeffrey, *Frontier Women,* pp. 12, 95–98, 106–107 ff., 135.

58. Degler, *At Odds,* pp. 300–325. John Cumbler contrasted male- and female-dominated charity societies in Massachusetts and found female-dominated organizations more sympathetic to the poor and less concerned with rooting out the unworthy: "The Politics of Charity: Gender and Class in Late Nineteenth-Century Charity Policy," *Journal of Social History,* 14 (Fall 1980): 99–112.

## *2. Divorce Documents and Divorce Seekers*

1. *Statutes of California: Second Session, 1851* (Eugene Casserly: State Printer, 1851), pp. 186–87.

2. *Statutes of California: Eighteenth Session, 1869–1870* (D. W. Glewicks: State Printer, 1870), p. 291; *West's Annotated California Codes: Civil Code, Sections 1 to 192* (St. Paul: West Publishing Company, 1954), p. 337. On divorce laws, see also Wright, *A Report on Marriage and Divorce in the United States, 1867 to 1886* p. 91; U.S. Bureau of the Census, *Special Reports: Marriage and Divorce, 1867–1906,* Part 1, pp. 280–81; Blake, *Road to Reno,* pp. 34–79; Morris, *Studies in American Law,* chapter 3.

3. After 1872, impotency and fraud were still valid grounds for marital dissolution: in a new marriage, impotency brought an annulment; otherwise, it would be included in desertion allegations. Proof of fraud brought an annulment. The three annulments in this sample were treated in the statistics as grants of divorce. The first California constitution, drafted in 1849, included a provision for the separate property of married women. All

property the wife brought to the marriage, or acquired by gift or otherwise after the marriage, remained her property. California passed a community property law in 1850: all property of the family acquired after marriage was considered to be held equally by the husband and the wife.

4. In this study, 45.8 percent of the female plaintiffs but only 20.8 percent of the male plaintiffs included cruelty allegations in their complaint.

5. Henry J. Labatt, *Reports of Cases Determined in the District Courts of the State of California,* I (San Francisco: Whitton, Towne, & Co., 1858), p. 52.

6. Ibid., II: 32.

7. Ibid., I: 384.

8. *Reports of Cases Determined in the Supreme Court of the State of California,* XIX (Sacramento, 1862), p. 628.

9. Ibid., XXII (San Francisco: H. H. Bancroft Co., 1864), pp. 360–61; *Statutes of California: Eighteenth Session, 1869–1870,* p. 291.

10. Quoted in Morton Keller, *Affairs of State: Public Life in Late Nineteenth-Century America* (Cambridge: Harvard University Press, 1977), p. 469. (Emphasis in the original.) On the improving legal status of nineteenth-century women, see Eleanor Flexner, *Century of Struggle: The Woman's Rights Movement in the United States* (New York: Atheneum, 1970), pp. 64–65, 93; Lawrence M. Friedman, *A History of American Law* (New York: Simon & Schuster, 1973), pp. 184–86; Degler, *At Odds,* p. 332. For the fullest treatment of law and the nineteenth-century family, see Michael Grossberg, "Law and the Family in Nineteenth Century America," Ph.D. diss., Brandeis University, Waltham, Mass., 1979. Grossberg argues that from 1790 to 1860, courts and state legislatures refashioned family law to promote the rights of individuals at the expense of traditional familial and community controls. Thereafter, fearing that rising divorce, falling fertility, women's rights, new sexual standards, the avoidance of marriage, and Mormon polygamy all threatened family cohesion, lawmakers and courts again shifted the focus of family law, this time to allow greater public control over family life.

11. Up until 1880, litigants filed divorce suits in district court, thereafter in superior court. The change came, not from any alteration in divorce law, but from a change in the California court system.

12. *West's Annotated California Codes,* p. 379. In this study, 69.7 percent (147) of the male defendants defaulted and 30.3 percent (64) answered; sixty-five cases lacked information on whether the summons was answered or ignored. Among female defendants, 70.6 percent (60) defaulted and 29.4 percent (25) answered; forty cases lacked such information.

13. The referee usually requested general information; for example, "Please describe the general character of the plaintiff." Other times (happily more rare) the referee would ask rather leading questions: "Would you describe the defendant as a man of good, frugal habits?" But the court, it should be emphasized, emphatically rejected the use of leading questions; in an 1867 case, Judge McKee registered disapproval with the referee's questioning and dismissed the case. He also bemoaned the lack of facts in the testimony and wrote that the witnesses "seem to have determined the question for themselves: for they give us their opinions and conclusions without

stating any facts or circumstances to sustain them." See Martin v. Sarah Daves, Case 2546, Santa Clara County, 1867. For reasons that remain unclear, the inclusion of testimony became infrequent by the mid-1880s, and its virtual disappearance by 1890 was one reason why this study stopped in that year.

14. The ratio of divorces per 1000 existing marriages in the United States was 1.2 in 1860, 1.5 in 1870, 2.2 in 1880, and 3.0 in 1890; see Paul H. Jacobson, *American Marriage and Divorce* (New York: Rinehart & Company, 1959), p. 90.

15. The divorce records also reflect the kinds of tensions present in thousands of other marriages; surely, without indulging in excessive speculation, the actual number of divorces represented only a small fraction of the couples suffering serious marital difficulties.

16. *San Jose Daily Mercury,* 10 Feb. 1886. Emphasis in original.

17. Women received 72 percent of the judgments for divorce; men, 28 percent. However, I want to emphasize that this study is based on 401 cases brought into court, not 401 divorces granted. Of the 401 cases, 265 ended in a divorce for the plaintiff and eight cases ended with an award to the defendant by cross-complaint. The judge dismissed eleven cases, plaintiffs dismissed another fifty-six, and the fate of sixty-one couples was unknown. In other words, of the 401 cases, 68 percent ended in a divorce for one party or the other. I used information from all 401 suits—often dismissed cases or those with no settlement contained all the information of completed cases save the final judgment—and thus the focus is at all times on the 401 suits filed, not the 273 that actually ended in divorce.

18. Of course, unless we know the full occupational structure of the two counties, we do not know whether one class or another was over- or under-represented. But even without this detailed analysis—an analysis that could be done with the manuscript census—the high number of working-class people is nevertheless striking.

19. Most of the occupations were found in the divorce records, but several others came to light in county directories of the time. Positively matching names between divorce cases and directory entries required caution, and I counted the occupation only if there was sufficient unambiguous evidence that the person in the directory was indeed the person in the divorce case. Several others came from two Santa Clara County histories: J. P. Munro-Fraser, *History of Santa Clara County, California* (San Francisco: Alley, Bowen, & Co., 1891); and Eugene T. Sawyer, *History of Santa Clara County, California* (Los Angeles: Historic Record Co., 1922). Both volumes are "booster histories" of the county, with the back two-thirds of each book taken up with brief biographies of early county residents. On the occupational classification scheme, see Michael B. Katz, *The People of Hamilton, Canada West: Family and Class in a Mid-Nineteenth Century City* (Cambridge: Harvard University Press, 1975), pp. 343–48.

20. The national figures are from U.S. Bureau of the Census, *Special Reports: Marriage and Divorce, 1867–1906,* p. 43.

21. The 1850s and 1860s were combined because of the small number of cases in the 1850s.

22. The division between white collar and blue collar is made between the upper and middle class on one hand and the farmers, skilled trades, unskilled trades, and laborers on the other.

23. Modernization theorists all include literacy as a key component of modern, in contrast to traditional, consciousness; see, for example, Richard D. Brown, *Modernization: The Transformation of American Life* (New York: Hill & Wang, 1976), pp. 13, 18, 40. Linda Kerber has suggested that high rates of female illiteracy in eighteenth-century America had important implications for gender relations: "To the extent that female culture had relied on the spoken word, it was premodern at a time when male culture was increasing its dependence on written communication." So long as this disparity prevailed, women were largely cut off from outside information and different viewpoints, thereby prolonging their dependence on and inferior status to men. (Kerber, *Women of the Republic,* pp. 192–93.) Illiteracy, of course, is only one facet of traditional culture: others include a sense of resignation, fatalism, and personal inefficacy. What is striking about the illiterate women in this study, then, is their willingness to act and to change their lives despite their lack of a basic element of modern consciousness.

24. On the racial composition for both counties, see the appropriate tables from the following U.S. Bureau of the Census publications: *The Statistics of the Population of the United States: The Ninth Census* (Washington, D.C.: Government Printing Office, 1872), p. 15; *The Statistics of the Population of the United States at the Tenth Census* (Washington, D.C.: Government Printing Office, 1883), p. 382; *Statistical View of the United States: Compendium of the Eleventh Census, 1890, Part 1: Population* (Washington, D.C.: Government Printing Office, 1892), pp. 477, 541, 668.

25. U.S. Bureau of the Census, *Compendium of Eleventh Census, 1890, Part 2* (Washington, D.C.: Government Printing Office, 1894), p. 615. In terms of visibility, the exceptions, of course, were the Chinese, who were highly visible and very oppressed; but they did not contribute to the divorce sample. A good starting point for the study of Chinese–white relations in California is Alexander Saxton, *The Indispensable Enemy: Labor and the Anti-Chinese Movement in California* (Berkeley: University of California Press, 1971).

26. Other people have also argued that the rise in divorce in the nineteenth century signified a rise in marital expectations; see O'Neill, *Divorce in the Progressive Era,* especially chapter 1.

27. On the rise in divorce, and for the figures in Table 5, see Wright, *Marriage and Divorce,* pp. 144, 148. The rate of divorce in San Francisco city and county was higher than that for the rest of the state. In 1880, San Francisco had 183 married couples to each divorce, whereas the remainder of the state, including San Francisco County, had 270 married couples to each divorce. Ibid., p 161.

28. Because the Santa Clara data is a sample based on every fifth case, the data in Table 7 are an estimate. Figures from the census, however, confirm the reliability of these figures: compared to the previous ten-year period, San

Mateo County from 1877 to 1886 had a 104 percent increase in the number of divorces granted and Santa Clara County a 106 percent increase. See U.S. Bureau of the Census, *Special Reports: Marriage and Divorce, 1867–1906: Part II, General Tables* (Washington, D.C., 1908), pp. 748–49.

29. Ibid., p. 82.

30. Cott, "Divorce and the Changing Status of Women," pp. 593, 602–14.

31. Both counties lie just south of San Francisco and are in what is called today the Bay Area. San Mateo County is contiguous with and lies directly south of the city of San Francisco; Santa Clara County borders on part of San Mateo County and encompasses the land directly south of the tip of the bay.

32. The figures in Table 12 are from U.S.Bureau of the Census, *Statistical View of the United States, Compendium of the Eleventh Census, 1890, Part 1: Population* (Washington, D.C.: Government Printing Office, 1892), p. 9.

33. These figures on San Jose come from U.S. Bureau of the Census, *Statistics: Ninth Census,* p. 92; U.S. Bureau of the Census, *Compendium of the Eleventh Census, 1890, Part 1, Population,* p. 74. There are no population figures for San Jose prior to 1870.

34. The figures in Table 13 are from the following U.S. Bureau of the Census publications: *Statistics: Ninth Census,* p. 92; *Statistics at Tenth Census,* p. 109; *Compendium of Eleventh Census, 1890, Part 1, Population,* p. 74.

35. Munro-Fraser, *History of Santa Clara County, California,* p. 23. On the history of Santa Clara County, see also Sawyer, *History of Santa Clara County, California.* See also a volume produced by the *San Jose Mercury* in 1895, called *Santa Clara County and Its Resources* (San Jose: *San Jose Mercury,* 1895). On San Mateo County, there is even less information, but of some help is Frank Stanger, *South from San Francisco: San Mateo County, California: Its History and Heritage* (San Mateo County Historical Association, 1963).

36. Once one moves away from San Francisco County, the dominance of agriculture becomes immediately apparent. As late as 1890, most California counties had fewer than one hundred manufacturing establishments, many recorded fewer than fifty, and a good number listed fewer than twenty-five. The vast majority of these establishments were small, employed a handful of people, and consisted of blacksmith, saddle, and harness shops, some small flour mills, cheese and butter factores, canning establishments, and the like. In the same year, twenty counties recorded at least one thousand farms and another twenty recorded over five hundred farms. See U.S. Bureau of the Census, *Report on Manufacturing Industries in the United States at the Eleventh Census, 1890, Part I: Totals for States and Industries* (Washington, D.C.: Government Printing Office, 1895), pp. 352–55; U.S. Bureau of the Census, *Report on the Statistics of Agriculture in the United States at the Eleventh Census: 1890* (Washington, D.C.: Government Printing Office, 1895), p. 200.

37. *San Jose Mercury, Santa Clara County and Its Resources,* p. 12.

38. U.S. Bureau of the Census, *Agriculture of the United States in 1860: The Eighth Census* (Washington, D.C.: Government Printing Office, 1865), p. 10.

39. U.S. Bureau of the Census, *Manufactures of the United States in 1860: The Eighth Census* (Washington, D.C.: Government Printing Office, 1865), p. 28.

40. U.S. Bureau of the Census, *Report on Manufacturing Industries at the*

*Eleventh Census, 1890, Part 1, Totals for States and Industries* (Washington, D.C.: Government Printing Office, 1895), pp. 354–55; U.S. Bureau of the Census, *Census Reports: Manufacturers: States and Territories,* VIII, Part 2 (U.S. Census Office, 1902), pp. 56, 390.

41. U.S. Bureau of the Census, *Manufacturing at Eleventh Census, 1890: Part l,* p. 355.

42. U.S. Bureau of the Census, *Manufactures 1860: Eighth Census,* p. 30.

43. U.S. Bureau of the Census, *Industry and Wealth at the Ninth Census,* III (Washington, D.C.: Government Printing Office, 1872), p. 640; U.S. Bureau of the Census, *Report on the Manufactures of the United States at the Tenth Census* (Washington, D.C.: Government Printing Office, 1883), p. 198.

44. U.S. Bureau of the Census, *Report on the Production of Agriculture: Tenth Census* (Washington, D.C.: Government Printing Office, 1883), pp. 34–35.

45. U.S. Bureau of the Census, *Manufacturing at Eleventh Census, 1890: Part I,* pp. 354–55.

## *3. Ideal Womanhood in California*

1. Abigail v. William Bennett, Case 3351, Santa Clara County, 1870 (testimony of George Bennett, Mary Barker, and Laura Bennett).

2. Ann Douglas, *The Feminization of American Culture* (New York: Alfred Knopf, 1977), pp. 61, 77. Two of the best treatments of the rise of woman's sphere are Cott, *The Bonds of Womanhood,* chapters 1 and 2, and Sklar, *Catharine Beecher,* pp. 135–37, 151–67. Carl Degler analyzes how the assumptions of domesticity functioned in reform politics in *At Odds,* pp. 298–327. Cott, Sklar, and Degler, however, do not share Douglas's and others' general pessimism about the separation of society into two distinct spheres.

3. Barbara Berg, *Remembered Gate,* 75 ff., 102, 106–7.

4. The quotation is from Barbara J. Harris, *Beyond Her Sphere: Women and the Professions in American History* (Westport, Conn.: Greenwood Press, 1978), p. 35. On women's character traits, see Ann Firor Scott, *The Southern Lady: From Pedestal to Politics, 1830–1930* (Chicago: University of Chicago Press, 1970), p. 17; Barbara Welter, "The Cult of True Womanhood: 1820–1860," *American Quarterly,* 18 (1966), pp. 151–74; Cott, *Bonds of Womanhood,* pp. 146–47; and Regina Morantz, "The Lady and Her Physician," in Mary Hartman, Lois Banner, eds., *Clio's Consciousness Raised: New Perspectives on the History of Women* (New York: Harper & Row, 1974), p. 42.

5. Harris, *Beyond Her Sphere,* p. 34.

6. Berg, *Remembered Gate,* p. 104. On education, also see Cott, *Bonds of Womanhood,* pp. 101–25.

7. Morantz, "Lady and Her Physician," p. 38.

8. Berg, *Remembered Gate,* p. 72. The following are representative of those who stress the negative implications of domesticity for woman: Faragher, *Women and Men on the Overland Trail,* p. 177; Douglas, *Feminization of American Culture,* pp. 48 ff. 54, 60–61, 77; Harris, *Beyond Her Sphere,* pp. 21, 34, 56–57, 75 ff., 86, 102 7; Carroll Smith Rosenberg, "The Hysterical Woman: Sex

Roles and Role Conflict in Nineteenth Century America," *Social Research,* 39 (1972): 652–78; and Carroll Smith-Rosenberg and Charles Rosenberg, "The Female Animal: Medical and Biological Views of Woman and Her Role in Nineteenth-Century America," *Journal of American History,* 60 (1973): 332–56.

9. For example, contrast Linda Kerber's well-documented analysis of the Enlightenment's general indifference or even hostility to women with Barbara Berg's claims to the contrary in Kerber, *Women of the Republic,* pp. 15–27, 32, and Berg, *Remembered Gate,* p. 16.

10. Norton, *Liberty's Daughters,* pp. 61–63, 117–19; Norton, "Eighteenth-Century American Women in Peace and War," pp. 386–409; Kerber, *Women of the Republic,* pp. 120–36; Wells, "Demographic Change and the Life Cycle of American Families," pp. 273–82.

11. Norton, *Liberty's Daughters,* pp. 228-55 and Chapters 6 and 7.

12. Ibid., pp. 197–98, 243, 256–65; Kerber, *Women of the Republic,* pp. 47, 204–10, 227–29, 283–87. Kerber quote p. 283. Jacqueline S. Reinier also explores the impact of republicanism on motherhood and childrearing in "Rearing the Republican Child: Attitudes and Practices in Post-Revolutionary Philadelphia," *William and Mary Quarterly,* 39, (1982): 150-63.

13. Ryan's recent book, *Cradle of the Middle Class: The Family in Oneida County, New York, 1790–1865* (Cambridge, Eng.: Cambridge University Press, 1981), provides an insightful and much needed case study of the relationship between economic change and the origins of domesticity; see chapters 2–5. The quotation is from p. 153. Women's potential as a source of national unity is discussed in Sklar, *Catharine Beecher,* pp. 132, 134–35, 172–74; the home as sanctuary is noted in Jeffrey, "Family History," pp. 74–76, 96, 101–37; and women's civilizing role in the West by Jeffrey, *Frontier Women,* pp. 12, 20ff, 87–95, 107ff, 135.

14. Why women's power within the family increased is linked to the emergence of domesticity, which, in turn, was tied to concerns about social order and the rise of an urban market economy in which increasing numbers of women were without a direct economic role. But the assumptions of domesticity, although inflating women's social and moral importance, would not necessarily have required an elevation of female power vis-à-vis that of males. More generalized changes in women's status were necessary before domesticity could translate into increased power within the home. Carl Degler suggests that the roots of such changes go back to the emergence of individualism in the West, but more specifically, in women's case, to the Reformation and the Enlightenment: the former underscored the importance of the family and the wives' right to respect and affection; the latter emphasized the ideas of individualism and equality, thus offering a favorable climate for the first cautious and tentative statements on women's rights. In short, women slowly became conscious of themselves as individuals, an attitude "that underlay," as Degler explained, "the drive for autonomy for women within the family." This drive was central to the emergence of the companionate family because as women's self-conceptions changed, so, too, did family relations. Degler's general theory fits well with Kerber's and

Norton's work on the elevation of women's status in society and in the family in the Revolutionary and post-Revolutionary years. In the wake of the Revolution, women demanded better educational opportunities, criticized the sexual double standard, and, in keeping with republican egalitarianism, desired greater authority within the home and more control over their own fertility. See Degler, *At Odds,* pp. 188–94; Norton, *Liberty's Daughters,* pp. 228–42, 256–94; and Kerber, *Women of the Republic,* chapters 7 and 8.

15. *Santa Clara Argus,* 21 July 1866.
16. *San Mateo County Journal,* 5 August 1880.
17. *Weekly Argus,* 4 July 1874.
18. *San Mateo County Gazette,* 31 March 1880.
19. Ibid., 11 June 1859.
20. *San Mateo County Journal,* 15 July 1880.
21. Ibid.
22. Ibid., 29 April 1880.
23. *San Jose Daily Mercury,* 2 November 1886. Emphasis in original.
24. *San Mateo County Gazette,* 20 August 1859.
25. *Weekly Argus,* 28 March 1874.
26. *San Jose Daily Mercury,* 25 December 1886.
27. *Santa Clara Argus,* 5 May 1866.
28. *San Jose Daily Mercury,* 1 August 1886. Emphasis in original.
29. Cott makes a similar argument in her book, *Bonds of Womanhood,* p. 200. The ideology of domesticity has both conservative and reformist implications. As we have seen, it could function to increase women's status in the home and to legitimate reformist political activity ranging from temperance and anti-prostitution campaigns to the settlement house movement. But the same ideology could and still does hamper women's drive for full political and economic equality, as the early opposition to women's suffrage and today's battle against the Equal Rights Amendment attests. On domesticity and suffrage, the following are helpful: Ellen DuBois, "The Radicalism of the Woman Suffrage Movement: Notes toward the Reconstruction of Nineteenth-Century Feminism," *Feminist Studies,* 3 (Fall 1975): 63–71; Aileen S. Kraditor, *The Ideas of the Woman Suffrage Movement, 1890–1920* (Garden City, N.Y.: Anchor Books, 1971), pp. 38–63; and Degler, *At Odds,* pp. 328–61.

Although the domestic ideal may have first arisen among the middle class, the divorce evidence suggests that its influence soon transcended class lines, a point also made by Elizabeth Jameson in her study of Colorado miners' wives. These workingclass wives—married to class conscious, radical men—took the canons of domesticity as their ideal; see "Imperfect Unions: Class and Gender in Cripple Creek, 1894–1904," in Milton Cantor, Bruce Laurie, eds., *Class, Sex, and the Woman Worker* (Westport, Conn.: Greenwood Press, 1977), pp. 166-202. Such evidence may mean that the cult of domesticity not only provided a sense of identity for all women but a measure of national unity as well.

30. Catherine v. Isaac Court, Case 1752, Santa Clara County, 1862 (formal complaint).

31. Ellen v. A. J. Collamere, Case 575, San Mateo County, 1868 (formal complaint). For similar language, see the complaints in May v. William Short, Case 2026, Santa Clara County, 1864; Vicenta v. Daniel Wilson, Case 2353, Santa Clara County, 1866; Polly v. James Haun, Case 2417, Santa Clara County, 1866; Elaika v. Marlin Mattson, Case 214, San Mateo County, 1880; Sarah v. James White, Case 276, San Mateo County, 1881; Adelle v. Harvey Kincaid, Case 281, San Mateo County, 1881.

32. Greenburg v. Susan McMahill, Case 1850, Santa Clara County, 1863 (defendant's answer).

33. Ann v. Thomas Warhurst, Case 2231, Santa Clara County, 1865 (formal complaint). For similar language, see Frances v. Hiram Springett, Case 2985, Santa Clara County, 1869 (formal complaint); Bridget v. Dennis Hanagan, Case 634, San Mateo County, 1885 (formal complaint); Mary v. James Grey, Case 635, San Mateo County, 1885 (formal complaint).

34. Julia v. John Demartini, Case 6981, Santa Clara County, 1884 (formal complaint); Katharina v. William Wahl, Case 654, San Mateo County, 1885 (formal complaint).

35. Levi v. Nellie Rathburn, Case 3863, Santa Clara County, 1873 (defendant's answer).

36. William v. May Stewart, Case 424, San Mateo County, 1882 (defendant's answer).

37. Grace v. George Weston, Case 4668, Santa Clara County, 1876 (formal complaint); Caroline v. Archibald White, Case 5419, Santa Clara County, 1878 (formal complaint). For other references to sexual modesty and propriety in the formal legal documents, see Elizabeth v. Johann Baumgartner, Case 8187, Santa Clara County, 1888 (formal complaint); Catharina v. Martin Spitzer, Case 792, San Mateo County, 1887 (formal complaint); Catharine v. H. F. Thurston, Case 806, San Mateo County, 1887 (formal complaint); and May v. James Grey, Case 896, San Mateo County, 1888 (formal complaint).

38. Amilla v. Joseph Kelly, Case 1375, Santa Clara County, 1860 (formal complaint).

39. Ann v. Thomas Warhurst, Case 2231, Santa Clara County, 1865 (formal complaint).

40. Sarah v. Euclid Isbill, Case 402, San Mateo County, 1882 (testimony of Sarah Isbill and Isaac Wixam).

41. Melissa v. Hiram Ray, Case 320, San Mateo County, 1882 (testimony of Melissa Ray).

42. Ellen v. Minor Havely, Case 3024, Santa Clara county, 1869 (testimony of Ellen Havely).

43. Julia v. Scott Sabine, Case 734, San Mateo County, 1871 (testimony of Julia Sabine).

44. Annie v. Edwin Parker, Case 403, San Mateo County, 1882 (testimony of Annie Parker); Maria v. W. B. Estes, Case 447, San Mateo County, 1883 (testimony of Maria Estes).

45. Ellen DuBois and Carl Degler contend that the suffrage was radical and therefore threatening to nineteenth-century Americans, because it was at

odds with the assumptions of the separation of the spheres. Suffrage for women implied that husbands did not represent the political interests of the family and that women were indeed individuals who deserved to vote in their own right. This desire to vote as an individual did not comport with women's other-serving roles as mother, wife, and bastion of morality. See DuBois, "The Radicalism of the Woman Suffrage Movement," pp. 63–71, and Degler, *At Odds,* pp. 341–61.

46. Welter, "Cult of True Womanhood," pp. 158–62.

47. Ibid., p. 159.

48. *San Mateo County Gazette,* 3 Sept. 1859.

49. Jeffrey, "Family History," chapter 5.

50. Elaika v. Marlin Mattson, Case 214, San Mateo County, 1880 (formal complaint).

51. Emma v. Joseph Tuers, Case 2161, Santa Clara County, 1865 (testimony of Hannah Marrs).

52. Elaika v. Marlin Mattson, Case 214, San Mateo County, 1880 (testimony of F. M. Hale).

53. Ellen v. Minor Havely, Case 3024, Santa Clara County, 1869 (testimony of Zenas Churchill).

54. Sarah v. Summerville Forbes, Case 2959, Santa Clara County, 1869 (testimony of C. D. Davidson).

55. Martha v. Calvin Putman, Case 692, San Mateo County, 1870 (testimony of Martha Putman); Grace v. Manuel Thomas, Case 8526, Santa Clara County, 1889 (testimony of Grace Thomas).

56. John v. Sarah Cardinell, Case 650, San Mateo County, 1870 (testimony of John Cardinell).

57. Cornelius v. Anne Paddock, Case 1276, San Mateo County, 1877 (testimony of Cornelius Paddock).

58. The companionate marriage was grounded in mutual respect or as the *San Mateo County Journal* (15 July 1880) wrote: "It is a community of feelings and of interests that draws close the marriage bond, and gets perfection when the common feeling and interest are staked in what is most precious and most permanent."

59. Emma v. Joseph Tuers, Case 2161, Santa Clara County, 1865 (defendant's answer); William v. May Stewart, Case 424, San Mateo County, 1887 (testimony of Samantha Kelly).

60. Joseph v. Arena Gardner, Case 794, San Mateo County, 1887 (testimony of Samantha Kelly).

61. Annie v. Edwin Parker, Case 403, San Mateo County, 1882 (letter of Edwin Parker to Annie Parker dated 21 Dec. 1882).

62. The following studies emphasize the medical community's seeming hostility to women: Ben Barker-Benfield, "The Spermatic Economy: A Nineteenth-Century View of Sexuality," *Feminist Studies,* 1 (Summer 1972): 45–74; Ann Douglas Wood, " 'The Fashionable Diseases': Women's Complaints and Their Treatment in Nineteenth-Century America," *Journal of Interdisciplinary History,* 4 (Summer 1973): 25–52; Carroll Smith-Rosenberg, "Puberty to Menopause: The Cycle of Femininity in Nineteenth-Century

America," in Hartman and Banner, eds., *Clio's Consciousness Raised,* pp. 23–37; and Carroll Smith-Rosenberg, Charles Rosenberg, "Female Animal," pp. 332–56. Barker-Benfield and Wood are far less cautious than Smith-Rosenberg and Rosenberg in their appraisal of the medical profession's distrust and oppression of women.

63. Regina Morantz views the medical community's attitude toward women more positively than the authorities cited in the previous note; see "The Lady and Her Physician," in Hartman and Banner, eds., *Clio's Consciousness Raised,* pp. 38–53. Carl Degler's article on nineteenth-century female sexuality likewise views the medical community as relatively enlightened regarding women and sex, a view in sharp contrast to Barker-Benfield's denunciation of doctors: "What Ought To Be and What Was: Women's Sexuality in the Nineteenth Century," *American Historical Review,* 79 (December 1974): 1467–90.

64. Carroll Smith-Rosenberg, "The Hysterical Woman: Sex Roles and Role Conflict in Nineteenth-Century America," *Social Research,* 39 (Winter 1972): 652–78.

65. Sklar, *Catharine Beecher,* p. 214.

66. On the division of women's occupations, see Table 21, p. 81. Most of the women who listed a job were forced to work because their husbands had deserted them or refused to support them.

67. Catharine v. H. F. Thurston, Case 806, San Mateo County, 1887 (defendant's answer).

68. Katharina v. William Wahl, Case 688, San Mateo County, 1886 (formal complaint).

69. Charles v. Ellen King, Case 245, San Mateo County, 1881 (testimony of James L. Crossett and defendant's answer).

70. Seward v. Nellie Jones, Case 366, San Mateo County, 1882 (testimony of Nellie Jones).

71. Vicenta v. Daniel Wilson, Case 2353, Santa Clara County, 1866 (testimony of E. F. Wilcox).

72. Eugenia v. William Duncombe, Case 444, San Mateo County, 1883 (letter of William Duncombe to lawyer J. K. Finley); Antoinette v. Joseph Johnson, Case 3993, Santa Clara County, 1874 (testimony of Dr. A. B. Caldwell).

73. Annie v. Vassily Semenoff, Case 580, San Mateo County, 1884 (formal complaint).

74. Jennie v. Stillman Moulton, Case 4132, Santa Clara County, 1874 (formal complaint). Stillman was unemployed.

75. Antoinette v. Joseph Johnson, Case 3993, Santa Clara County, 1874; Maria v. Benedict Schwab, Case 5517, Santa Clara County, 1878; Martha v. William Rinehart, Case 7264, Santa Clara County, 1885; Alice v. Edward Kilday, Case 736, San Mateo County, 1886; Caroline v. John Planer, Case 1002, San Mateo County, 1874. Johnson's and Schwab's husbands were businessmen, Planer's was a baker, and the occupations of the others were unknown. Many other legal documents contained information on female

health: child custody motions, alimony requests, affidavits for alimony, and defendants' answers all might contain reference to a woman's physical condition. For various examples, see Frank v. Susan Gilbert, Case 1134, San Mateo County, 1875 (child custody motion); Thomas v. Harriet Yates, Case 343, San Mateo County, 1875 (alimony request); Stephen v. Alice Burdick, Case 604, San Mateo County, 1885 (affidavit for alimony).

76. Ellen v. Minor Havely, Case 3024, Santa Clara County, 1869 (formal complaint).

77. Eleanor v. James Chesley, Case 758, San Mateo County, 1887 (formal complaint); Louisa v. J. C. Koppell, Case 8332, Santa Clara County, 1889 (formal complaint). Emphasis in original.

78. Annie v. Vassily Semenoff, Case 580, San Mateo County, 1884 (formal complaint).

79. Martha v. Samuel Brisbine, Case 3623, Santa Clara County, 1872 (formal complaint).

80. Vicenta v. Daniel Wilson, Case 2353, Santa Clara County, 1866 (testimony of Sarah Wilcox and Lucretia Miller).

81. Abigail v. William Bennett, Case 3351, Santa Clara County, 1870 (testimony of Eunice Bennett).

82. Esther v. George Philbrick, Case 6742, Santa Clara County, 1883 (testimony of Esther Philbrick).

83. Antoinette v. Joseph Johnson, Case 3993, Santa Clara County, 1874 (testimony of Antoinette Johnson). Many other cases alleged that the husband had caused his wife's poor health; see, for example, Ellen v. Robert Pollett, Case 500, San Mateo County, 1883 (formal complaint); Mary v. John Kribler, Case 379, San Mateo County, 1882 (formal complaint); Jennie v. Stillman Moulton, Case 4132, Santa Clara County, 1874 (formal complaint); Mary v. Thornton Sharp, Case 367, San Mateo County, 1882 (testimony of Mary Sharp); Maggie v. George Cottrell, Case 5075, Santa Clara County, 1877 (testimony of Sara Tedford).

84. These figures represent a breakdown of the various permutations of sources of support and therefore add up to more than 100 percent. Many women mentioned supporting themselves and/or receiving help from friends, relatives, and neighbors.

85. Mary v. George Dale, Case 594, San Mateo County, 1868 (testimony of Mary Dale and Albert Vincent).

86. Harriet v. David Shupe, Case 678, San Mateo County, 1870 (testimony of Harriet Shupe).

87. Jane v. Fred Sayers, Case 595, San Mateo County, 1868 (testimony of Clara Spaulding).

88. Mary v. James Glover, Case 1272, San Mateo County, 1878 (testimony of Kate Williams).

89. The small number of women involved stems from the fact that these figures refer only to unhealthy women and then only to those whose sources of support we know.

90. Margaret v. John McClelland, Case 1207, San Mateo County, 1877

(formal complaint).

91. Susan v. Frank Gilbert, Case 1125, San Mateo County, 1876 (testimony of Dr. J. A. Miller).

92. Elizabeth v. Egbert Etts, Case 684, San Mateo County, 1870 (testimony of Elizabeth Etts and A. R. Sansman).

93. May v. William Short, Case 2026, Santa Clara County, 1864 (formal complaint); Ann v. Thomas Warhurst, Case 2231, Santa Clara County, 1865 (formal complaint); Harriet v. David Shupe, Case 678, San Mateo County, 1870 (testimony of Harriet Shupe); Ottilia v. Herman Kottinger, Case 4505, Santa Clara County, 1876 (testimony of Ottilia Kottinger).

94. Martha v. Robert Lucas, Case 2298, Santa Clara County, 1866 (formal complaint). For further evidence on the connection between poor health and limited economic opportunities, see Catharine v. Daniel Cleal, Case 3433, Santa Clara County, 1871 (formal complaint); Nellie v. Frank Chadivick, Case 7367, Santa Clara County, 1885 (formal complaint); Josephine v. William Stayton, Case 3686, Santa Clara County, 1872 (formal complaint); Martha v. Calvin Putnam, Case 692, San Mateo County, 1870 (formal complaint); Martha v. Isaac Gifford, Case 6810, Santa Clara County, 1883 (formal complaint); Katharine v. Alfred Cole, Case 644, San Mateo County, 1885 (answer to demurrer); Ortency v. Louis Franklyn, Case 1011, San Mateo County, 1889 (judge's findings).

95. Vincenta v. Daniel Wilson, Case 2353, Santa Clara County, 1866 (testimony of Mrs. H. S. Hanover).

96. *San Jose Daily Mercury,* 10 Feb. 1886.

## *4. Dimensions of Womanhood: Domesticity, Chastity, and Independence*

1. Carole Shammas, "The Domestic Environment in Early Modern England and America," *Journal of Social Hisotry,* 14 (1980): 3.

2. Ibid., p. 11.

3. Norton, *Liberty's Daughters,* pp. 34–38.

4. Ibid., p. 155.

5. Ibid., p. 243. Also see Kerber, *Women of the Republic,* 210, 252–53, 269, and Cott, *The Bonds of Womanhood,* pp. 104–5.

6. Cott, "Divorce and Changing Status," pp. 592–93, 602–6, 613–14.

7. On the relationship between economic change and the rise of domesticity see Ryan, *Cradle of the Middle Class,* chapters 2–5, and Cott, *Bonds of Womanhood,* chapters 1 and 2.

8. On the home as refuge see Cott, *Bonds of Womanhood,* pp. 69–70; Jeffrey, "Family History," pp. 101, 117–35; Berg, *Remembered Gate,* p. 67; Sklar, *Catharine Beecher,* pp. 135–37, 156–59; and Richard Sennett, *Families against the City: Middle Class Homes of Industrial Chicago, 1872–1890* (Cambridge, Mass.: Harvard University Press, 1970).

9. On Southern women, see Scott, *Southern Lady,* pp. 3–44.

10. Jeffrey, *Frontier Women,* pp. 9, 24, 177–78.

11. Faragher, *Women and Men on The Overland Trail,* pp. 170 ff.

12. *San Jose Daily Mercury,* 12 Feb. 1886.

13. Cott, *Bonds of Womanhood,* p. 73. In making women's domestic work a vocation, moralists, argued Cott, prescribed work values for women that looked strikingly like those urged on men (pp. 71–74). Cott writes (p. 98), "The accent on individual character and self-control in the canon of domesticity simulated—and underpinned—individual economic struggle, just as women's vocation simulated men's." Also see Sklar, *Catharine Beecher,* pp. 151–67, and Patricia Branca, *Silent Sisterhood: Middle Class Women in Victorian Home* (London: Croom Helm, 1975), pp. 25–35. Both Sklar and Branca note the rise of housework as a vocation, and though their evidence is from middle-class prescriptive literature, the divorce evidence suggests that women and men from all social classes saw housework in purposeful, instrumental terms.

14. Frances v. Frank Cory, Case 777, San Mateo County, 1871 (formal complaint).

15. Nicholas v. Annie Holden, Case 5116, Santa Clara County, 1877 (testimony of Margaret Peterson, Annie Holden, and Annie Leddy).

16. Antoinette v. Joseph Johnson, Case 3993, Santa Clara County, 1874 (testimony of A. W. Saxe).

17. Sarah v. Henry Simonds, Case 377, San Mateo County, 1864 (testimony of Abner Colburn and George Troop).

18. Emma v. Joseph Tuers, Case 2161, Santa Clara County, 1865 (testimony of Joseph Winterbarn, John Patterson, William Stewart, C. D. Rodgers, and William Spencer).

19. Abigail v. Wiliam Bennett, Case 3351, Santa Clara County, 1870 (testimony of Mary Barker and Laura Bennett).

20. Catharine v. Daniel Cleal, Case 4106, Santa Clara County, 1874 (testimony of Kate Weller).

21. Sarah v. Euclid Isbill, Case 402, San Mateo County, 1882 (testimony of Mary Wixam).

22. Mary v. Thornton Sharp, Case 367, San Mateo County, 1882 (testimony of Alice Crane). Also see Armenia v. Richard Parker, Case 4173, Santa Clara County, 1874 (testimony of W. H. Collins).

23. Grace v. Manuel Thomas, Case 8526, Santa Clara County, 1889 (testimony of Timeteo Sierra); Maria v. Rafael Alviso, Case 1960, Santa Clara County, 1864 (testimony of Tadeo Lopez).

24. Martha v. Robert Lucas, Case 2298, Santa Clara County, 1866 (defendant's answer).

25. Ortency v. Louis Franklyn, Case 1011, San Mateo County, 1889 (defendant's answer). Tamara Hareven makes some interesting speculations on the relations among modernization, housework, and women's roles in her article, "Modernization and Family History: Perspectives on Social Change," *Signs,* 2 (1976): 190–206. In contrasting housework with the emergence of industrial work, Cott notes that domestic work was "unsystematized, inefficient, nonurgent." Later, Cott describes efforts to modernize housework by making home duties "a discrete, specialized, and objective work-role." Cott, *Bonds of Womanhood,* pp. 61–62, 71–74. Also seen Tamara Hareven, "Family

Time and Industrial Time: Family and Work in a Planned Corporation Town, 1900–1924," *Journal of Urban History*, 1 (1975): 365–89.

26. William v. Addie Gray, Case 480, San Mateo County, 1883 (testimony of Carrie Gray).

27. Henry v. Clara Conners, Case 909, San Mateo County, 1888 (formal complaint).

28. Louisa v. J. C. Koppell, Case 8332, Santa Clara County, 1889 (defendant's answer).

29. Emma v. Joseph Tuers, Case 2161, Santa Clara County, 1865 (testimony of William Tuers and John Tuers).

30. Neither of Nancy Cott's articles on divorce contain evidence of praise or criticism of women's domestic duties: see "Eighteenth-Century Family and Social Life" and "Divorce and the Changing Status of Women." Nor does Kerber's work on eighteenth-century Connecticut divorces contain such references, although wives who refused to help the family improve economically or who misused the family estate were sometimes mentioned in divorce petitions. (Kerber, *Women of the Republic*, pp. 159–84.)

31. Nancy Cott, "Passionlessness," pp. 219–36. The quotation is from Welter, "Cult of True Womanhood," p. 156. On women's sexuality in the nineteenth-century, see Carl Degler's essay, "What Ought To Be and What Was," pp. 1467–90 and chapter 11 in *At Odds*. Degler's findings reveal that "passionlessness" was not universally accepted: the late-nineteenth-century medical community generally took it for granted that women possessed sexual desires. Also useful are John S. Haller, Jr., and Robin M. Haller, *The Physician and Sexuality in Victorian America* (Urbana: University of Illinois Press, 1974); Michael Gordon, "From an Unfortunate Necessity to a Cult of Mutual Orgasm: Sex in American Marital Education Literature, 1830–1940," in James M. Henslin, ed., *Studies in the Sociology of Sex* (New York: Appleton-Century Crofts, 1971), pp. 53–80; David J. Pivar, *Purity Crusade: Sexual Morality and Social Control, 1868–1900* (Westport, Conn.: Greenwood Press, 1973).

32. Berg, *Remembered Gate*, p. 84.

33. Ibid., p. 85.

34. Welter, "Cult of True Womanhood," pp. 154–58; Berg, *Remembered Gate*, p. 85.

35. Cott, "Passionlessness," pp. 233–36. In the article, Cott suggests (pp. 228–32) that a decline in parental control over mate selection, a rise in the age of marriage, an increase in the number of prebridal pregnancies, and an increase in the number of women never married all signified women's increased sexual vulnerability in the late eighteenth and early nineteenth centuries. Also see Sklar, *Catharine Beecher*, pp. 210–11.

36. Louise v. James Butchart, Case 1415, San Mateo County, 1879 (formal complaint). The importance of a woman's sexual reputation for chastity is evidenced by the fact that Louise was granted the $20,000 in damages. Lawrence Stone has written: "Among the plebs, sex within marriage—which is where sex inevitably took place—is a world closed to the historian." See

Stone, *Family, Sex, and Marriage,* p. 603. The divorce evidence provides a way to gain a glimpse—however fleeting—through the bedroom keyhole.

37. Maria v. James Quentin, Case 596, San Mateo County, 1868 (formal complaint); Jennie v. Elhyder Hammond, Case 2642, Santa Clara County, 1868 (formal complaint).

38. Grace v. George Weston, Case 4668, Santa Clara County, 1876 (formal complaint).

39. Elizabeth v. Egbert Etts, Case 684, San Mateo County, 1870 (formal complaint); Mary Ann v. Edward Evans, Case 1360, San Mateo County, 1878 (formal complaint); Vicenta v. Daniel Wilson, Case 2353, Santa Clara County, 1866 (formal complaint); and E. M. v. Isadore Keller, Case 1239, San Mateo County, 1877 (formal complaint). Many other complaints included charges that husbands used abusive sexual epithets; see, for example, Annie v. W. J. McKee, Case 7431, Santa Clara County 1885 (formal complaint); Caroline v. Archibald White, Case 5419, Santa Clara County, 1878 (amended complaint); Maria v. Benedict Schwab, Case 5517, Santa Clara County, 1878 (formal complaint); Ugolina v. Cesare Nicora, Case 6565, Santa Clara County, 1882 (formal complaint); Mary v. Lyman Avery, Case 7783, Santa Clara County, 1887 (formal complaint).

Women did not receive divorces solely on the ground of their husbands' indignities, but such allegations functioned to support wive's complaints of systematic cruelty on the part of husbands. While California was more progressive than many states in what it considered cruel behavior, as late as 1890 the State Supreme Court ruled that epithets and indignities that did not potentially or actually injure the health failed to constitute cruelty. However, in 1892 the court overruled the 1890 decision and contended that indignities that humiliated the wife need not potentially or actually injure her health in order to constitute cruelty. This decision included a ringing declaration that marriages in "advanced civilization" were based on "mutual sentiments of love and respect" and that indignities could destroy the basis of marriage even if no physical threat to the wife's body or health was evident. For the 1890 case, see Waldron v. Waldron, *The Pacific Reporter,* vol. 24 (St. Paul: West Publishing Co., 1891), pp. 649–54, and for the 1892 case, Barnes v. Barnes, *The Pacific Reporter,* vol. 30 (St. Paul: West Publishing Co., 1892), pp. 298–99.

40. Antoinette v. Joseph Johnson, Case 3993, Santa Clara County, 1874 (testimony of Antoinette Johnson).

41. Abigail v. William Bennett, Case 3351, Santa Clara County, 1870 (testimony of Abigail Bennett, William Bennett, and George Bennett).

42. Ibid., (testimony of L. Archer).

43. Mary v. James Gray, Case 896, San Mateo County, 1888 (formal complaint).

44. Sarah v. James White, Case 276, San Mateo County, 1881 (formal complaint); Greenburg v. Susan McMahill, Case 1850, Santa Clara County, 1863 (defendant's answer and cross-complaint).

45. Caroline v. Archibald White, Case 5419, Santa Clara County, 1878 (amended complaint); Winnifred v. Michael Fay, Case 945, San Mateo

County, 1874 (testimony of Winnifred Fay). On other public accusations of adultery, see Joanna v. Henri Vandervorst, Case 4980, Santa Clara County, 1877 (formal complaint); Mary v. James Coyl, Case 6184, Santa Clara County, 1880 (formal complaint); Esther v. George Philbrick, Case 6742, Santa Clara County, 1883 (formal complaint); Elizabeth v. Johann Baumgartner, Case 8187, Santa Clara County, 1888 (formal complaint); Catherine v. Michael Comerford, Case 484, San Mateo County, 1883 (formal complaint); Sarah v. James White, Case 276, San Mateo County, 1881 (formal complaint).

46. Frank v. Susan Gilbert, Case 1134, San Mateo County, 1875 (formal complaint and amended complaint).

47. Ibid., (defendant's answer). Also see Susan v. Frank Gilbert, Case 1125, San Mateo County, 1876. In this case, Susan sued successfully for divorce on grounds of desertion and non-support.

48. Levi v. Nellie Rathburn, Case 3863, Santa Clara County, 1873 (testimony of Michael Barney).

49. Ibid., (testimony of Mary Barney). Her husband offered a similar comment: "I have no ill will towards Mrs. Rathburn."

50. *San Mateo County Journal,* 5 Aug. 1880.

51. Annie v. Edwin Parker, Case 403, San Mateo County, 1882 (letter of December 1882 from Edwin to Annie Parker).

52. Cott, "Divorce and the Changing Status of Women in Eighteenth-Century Massachusetts," pp. 586–614; see also her article, "Eighteenth-Century Family and Social Life Revealed in Massachusetts Divorce Records," pp. 20–43.

53. Kerber, *Women of the Republic,* p. 163.

54. Degler, *At Odds,* 372–73, 377. Nationally, over 95 percent of white married women did not work outside the home in the nineteenth century. See Smith, "Family Limitation, Sexual Control, and Domestic Feminism in Victorian America," pp. 42–43.

55. U.S. Bureau of the Census, *Report on Manufacturing Industries in the United States at the 11th Census, 1890, Part I: Totals for States and Industries* (Washington, D.C.: Government Printing Office, 1895), p. 355.

56. William v. Sophia Hendrickson, Case 382, San Mateo County, 1882 (testimony of J. W. Landon).

57. Annie v. Edwin Parker, Case 403, San Mateo County, 1882 (testimony of Annie Parker).

58. Walter v. Susan Battey, Case 1404, Santa Clara County, 1860 (defendant's answer); Mary v. James Gray, Case 635, San Mateo County, 1885 (formal complaint).

59. Elaika v. Marlin Mattson, Case 214, San Mateo County, 1880 (testimony of Elaika Mattson).

60. The records generally indicate that most women supported themselves and, in addition, received help from various people. The evidence does not, however, reveal the pattern of support. Thus, for example, it is impossible to determine whether women who supported themselves received steady additional aid from their parents or friends or received such help only in times of

crisis. Nor can it be determined if children volunteered support or were requested to do so by their mother or her concerned friends. For 229 cases, there was no information whatsoever on the wife's economic situation.

61. These figures came only from those cases which included information about the woman's source(s) of support, regardless of whether she was the plaintiff or the defendant. Not surprisingly, most cases in which the defendants were wives contained no information about their economic situations, but these cases were not included in the comparison above.

62. On the purposeful, instrumental nature of wives' domestic labor, see Cott, *Bonds of Womanhood,* pp. 42, 54–58, 63–100; and Sklar, *Catharine Beecher,* pp. 151–67.

63. Carroll Smith-Rosenberg, "The Female World of Love and Ritual," *Signs: A Journal of Women in Culture and Society,* I (1975): 1–30.

64. Cott, "Passionlessness," p. 233.

65. Jeffrey, *Frontier Women,* pp. 41–42, 69, 74–75. Also on sororal ties, see Cott, *Bonds of Womanhood,* pp. 160–96; Norton, *Liberty's Daughters,* pp. 102, 105–9; Smith, *Inside the Great House,* pp. 73–74; and Cumbler, "Politics of Charity," p. 107.

66. Elisha v. Samantha Hughes, Case 1810, Santa Clara County, 1863 (letter of Samantha Hughes to Elisha Hughes). Emphasis in original. Samantha's friend Arena Gardner also testified that Samantha had no intention of living with her husband: "I have heard her say she never would live with him. Had heard her say so frequently. We had several conversations about it. She told me she would starve before she would live with him."

67. John v. Margaret Tanner, Case 8168, Santa Clara County, 1888 (testimony of C. Archer, Louise Ord, and Carrie Ennor).

68. Annie v. Edwin Parker, Case 403, San Mateo County, 1882 (letters of Edwin Parker to his wife and to the superior court judge). On the importance of mediums in many women's lives in the nineteenth century, see R. Laurence Moore, *In Search of White Crows: Spiritualism, Parapsychology and American Culture* (New York: Oxford University Press, 1977).

69. Faragher, *Women and Men on the Overland Trail,* pp. 163–64.

70. Jeffrey, *Frontier Women,* pp. 30–31.

71. Richard v. Jennie Denson, Case 1268, San Mateo County, 1878 (formal complaint).

72. Mills v. Zilpha Plumb, Case 364, San Mateo County, 1882 (testimony of Mills Plumb).

73. William v. Addie Gray, Case 480, San Mateo County, 1883 (testimony of Carrie Gray).

74. Park v. Ella Henshaw, Case 837, San Mateo County, 1887 (testimony of Cora Kennedy). Ella was married in Missouri.

75. William v. Emma Waterbury, Case 419, San Mateo County, 1882 (testimony of William Waterbury).

76. Will v. Mary King, Case 375, San Mateo County, 1882 (formal complaint).

77. Joseph v. Jane Keith, Case 385, San Mateo County, 1865 (testimony of Elisha Keith).

78. Ruell v. Emily Merrill, Case 895, San Mateo County, 1873 (formal complaint). For other cases of wives preferring to live in the state where they married, see Joseph v. Helen Gilpatrick, Case 633, San Mateo County, 1869 (formal complaint); John v. Annie Bradbury, Case 461, San Mateo County, 1883 (formal complaint); Charles v. Kate Leszynsky, Case 228, San Mateo County, 1881 (formal complaint).

79. Although the cult of feminine purity is generally associated with middle-class women, Carl Degler is surely correct in arguing that middle-class women—and hence middle-class values—"undoubtedly set the tone and provided the models for most women." See Degler, "What Ought To Be and What Was: Women's Sexuality in the Nineteenth Century," p. 1469. The divorce records, as we saw earlier, also reveal that women from all social classes were expected to follow middle-class ideas about sexual propriety.

80. Lew v. Ann Stevens, Case 517, San Mateo County, 1883 (letter of 4 May 1882 from Ann Stevens to Walter Knight).

81. Acton is quoted in Degler, "What Ought To Be and What Was," p. 1467.

82. Lew v. Ann Stevens, Case 517, San Mateo County, 1883 (letter of 4 may 1882 from Ann Stevens to Walter Knight).

83. Ibid., (letter of 23 May 1882 from Ann Stevens to Walter Knight).

84. Camille v. Julia Grosjean, Case 345, San Mateo County, 1882 (testimony of Camille Grosjean). "Making love" here apparently refers to flirting and not sexual intercourse; adultery was not charged against Julia.

85. Ibid., (testimony of Camille Grosjean).

86. Cornelius v. Ann Paddock, Case 1276, San Mateo County, 1877 (amended complaint). This case provides good evidence that middle-class ideas about sexual propriety infused working-class values as well. The point of this testimony is to reveal that Ann, a teamster's wife, did not adhere to proper notions of female decorum despite social expectations that she do so.

87. Ibid., (testimony of Charles Peterson).

88. Ibid., (judge's order dismissing the case).

89. Ibid.

## 5. *Ideal Manhood in California*

1. John v. Mary Henning, Case 2463, Santa Clara County, 1867 (testimony of George Elliot).

2. Vicenta v. Daniel Wilson, Case 2353, Santa Clara County, 1866 (defendant's answer).

3. Jeffrey, "Family History," p. 168.

4. Daniel Rodgers, *The Work Ethic in Industrial America, 1850-1920* (Chicago: University of Chicago Press, 1978), p. xi.

5. Ibid., chapters 1–3. Recently, several studies of nineteenth-century working-class culture and ideology have appeared, most of them focusing on the impact of industrialization on pre-industrial, artisanal values; see, for example, Herbert Gutman, "Work, Culture, and Society in Industrializing America, 1815–1919," *American Historical Review,* 78 (1973): 531–88; Paul

Faler, "Cultural Aspects of the Industrial Revolution: Lynn, Massachusetts, Shoemakers and Industrial Morality, 1826–1860," *Labor History,* 15 (1974): 367–94; Paul Faler and Alan Dawley, "Working-Class Culture and Politics in the Industrial Revolution: Sources of Loyalism and Rebellion," *Journal of Social History,* 9 (1976): 466–80; Daniel T. Rogers, "Tradition, Modernity, and the American Industrial Worker: Reflections and Critique," *Journal of Interdisciplinary History,* 7 (1977): 655–82; and Milton Cantor, ed., *American Working-Class Culture: Explorations in American Labor and Social History,* (Westport, Conn.: Greenwood Press, 1979).

6. *Weekly Argus,* 26 Sept. 1874. Nineteenth-century newspapers abound with exhortations, epigrams, and moralistic stories urging men to infuse their lives with Calvinist virtues. What follows is just a sample of the daily barrage of such advice. Daniel Rodgers also noted the ubiquity of such advice. *Work Ethic,* p. 6.

7. *Weekly Argus,* 12 Dec. and 23 May 1874.

8. *San Jose Daily Mercury,* 15 Aug. 1886.

9. *Weekly Argus,* 22 Aug. 1874.

10. *Santa Clara Argus,* 7 July 1866.

11. *San Jose Daily Mercury,* 4 July 1886.

12. Ibid., 25 Dec. 1886. A similar analysis of the nineteenth-century "ideology of mobility" appears in Stephen Thernstrom, *Poverty and Progress: Social Mobility in a Nineteenth Century City* (New York: Atheneum, 1971), pp. 57–79. Also see Irvin G. Wylie, *The Self-Made Man in America: The Myth of Rags to Riches* (New Brunswick, N.J.: Rutgers University Press, 1954); John G. Cawelti, *Apostles of the Self-Made Man: Changing Concepts of Success in America* (Chicago: University of Chicago Press, 1965), pp. 39–166; and Sidney Fine, *Laissez Faire and the General Welfare State: A Study of Conflict in American Thought, 1865–1901* (Ann Arbor: University of Michigan Press, 1967). Fine's book is useful in exploring intellectual currents that ran counter to the extreme emphasis on individual responsibility for success and failure. Daniel Rodgers also notes the rise of hireling-to-capitalist literature and sees it as a response to anxieties over the rise of industrial wage labor and the consequent degradation of work. See *Work Ethic,* pp. 30-64.

13. *San Jose Daily Mercury,* 25 Dec. 1886. Emphasis in the original.

14. Thernstrom, in *Poverty and Progress,* lamented that only inferences could be made about the relationship between the "ideology of mobility" and actual attitudes held by common people: "Direct evidence on lower class attitudes about mobility opportunities is unobtainable: dead men cannot be interviewed, and humble workmen left no written testimony behind for the historian's use." See *Poverty and Progress,* pp. 58–59. This section attempts to reconstruct work attitudes from the divorce testimony of dead men and women, testimony that is not without limitations but that does offer one window on the work attitudes of nineteenth-century men.

15. Cornelius v. Anne Paddock, Case 1276, San Mateo County, 1877 (testimony of Oliver Paddock).

16. William v. Sophia Hendrickson, Case 382, San Mateo County, 1882 (testimony of J. W. Landon).

17. Martin v. Sarah Daves, Case 2546, Santa Clara County, 1867 (testimony of Charles Parr).

18. John v. Mary Ann Henning, Case 2463, Santa Clara County, 1867 (testimony of James Williams). For similar evidence see Eli v. Helen Randell, Case 1646, Santa Clara County, 1862 (testimony of H. D. Bartlett).

19. William v. Emma Waterbury, Case 419, San Mateo County, 1882 (testimony of Ansel Robison).

20. Catharine v. H. F. Thurston, Case 806, San Mateo County, 1887 (defendant's answer).

21. Adelle v. Harvey Kincaid, Case 281, San Mateo County, 1881 (defendant's answer). The widespread adherence of these Californians to the work ethic was not, I believe, a pandering to the sensibilities of middle-class judges or to bourgeois public opinion. As Paul Faler and others have shown, key values of the work ethic were adopted by workingmen themselves, some because they accepted the basic worldview and assumptions of middle-class reformers, others because they saw in sobriety, frugality, self-reliance, and self-discipline a way to maintain their own sense of dignity and respect and to preserve, as best they could, their independence in a changing economic world. See Faler, "Cultural Aspects of the Industrial Revolution," pp. 391–94. On this point, also see Dawley and Faler, "Working-Class Culture and Politics," pp. 467–473 and Johnson, *Shopkeeper's Millennium,* pp. 119–28. On the dignity of labor as a partisan creed, Eric Foner's *Free Soil, Free Labor, Free Men: The Ideology of the Republican Party before the Civil War* is most useful, especially pp. 1–39. (New York: Oxford University Press, 1970).

22. May, *Great Expectations,* pp. 27, 137–55.

23. Joseph v. Arena Garner, Case 794, San Mateo County, 1887 (testimony of Samantha Hughes).

24. Camille v. Julia Grosjean, Case 345, San Mateo County, 1882 (testimony of Eugene Pasquard).

25. Emma v. Joseph Tuers, Case 2161, Santa Clara County, 1865 (testimony of John Tuers).

26. Abigail v. William Bennett, Case 3351, Santa Clara County, 1870 (testimony of D. S. McLelland).

27. Park v. Ella Henshaw, Case 837, San Mateo County, 1887 (deposition of Mrs. E. R. Wayland and Cora Kennedy). For other cases that stressed the man's ability to provide something more than a subsistence existence, see Elisha v. Samantha Hughes, Case 1810, Santa Clara County, 1863 (testimony of Jonathan Smith); John v. Mary Ann Henning, Case 2463, Santa Clara County, 1867 (testimony of George Harrell); John v. Harriet Hickey, Case 422, San Mateo County, 1882 (testimony of John Quinn); Eli v. Helen Randell, Case 1646, Santa Clara County, 1887 (testimony of H. D. Bartlett).

28. William v. Emma Waterbury, Case 419, San Mateo County, 1882 (testimony of William Waterbury and John Brockwell). My emphasis.

29. Camille v. Julia Grosjean, Case 345, San Mateo County, 1882 (testimony of Camille Grosjean).

30. Aaron v. Henrietta Van Valkenburg, Case 3474, Santa Clara County, 1871 (testimony of Aaron Van Valkenburg).

31. On the linkage of moral autonomy and economic independence to Victorian morality, see May, *Great Expectations,* pp. 17 ff. Don H. Doyle discusses the role of small-town voluntary organizations in promoting proper work habits and character attributes in *The Social Order of a Frontier Community: Jacksonville, Illinois, 1825–1870* (Urbana: University of Illinois Press, 1978), pp. 178–93.

32. Even on the overland trail, where neither homes nor an established society existed, women tried to establish a proper moral tone and frequently complained about men's too frequent drinking, gambling, and cursing. See Faragher, *Women and Men on The Overland Trail,* p. 93.

33. Mary Ann v. Marcellus Knowles, Case 870, San Mateo County, 1888 (formal complaint); Emma v. Henry Ramey, Case 349, San Mateo County, 1882 (formal complaint); Celeste v. Elcano Britton, Case 446, San Mateo County, 1883 (formal complaint); Melissa v. Hiram Ray, Case 320, San Mateo County, 1882 (formal complaint).

34. Tillie v. William Jordan, Case 5023, Santa Clara County, 1877 (formal complaint); Sarah v. Euclid Isbill, Case 402, San Mateo County, 1882 (court findings); for other divorce complaints using similar language, see Mary v. David Savage, Case 6065, Santa Clara County, 1880 (formal complaint); Georgia v. James Johnson, Case 5813, Santa Clara County, 1879 (formal complaint); and Hannah v. Robert Whiteside, Case 7054, Santa Clara County, 1884 (formal complaint).

35. Elizabeth v. Egbert Etts, Case 684, San Mateo County, 1870 (testimony of A. R. Sansman, Elizabeth McCoy, and Elizabeth Etts).

36. Mary v. George Dale, Case 594, San Mateo County, 1868 (testimony of Albert Vincent and Elizabeth Ray).

37. Annie v. Edwin Parker, Case 403, San Mateo County, 1882 (testimony of William Robinson and Annie Parker).

38. Sarah v. Euclid Isbill, Case 402, San Mateo County, 1882 (testimony of Sarah Isbill).

39. Ibid., (testimony of Isaac Wixam).

40. Mary v. Thornton Sharp, Case 367, San Mateo County, 1882 (testimony of Alice Crane).

41. Jane v. Fred Sayers, Case 595, San Mateo County, 1868 (testimony of Clara Spaulding). Emphasis in the original.

42. Rodgers, *Work Ethic,* p. xi.

43. Ellen v. John Diehl, Case 96, San Mateo County, 1880 (formal complaint); Emma v. Henry Ramey, Case 349, San Mateo County, 1882 (formal complaint).

44. Elizabeth v. Egbert Etts, Case 684, San Mateo County, 1870 (testimony of A. R. Sansman).

45. Mary v. George Dale, Case 594, San Mateo County, 1868 (testimony of Albert Vincent); Winnifred v. Michael Fay, Case 945, San Mateo County, 1874 (testimony of Jacob Bryan).

46. Martha v. Robert Lucas, Case 2298, Santa Clara County, 1866 (formal complaint); Martha v. Samuel Brisbine, Case 3623, Santa Clara County, 1872 (formal complaint). For other references to "healthy, robust, able-bodied"

husbands, see Tillie v. William Jordan, Case 5023, Santa Clara County, 1877 (formal complaint); Mary v. George Dale, Case 594, San Mateo County, 1868 (testimony of Elizabeth Ray); Annie v. Edwin Parker, Case 403, San Mateo County, 1882 (testimony of William Robinson); Sarah v. Euclid Isbill, Case 402, San Mateo County, 1882 (testimony of Sarah Isbill); Jennie v. Elhyder Hammond, Case 2642, Santa Clara County, 1868 (testimony of Lutricia Burton); and Apphia v. Lorenzo Milliken, Case 317, San Mateo County, 1882 (testimony of E. E. Staples).

47. Jeffrey, *Frontier Women,* p. 180. Jeffrey noted that "Saloons were a threat to the whole structure of domesticity" (p. 135).

48. Jon M. Kingsdale, "The 'Poor Man's Club': Social Functions of the Urban Working-Class Saloon," in Elizabeth Pleck and Joseph Pleck, eds., *The American Man* (Englewood Cliffs: Prentice-Hall, 1980), pp. 257–83. Although Kingsdale's article focuses on urban saloons, many of his findings are applicable to rural taverns as well. W. J. Rorabaugh's recent book offers a perceptive analysis of drinking and group social life; see *The Alcoholic Republic: An American Tradition* (New York: Oxford University Press, 1979), pp. 149–55.

49. Degler, *At Odds,* pp. 316–17. On this point, also see Doyle, *Social Order,* pp. 218–26.

50. Harriett v. Stephen Purdy, Case 3298, Santa Clara County, 1870 (testimony of A. Chubbuck). On the relationship between poverty and intemperance, see David Rothman, *The Discovery of the Asylum: Social Order and Disorder in the New Republic* (Boston: Little, Brown, 1971), pp. 163 ff.; Thernstrom, *Poverty and Progress,* p. 66; and Raymond A. Mohl, *Poverty in New York, 1783–1825* (New York: Oxford University Press, 1971), pp. 210–21.

51. Polly v. James Haun, Case 2417, Santa Clara County, 1866 (testimony of J. M. Owen).

52. Susan v. Nicholas Dodge, Case 2829, Santa Clara County, 1869 (testimony of Deborah McGowan); Martha v. Samuel Brisbine, Case 3623, Santa Clara County, 1872 (testimony of George and Exa Loss).

53. Kate v. Edward Bliven, Case 4574, Santa Clara County, 1876 (testimony of Kate Bliven and John Turner); Elaika v. Marlin Mattson, Case 214, San Mateo County, 1876 (testimony of F. M. Hale); Thomas v. Harriet Yates, Case 343, San Mateo County, 1882 (defendant's answer); Michael v. Catharine Ryan, Case 931, San Mateo County, 1888 (defendant's cross-complaint). For other cases linking poverty and character deficiencies, see Mary v. Kendall Sanborn, Case 6485, Santa Clara County, 1881 (formal complaint); Susan v. Nicholas Dodge, Case 2829, Santa Clara County, 1869 (testimony of William Hughes); Vicenta v. David Hildebrand, Case 2866, Santa Clara County, 1869 (testimony of Albert Warther).

54. Mary v. William Allen, Case 823, San Mateo County, 1872 (testimony of Michael Larkin, George Wyman, and Charles Kelly).

55. The working class here refers to the bottom four occupational categories—farmers, high trades, low trades, and laborers.

56. On nineteenth-century charity, see Rothman, *Discovery of the Asylum,*

pp. 155–205; Benjamin J. Klebaner, "Poverty and Its Relief in American Thought, 1815–1861," *Social Science Review,* 38 (1964): 382–89; Mohl, *Poverty in New York,* pp. 121–72.

57. Berg, *Remembered Gate,* p. 72. On the crisis in male self-esteem brought on by changing urban social relations, see ibid., pp. 30–59. For similar views of men as cold and authoritarian, see Ersel E. LeMasters, "The Passing of the Dominant Husband Father," in Hans Peter Dreitzel, ed., *Recent Sociology, no. 4: Family, Marriage, and the Struggle of the Sexes* (New York: Macmillan Co., 1972), pp. 107–20, and Peter Cominos, "Late Victorian Sexual Respectability and the Social System," *International Review of Social History,* 8 (1963): 18–48, 216–50.

58. Faragher, *Women and Men on the Overland Trail,* pp. 74, 102, 105, 114, 182–83.

59. Jeffrey, "Family History," pp. 138, 146, 164—68.

60. *Weekly Argus,* 11 July 1874.

61. Ibid.

62. *San Jose Daily Mercury,* 22 Aug. 1886.

63. Again, I am making explicit the class bases of the evidence; lawyers (middle class) penned the formal divorce documents. People from all social backgrounds testified.

64. Catharine v. H. F. Thurston, Case 806, San Mateo County, 1887 (defendant's answer).

65. William v. May Stewart, Case 424, San Mateo County, 1882 (defendant's answer).

66. Charles v. Ellen King, Case 245, San Mateo County, 1881 (formal complaint); Emma v. Joseph Tuers, Case 2161, Santa Clara County, 1865 (defendant's answer).

67. Stephen v. Alice Burdick, Case 604, San Mateo County, 1885 (formal complaint); Seward v. Nellie Jones, Case 366, San Mateo County, 1882 (formal complaint). Many other documents included references to male kindness, affection, and love: see Mary v. Lyman Avery, Case 7783, Santa Clara County, 1887 (defendant's demurrer); Albert v. Alice Hammond, Case 8009, Santa Clara County, 1888 (answer to cross-complaint); Louisa v. J. C. Koppell, Case 8332, Santa Clara County, 1889 (defendant's answer); Park v. Ella Henshaw, Case 837, San Mateo County, 1887 (judge's findings); and William v. Hattie Newhall, Case 757, San Mateo County, 1887 (formal complaint).

68. W. H. v. Bridget Russell, Case 368, San Mateo County, 1882 (testimony of W. H. Russell).

69. Joseph v. Jeannette Shepherd, Case 3793, Santa Clara County, 1873 (testimony of Joseph Shepherd).

70. Camille v. Julia Grosjean, Case 345, San Mateo County, 1882 (testimony of Camille Grosjean); Aaron v. Henrietta Van Valkenburg, Case 3474, Santa Clara County, 1871 (testimony of Aaron Van Valkenburg). For other testimony as to men's affection and kindness, see William v. Emma Waterbury, Case 419, San Mateo County, 1882 (testimony of William Waterbury); John v. Harriet Hickey, Case 422, San Mateo County, 1882 (testimony of

John Hickey); and Cornelius v. Mary Young, Case 429, San Mateo County, 1882 (testimony of Cornelius Young).

71. Edith v. John Harris, Case 1016, San Mateo County, 1889 (prison letter of 3 Nov. 1889). Emphasis in the original.

72. Ibid., letter of 30 Nov. 1889.

73. Park v. Ella Henshaw, Case 837, San Mateo County, 1887 (deposition of Mrs. E. R. Wayland).

74. Emma v. Joseph Tuers, Case 2161, Santa Clara County, 1865 (testimony of Hannah Marrs).

75. Eli v. Helen Randell, Case 1646, Santa Clara County, 1862 (testimony of H. D. Bartlett and A. W. Bell).

76. Elisha v. Samantha Hughes, Case 1810, Santa Clara County, 1863 (testimony of Jonathon Smith and Andrew Gordon). Emphasis in the original.

77. Cominos, "Late Victorian Sexual Respectability," p. 42.

78. Camille v. Julia Grosjean, Case 345, San Mateo County, 1882 (testimony of Eugene Pasquard).

79. William v. Addie Gray, Case 480, San Mateo County, 1883 (testimony of Carrie Gray).

80. Augustus v. Hannah Belknap, Case 144, San Mateo County, 1850 (testimony of William Smith, A. M. White, and George Sniffen). For other testimonials as to a husband's general warmth and emotion, see Annie v. Edwin Parker, Case 403, San Mateo County, 1882 (testimony of Annie Parker); Abigail v. William Bennett, Case 3351, Santa Clara County, 1870 (testimony of Paul Reynaud); and W. H. v. Bridget Russell, Case 368, San Mateo County, 1882 (testimony of W. J. Hasking).

81. Stephen v. Alice Burdick, Case 604, San Mateo County, 1885 (testimony of Charles Bowles and affidavit of Stephen Burdick).

82. Abigail v. William Bennett, Case 3351, Santa Clara County, 1870 (testimony of Paul Reynaud). In the same case, also see the testimony of D. S. McLelland, Mary Williams, and Green Hanna.

83. James v. Eliza Megannon, Case 1316, San Mateo County, 1878 (testimony of William Cook).

84. Cornelius v. Anne Paddock, Case 1276, San Mateo County, 1877 (testimony of F. M. Felt).

85. *Weekly Argus,* 28 Nov. 1874.

86. James Kett, *The Rites of Passage: Adolescence in America, 1790 to the Present* (New York: Basic Books, 1977), p. 107.

87. Degler, *At Odds,* pp. 257, 269–92.

88. Blanche Hersh, "A Partnership of Equals: Feminist Marriages in Nineteenth-Century America," in Pleck and Pleck, eds., *American Man,* pp. 202–4.

89. Ellen v. Minor Havely, Case 3024, Santa Clara County, 1869 (testimony of Ellen Havely). The emphasis here on injury to health indicates the status of legal definitions of cruelty in the second half of the nineteenth century. An examination of appellate court decisions from across the country reveals that the most conservative states (for example, Illinois) insisted on

actual bodily harm to prove cruelty whereas more liberal states, like California, maintained that actual or potential injury to the spouse's health was sufficient as proof of cruelty. After 1892, California would expand its definition still further and be in the vanguard of those states that recognized the legitimacy of mental cruelty even if no threat to the spouse's health was threatened or evident. The key case in California was Barnes v. Barnes, *Pacific Reporter,* vol. 30, pp. 298–99.

90. Mary v. James Coyl, Case 6184, Santa Clara County, 1880 (formal complaint).

91. Caroline v. Archibald White, Case 5347, Santa Clara County, 1884 (formal complaint).

92. Frank v. Susan Gilbert, Case 1134, San Mateo County, 1875 (answer to amended complaint).

93. Grace v. Manuel Thomas, Case 8526, Santa Clara County, 1889 (all quotations from testimony of Grace Thomas).

94. Charles v. Mary Seffens, Case 3756, Santa Clara County, 1873 (testimony of Charles Seffens).

95. Camille v. Julia Grosjean, Case 345, San Mateo County, 1882 (testimony of Eugene Pasquard).

96. Susan v. David Trayer, Case 4379, Santa Clara County, 1875 (testimony of George Plank).

97. Elizabeth v. Jerome Hill, Case 4295, Santa Clara County, 1875 (testimony of Sebastian Shaw and a lawyer named Gill).

98. Elizabeth v. Christian Bollinger, Case 5991, Santa Clara County, 1880 (defendant's answer and cross-complaint).

99. John v. Elizabeth Ennor, Case 672, San Mateo County, 1886 (formal complaint); William v. May Stewart, Case 424, San Mateo County, 1882 (formal complaint); Seward v. Nellie Jones, Case 366, San Mateo County, 1882 (formal complaint).

100. Mary v. Peter Flynn, Case 6211, Santa Clara County, 1880 (defendant's answer); Charles v. Ellen King, Case 245, San Mateo County, 1881 (formal complaint).

101. For the unsubstantiated claim that married men could visit prostitutes with impunity, see May, *Great Expectations,* p. 29.

102. Elizabeth v. Orrin Dennis, Case 623, San Mateo County, 1869 (testimony of D. Hoag, C. T. Fox, and R. S. Jenkins).

103. Seward v. Nellie Jones, Case 366, San Mateo County, 1882 (testimony of William Welles and P. M. Davenport).

104. Florence v. Douglas Woolley, Case 418, San Mateo County, 1882 (testimony of J. B. Mikan).

## 6. *Manhood and the Companionate Ideal*

1. *Santa Clara Argus,* 11 Aug. 1866.

2. Ellen v. Minor Havely, Case 3024, Santa Clara County, 1869 (formal complaint).

3. Ibid., (testimony of Washington Hopkins).

4. Ibid., (testimony of Ellen Havely). The divorce was not granted solely on the ground of his tyrannical conduct, but such conduct was included to reveal a pattern of systematic abuse that met the California statute's definition of cruelty.

5. Louisa v. J. C. Koppel, Case 8332, Santa Clara County, 1889 (formal complaint).

6. Abbie v. William Steele, Case 6260, Santa Clara County, 1881 (formal complaint); Mattie v. James Mitchell, Case 6535, Santa Clara County, 1882 (formal complaint).

7. Esther v. George Philbrick, Case 6742, Santa Clara County, 1883 (testimony of Esther Philbrick).

8. Ibid., (testimony of Esther Newton).

9. Josephine v. Salvadore Baldacci, Case 8105, Santa Clara County, 1888 (formal complaint).

10. Elizabeth v. Christian Bollinger, Case 5224, Santa Clara County, 1878 (formal complaint).

11. Abigail v. William Bennett, Case 3351, Santa Clara County, 1870 (testimony of Abigail Bennett).

12. Ibid., (testimony of Eunice Bennett).

13. Caroline v. John Peters, Case 784, San Mateo County, 1871 (formal complaint).

14. Ibid., (testimony of Peter Monotti).

15. Ibid., (testimony of William Nelson).

16. Vicenta v. Daniel Wilson, Case 2353, Santa Clara County, 1866 (formal complaint).

17. Alice v. Edward Kilday, Case 736, San Mateo County, 1886 (formal complaint).

18. Polly v. James Haun, Case 2417, Santa Clara County, 1866 (formal complaint).

19. William v. May Stewart, Case 424, San Mateo County, 1882 (answer to complaint).

20. *Santa Clara Argus,* 10 Nov. 1866.

21. Vicenta v. Daniel Wilson, Case 2353, Santa Clara County, 1866 (testimony of Mrs. H. S. Hanson).

22. Ann v. Thomas Warhurst, Case 2231, Santa Clara County, 1865 (formal complaint).

23. Annie v. Edwin Parker, Case 403, San Mateo County, 1882 (testimony of Annie Parker).

24. Elizabeth v. Jerome Hill, Case 4295, Santa Clara County, 1875 (testimony of Sebastian Shaw).

25. Emma v. Joseph Tuers, Case 2161, Santa Clara County, 1856 (testimony of William Spencer).

26. Sarah v. Henry Simonds, Case 377, San Mateo County, 1864 (testimony of Abner Colburn).

27. Joseph v. Arena Garner, Case 794, San Mateo County, 1887 (testimony of Joseph Garner).

28. Caroline v. John Planer, Case 1002, San Mateo County, 1874 (testimony of John Planer).

29. Cornelius v. Anne Paddock, Case 1276, San Mateo County, 1877 (testimony of Charles Peterson).

30. Maria v. James Quentin, Case 596, San Mateo County, 1869 (testimony of Margaret Finisty). All quotations in this paragraph are from Finisty's testimony.

31. Cott, *Bonds of Womanhood,* p. 20. Cott added (p. 62) that women's new influence came not without cost: "To be idealized, yet rejected by men—the object of yearning, and yet scorn—was the fate of the home-as-workplace."

32. Caroline v. John Peters, Case 784, San Mateo County, 1874 (formal complaint).

33. Ibid.

34. Ibid., (testimony of Joseph Coronett).

35. Ibid., (testimony of Mary Debernardi, Joseph Fowler, and Robert Evans).

36. Ibid., (testimony of Peter Monotti).

37. Ibid., (testimony of James Monotti).

38. Walter v. Susan Battey, Case 1404, Santa Clara County, 1860 (answer to formal complaint).

39. Mary v. James Glover, Case 1272, San Mateo County, 1878 (testimony of Mary Glover).

40. Ottilia v. Herman Kottinger, Case 4505, Santa Clara County, 1876 (testimony of S. Strauss).

41. Bridget v. Dennis Hanagan, Case 634, San Mateo County, 1885 (formal complaint).

42. Emma v. Joseph Tuers, Case 2161, Santa Clara County, 1865 (testimony of Emma Tuers).

43. Susan v. Nicholas Dodge, Case 2829, Santa Clara County, 1869 (testimony of Deborah McGowen).

44. Mary v. William Allen, Case 823, San Mateo County, 1872 (testimony of Mary Allen).

45. W. H. v. Bridget Russell, Case 368, San Mateo County, 1882 (testimony of Mary Allen).

46. Mary v. Christian Schumann, Case 1279, San Mateo County, 1878 (answer to formal complaint).

47. Adelle v. Harvey Kincaid, Case 281, San Mateo County, 1881 (answer to formal complaint).

48. Frank v. Susan Gilbert, Case 1134, San Mateo County, 1875 (formal complaint).

49. Emma v. Joseph Tuers, Case 2161, Santa Clara County, 1865 (testimony of William Spencer and Joseph Winterbarn).

50. Elizabeth v. Jerome Hill, Case 4295, Santa Clara County, 1875 (testimony of Elizabeth Hill).

51. Annie v. Edwin Parker, Case 403, San Mateo County, 1882 (letter from Edwin Parker to judge of Superior Court).

52. Kirk Jeffrey examined nineteenth-century moralists' emphasis on men

spending time in the home, a precondition if the "doctrine of companionship and collaboration" were to be realized. Jeffrey characterized this doctrine by describing it as a convergence of roles for men and women. See "Family History," especially chapter 5. The Alcott reference is in ibid., p. 170. The notion of "home as refuge" from urban chaos has been developed in several studies. See, for example, Kirk Jeffrey, "The Family as Utopian Retreat from the City," in Sallie Tesselle, ed., *The Family, Communes, and Utopian Societies* (New York: Harper & Row, 1972), pp. 21–41, and Richard Sennett, "Middle-Class Families and Urban Violence: The Experience of a Chicago Community in the Nineteenth Century," in Stephen Thernstrom and Richard Sennett, eds., *Nineteenth Century Cities: Essays in the New Urban History* (New Haven: Yale University Press, 1969), pp. 386–420.

53. *Santa Clara Argus,* 8 Sept. 1866.

54. Ibid.

55. Ibid., 12 May 1866. Though the serenity of rural life was idealized by moralists, rural areas were not without their fears and disorders. Home life as a refuge in these rural counties makes sense in light of the steady stream of articles on crime, labor strife, and particularly the "Chinese coolie" problem. For a sample of concern about the Chinese see *San Jose Daily Mercury,* 3 Feb. 1886; 5 Feb. 1886; 24 Feb. 1886; 7 March 1886; and 11 April 1886; on concern about criminal youth, see ibid., 3 Feb. 1886; and on labor strife in general see ibid., 4 May 1886.

56. Ibid., 25 Dec. 1886.

57. *Santa Clara Argus,* 8 Sept. 1866.

58. Jane v. Fred Sayers, Case 595, San Mateo County, 1869 (testimony of Clara Spaulding).

59. Mary v. Thornton Sharp, Case 367, San Mateo County, 1882 (testimony of Alice Crane).

60. Melissa v. Hiram Ray, Case 320, San Mateo County, 1882 (testimony of Melissa Ray).

61. Ibid., (testimony of H. C. Talbot).

62. Alice v. Edward Kilday, Case 736, San Mateo County, 1886 (formal complaint).

63. Elizabeth v. Jerome Hill, Case 4295, Santa Clara County, 1875 (testimony of Elizabeth Hill).

64. Catharine v. John Kennedy, Case 5922, Santa Clara County, 1880 (formal complaint).

65. Mary v. William Allen, Case 823, San Mateo County, 1872 (testimony of Mary Allen).

66. Ibid., (testimony of Mary Hull).

67. Katharina v. William Wahl, Case 654, San Mateo County, 1885 (formal complaint); Lizzie v. Robert Barnett, Case 5755, Santa Clara County, 1879 (formal complaint).

68. Elizabeth v. Egbert Etts, Case 684, San Mateo County, 1871 (formal complaint).

69. Eleanor v. James Chesley, Case 758, San Mateo County, 1887 (judge's findings).

70. Caroline v. John Peters, Case 784, San Mateo County, 1874 (formal complaint).

71. Katharina v. William Wahl, Case 654, San Mateo County, 1885 (formal complaint); Amilla v. Joseph Kelly, Case 1375, Santa Clara County, 1860 (formal complaint).

72. Ottilia v. Herman Kottinger, Case 4504, Santa Clara County, 1876 (testimony of Ottilia Kottinger); Elizabeth v. Egbert Etts, Case 684 San Mateo County, 1871 (formal complaint); Julia v. Scott Sabine, Case 734, San Mateo County, 1871 (formal complaint).

73. Jennie v. Stillman Moulton, Case 4132, Santa Clara County, 1874 (formal complaint).

74. Susan v. Nicholas Dodge, Case 2829, Santa Clara County, 1869 (testimony of Deborah McGowan).

75. Caroline v. John Peters, Case 784, San Mateo County, 1874 (testimony of Peter Monotti).

76. Ibid., (testimony of Mary Evans).

77. Susan v. Nicholas Dodge, Case 2829, Santa Clara County, 1869 (testimony of May Herd).

78. Grace v. Manuel Thomas, Case 8526, Santa Clara County, 1889 (testimony of Timeteo Sierras).

79. Ellen v. Minor Havely, Case 3024, Santa Clara County, 1869 (testimony of Carrie Armstrong).

80. Ibid., (testimony of Ellen Havely). This concern for women's limitations was not shared by seventeenth- and eighteenth-century Frenchmen, who, according to Lawrence Stone, selected their wives by "hard-headed common sense rather than emotion, with a view to obtaining a cook, a nurse, a housekeeper, an assistant in the field or the shop, and a sexual partner." Stone, *Family, Sex, and Marriage,* p. 54. Here, Stone is speaking of lower-class Frenchmen.

81. Louisa v. J. C. Koppel, Case 8332, Santa Clara County, 1889 (formal complaint). Emphasis in original.

82. Greenburg v. Susan McMahill, Case 1850, Santa Clara County, 1863 (answer to formal complaint).

83. Harriett v. Steven Purdy, Case 3298, Santa Clara County, 1870 (testimony of Alexander Luse).

84. Douglas, *Feminization of American Culture,* p. 6.

85. Mary v. William Allen, Case 823, San Mateo County, 1872 (testimony of Mary Allen).

86. Ibid., (testimony of Mary Hull and Charles Kelly).

87. Mary v. David Savage, Case 6065, Santa Clara County, 1880 (formal complaint).

88. Vicenta v. Daniel Wilson, Case 2353, Santa Clara County, 1866 (testimony of David Hildebrand).

89. Ibid.

90. Ibid., (testimony of James Stevens).

91. Mattie v. Albert Hoehner, Case 7812, Santa Clara County, 1887 (formal complaint).

92. Elizabeth v. Jerome Hill, Case 4295, Santa Clara County, 1875 (testimony of Mrs. E. J. Thompson).

93. Susie v. Enoch Ellis, Case 7358, Santa Clara County, 1885 (formal complaint).

94. Ellen v. Minor Havely, Case 3024, Santa Clara County, 1869 (testimony of Ellen Havely); Mary v. James Coyl, Case 6184, Santa Clara County, 1880 (formal complaint).

95. Caroline v. Archibald White, Case 5347, Santa Clara County, 1878 (formal complaint); Frank v. Susan Gilbert, Case 1134, San Mateo County, 1875 (answer to amended complaint).

96. Grace v. Manuel Thomas, Case 8526, Santa Clara County, 1889 (testimony of Grace Thomas). On proper male character in the Victorian era, see Cominos, "Late Victorian Sexual Respectability and the Social System," pp. 18–48, 216–50; Kett, *Rites of Passage,* pp. 103, 105–8, 112; Daniel Scott Smith and Michael Hindus, "Premarital Pregnancy in America, 1640–1971: An Overview and Interpretation," *Journal of Interdisciplinary History,* 5 (1975): 549; Kennedy, *Birth Control in America,* pp. 63–65; Charles Smith-Rosenberg, "Sexuality, Class and Role," *American Quarterly,* 25 (1973): 137, 139, 143.

97. Smith, "Family Limitation, Sexual Control, and Domestic Feminism," pp. 40–58.

98. Eugenia v. William Duncombe, Case 444, San Mateo County, 1883 (letter from William Duncombe to J. K. Finley).

99. Frank v. Susan Gilbert, Case 1134, San Mateo County, 1875 (formal complaint). For a general treatment of the rising opposition to abortion in the nineteenth century, see James C. Mohr, *Abortion in America: The Origins and Evolution of National Policy* (New York: Oxford University Press, 1978).

100. Ibid. All quotations in this paragraph from Susan's answer to Frank's amended complaint.

101. Lantz et al., "Changing American Family," pp. 406–21; Smith, "Parental Power and Marriage Patterns," pp. 419–28.

102. Cott, "Eighteenth-Century Family and Social Life," p. 32. Cott found that between 1736 and 1765, no divorce petitions (of 58) mentioned the loss of affections as a grievance, but that between 1766 and 1786, more than 10 percent of 121 divorce suits did so. Kerber found the same pattern in Connecticut suits; see *Women of the Republic,* pp. 175–77.

103. Stephen v. Alice Burdick, Case 604, San Mateo County, 1885 (judge's statement of findings).

104. John v. Sarah Cardinell, Case 650, San Mateo County, 1870 (all quotations in paragraph from testimony of John Cardinell).

105. Abbie v. William Steele, Case 6260, Santa Clara County, 1881 (formal complaint).

106. Caroline v. Archibald White, Case 5347, Santa Clara County, 1884 (formal complaint).

107. Joseph v. Mary Laine, Case 1244, San Mateo County, 1878 (all quotations in paragraph from testimony of George Thummel).

108. Eugenia v. William Duncombe, Case 444, San Mateo County, 1883

(all quotations in paragraph from a letter of William Duncombe to J. K. Finley).

109. Annie v. Edwin Parker, Case 403, San Mateo County, 1882 (all quotations in this paragraph from a letter of Edwin Parker to the Superior Court Judge).

110. Ibid. (All quotations in this paragraph from a letter of Edwin Parker to his wife).

## 7. *Parents and Children in Nineteenth-Century America*

1. Philip Greven, *The Protestant Temperament: Patterns of Child-Rearing, Religious Experience, and the Self in Early America* (New York: Alfred Knopf, Inc., 1977), pp. 265–95.

2. David E. Stannard, "Death and the Puritan Child," *American Quarterly,* 26 (1974): 456–76; Ross W. Beales, Jr., "In Search of the Historical Child: Miniature Adulthood and Youth in Colonial New England," *American Quarterly,* 27 (1975): 379–98.

3. Stannard, "Death and the Puritan Child," pp. 459–60; Greven, *Protestant Temperament,* chapters 2–4. On seventeenth-century children, also see Demos, *Little Commonwealth,* pp. 100–106, and Frost, *Quaker Family,* pp. 64–92.

4. Greven, *Protestant Temperament,* p. 37.

5. Ibid., p. 75.

6. Stannard, "Death and the Puritan Child," p. 462. Edmund Morgan, in *Puritan Family,* pp. 77, 168–86, emphasizes the love between parents and children.

7. Greven, *Protestant Temperament,* pp. 28–31.

8. Ibid., p. 30.

9. Ibid., p. 198.

10. Ibid., pp. 227, 231.

11. Ibid., pp. 152, 160, 164, 170–71, 178–79, 184, 227–33.

12. Philip J. Greven, Jr., *Four Generations: Population, Land, and Family in Colonial Andover, Massachusetts* (Ithaca: Cornell University Press, 1970) pp. 72–99, 133, 141–48.

13. Daniel Scott Smith, "Parental Power and Marriage Patterns: An Analysis of Historical Trends in Hingham, Massachusetts," *Journal of Marriage and the Family,* 35 (1973): 419–39.

14. Norton, *Liberty's Daughters,* p. 89.

15. Ibid., pp. 90–93, 101.

16. Ibid., pp. 235–38, 248–49. On this point also see Reiner, "Rearing the Republican Child," pp. 156-63.

17. Greven, *Protestant Temperament,* pp. 265, 268, 269–70, 274.

18. Smith, *Inside the Great House,* pp. 40–46, 49. Robert V. Wells argues that in the eighteenth century, parents began to respect rather than fear the unique qualities of their children. See "Family History and Demographic Transition," *Journal of Social History,* 9 (Fall 1975): 1–19. Evidence from

American family portraiture confirms the rising importance of children over the course of the eighteenth century. Karin Calvert's analysis of 334 family portraits from 1670 to 1810 found that the length of "visually expressed childhood doubled," that stages of girlhood and boyhood became more elaborate and distinct, that the perception of childhood "became increasingly distinct and positive, with virtues, activities, and artifacts of its own," and that interest in the nuclear family itself increased after 1770. See "Children in American Family Portraiture, 1670 to 1810," *William and Mary Quarterly,* 39 (1982): 87-113.

19. On the development of these new attitudes, a good starting point is Bernard Wishy, *The Child and the Republic: The Dawn of Modern American Child Nurture* (Philadelphia: University of Pennsylvania Press, 1968).

20. Sklar, *Catharine Beecher,* p. 261, Wishy, *Child and Republic,* pp. 11–13.

21. Ibid., pp. 95, 108. In post-Civil War child-rearing literature, Wishy noted a reluctance to even bring up the subject of religion.

22. Cott, *Bonds of Womanhood,* pp. 46, 84; Jeffrey, "Family History," p. 203. Carl Degler rightly suggests that the proliferation of antebellum books for and about children is another indicator of children's rising status (*At Odds,* pp. 68–69). The fullest treatment of nineteenth-century childhood is in Robert McGlone, "Suffer the Children: The Emergence of Modern Middle-Class Family life, 1820–1870," Ph.D. diss., University of California, Los Angeles, 1971.

23. Humphrey is quoted in Degler, *At Odds,* p. 89. Wishy also notes the nineteenth-century rejection of corporal punishment (*Child and Republic,* pp. 29, 32, 43). On proper discipline and character building, also see Degler, *At Odds,* pp. 71, 91, 98; Wishy, *Child and Republic,* pp. 23, 42 ff, 48; Jeffrey, "Family History," p. 205; Sklar, *Catharine Beecher,* pp. 127 ff.; Kett, *Rites of Passage,* pp. 105–8. Wishy argues (p. 24) that although the methods changed, the desired character was not "significantly different from long-established conceptions of the ideal American, Christian citizen."

24. Kett, *Rites of Passage,* p. 79; Degler, *At Odds,* pp. 68–69.

25. Norton argues that moralists directed most eighteenth-century child-rearing literature at fathers. See *Liberty's Daughters,* p. 95. The duties of republican motherhood, as we have already seen, increased mothers' importance in the Revolutionary and immediate post-Revolutionary era.

26. Degler, *At Odds,* p. 72.

27. Cott, *Bonds of Womanhood,* pp. 97–98.

28. Wishy, *Child and Republic,* pp. 38–40. Robert McGlone details these and similar nineteenth-century developments in his dissertation, "Suffer the Children"; for example, he describes middle-class parental concern with children's grooming and etiquette (pp. 104–6), diet (pp. 121–22), clothing (pp. 131–32 ff.), toilet training (p. 147), sleep habits (pp. 149–50), health and use of medicines (pp. 158–59), play and toys (pp. 266–69, 271), and social life (p. 276).

29. The post-Civil-War developments are traced in Wishy, *Child and Republic,* pp. 100–101, 106–20, 122–23. Daniel T. Rodgers describes the importance placed on parental love by late-nineteenth-century child nurturers in

"Socializing Middle-Class Children: Institutions, Fables, and Work Values in Nineteenth-Century America," *Journal of Social History,* 13 (1980): 354–67. Great interest in children's play developed among psychologists, behavioral scientists, anthropologists, and educational reformers after 1880, who studied play in order to explore socialization, health, morality, and language development; see Bernard Mergen, "The Discovery of Children's Play," *American Quarterly,* 27 (1975): 399–420.

30. Alexis de Tocqueville, *Democracy in America,* vol. 2 (New York: Vintage Books, 1945), p. 205. Writing in the 1830s, Tocqueville described American family relations as follows: "I think that in proportion as manners and laws become more democratic, the relation of father and son becomes more intimate and more affectionate; rules and authority are less talked of, confidence and tenderness are often increased, and it would seem that the natural bond is drawn closer in proportion as the social bond is loosened." On foreign travelers' negative opinion of American children, see Richard L. Rapson, *Britons View America: Travel Commentary, 1860–1935* (Seattle: University of Washington Press, 1971), pp. 93–105; William Bridges, "Family Patterns and Social Values in America, 1825–1875," *American Quarterly,* 17 (Spring 1965): 3–11.

31. Rapson, *Britons View America,* pp. 93–97, 103.

32. Rothman, *Discovery of the Asylum,* pp. 235–36, chapter 9. Rothman argues that the founders of children's asylums believed in the plasticity of human nature and contended that a strict and steady regimen would change children's character and behavior (pp. 213–14). In *Rites of Passage,* Joseph Kett argues (pp. 125–26) that the growth of cities, high population mobility, and a perception of social instability contributed to the idea that children's moral development must not be casual but rather regulated constantly.

33. Jeffrey, *Frontier Women,* p. 69.

34. Quoted in Degler, *At Odds,* p. 75.

35. Smith-Rosenberg, "Female World of Love and Ritual," pp. 1–30. Although Smith-Rosenberg's analysis extends from the 1760s to the 1880s, the overwhelming majority of her data on mother-daughter relations are from the nineteenth century.

36. Quoted in Degler, *At Odds,* p. 106.

37. Nineteenth-century naming practices also indicate new concern for the individuality of each child. Daniel Scott Smith found that the custom of naming first-born children after parents substantially declined from the seventeenth to the nineteenth centuries. Smith's unpublished findings are summarized in James A. Henretta, "Families and Farms: *Mentalité* in Pre-Industrial America," *William and Mary Quarterly,* 3rd ser., 35 (1978): 29 n.

38. *Santa Clara Argus,* 13 Jan. 1866.

39. *San Jose Daily Mercury,* 1 Aug. 1886.

40. *Santa Clara Argus,* 2 June 1866.

41. *San Jose Daily Mercury,* 14 Nov. 1886.

42. *Weekly Argus,* 14 Feb. 1874.

43. Ibid.,4 July 1874; for similar sentiments, see *Santa Clara Argus,* 10 Mar. 1866.

44. Ibid., 5 May 1866.

45. *San Jose Daily Mercury,* 14 Nov. 1886.

46. *Weekly Argus,* 4 July 1874.

47. Ibid.

48. *San Jose Daily Mercury,* 4 July 1886. An article in the *Weekly Argus* (18 Apr. 1878) urged fathers to spend time with their children. On the special beauty of motherhood, see *Santa Clara Argus,* 13 Jan. 1886; *San Mateo Gazette,* 21 May 1859; *Santa Clara Argus,* 5 May and 11 Aug. 1866; and *San Jose Daily Mercury,* 1 Aug. 1886.

49. Cott, "Eighteenth-Century Family and Social Life Revealed in Massachusetts Divorce Records," p. 28; also see Cott, "Divorce and the Changing Status of Women in Eighteenth-Century Massachusetts," pp. 586–614.

50. Cott, "Eighteenth-Century Family and Social Life," pp. 28–29.

51. Ibid., p. 29. The indispensable work on the history of childhood is Philippe Ariès, *Centuries of Childhood,* trans. Robert Baldick (New York: Vintage, 1962).

52. Forty-two percent of the female defendants (10 of 24) received custody but only five percent (1 of 19) of the male defendants did so.

53. *Santa Clara Argus,* 13 Jan. 1866.

54. *Reports of Cases Determined in the Supreme Court of the State of California, 1860,* XIV, 2d ed. (San Francisco: Bancroft & Whitney, 1887), pp. 513–19.

55. *West's Annotated California Codes: Civil Code,* Sections 1 to 192 (St. Paul: West Publishing Company, 1954), p. 502. The most extensive treatment of the relations among law, the family, and children is Grossberg's, "Law and the Family," chapters 7 and 14. Grossberg (p. 261) notes the "slow, halting, and incomplete" equalization of custody rights prior to the Civil War, but concludes that by mid-century, "paternal authority had been dethroned from its exalted common law stature." By the Civil War, courts extended broad custody rights to mothers, and in the late nineteenth century, women bringing successful divorce suits routinely received custody of their children. Sometimes even wives sued by their husbands and found guilty of moral transgressions were granted custody. This expansion of maternal prerogatives stemmed from both the heightened status of children—especially the young who in their "tender years" required a mother's guidance—and the celebration of motherhood itself (p. 257–79, 587–610). Grossberg later explained (pp. 625–42) how "the best interests of the child" argument legitimated greater state intervention in the affairs of the family.

56. Frances v. Hiram Springett, Case 2985, Santa Clara County, 1869 (formal complaint).

57. Levi v. Nelli Rathburn, Case 3863, Santa Clara County, 1873 (defendant's answer).

58. Charles v. Ellen King, Case 245, San Mateo County, 1881 (affidavit and answer).

59. Hannah v. Sheppard Obberson, Case 6510, Santa Clara County, 1882 (formal complaint); Frank v. Susan Gilbert, Case 1134, San Mateo County, 1875 (defendant's custody request); and Mary v. Peter Flynn, Case 6211, Santa Clara County, 1880 (formal complaint). For cases with similar lan-

guage, see Cynthia v. William Jarman, Case 8157, Santa Clara County, 1888 (formal complaint); Ann v. Thomas Warhurst, Case 2231, Santa Clara County, 1865 (formal complaint); and William v. Annie Zander, Case 998, San Mateo County, 1889 (affidavit of Elsie Warhurst).

60. Albert v. Alice Hammond, Case 8009, Santa Clara County, 1888 (settlement).

61. Apphia v. Lorenzo Milliken, Case 317, San Mateo County, 1882 (testimony of Mrs. E. E. Staples).

62. Polly v. James Haun, Case 2417, Santa Clara County, 1866 (testimony of J. M. Owen); for other cases showing the instrumental nature of motherhood, see Armenia v. Richard Parker, Case 4173, Santa Clara County, 1874 (testimony of W. H. Collins); Seward v. Nellie Jones, Case 366, San Mateo County, 1882 (testimony of P. M. Davenport).

63. Lovina v. Lee Taft, Case 318, San Mateo County, 1882 (testimony of Lovina Taft); Apphia v. Lorenzo Milliken, Case 317, San Mateo County, 1882 (testimony of Apphia Milliken).

64. Walter v. Susan Battey, Case 1404, Santa Clara County, 1860 (defendant's answer); Seward v. Nellie Jones, Case 366, San Mateo County, 1882 (testimony of Nellie Jones).

65. William v. Annie Zander, Case 998, San Mateo County, 1889 (affidavit of Annie Zander).

66. Abigail v. William Bennett, Case 3351, Santa Clara County, 1870 (testimony of Abigail Bennett).

67. Charles v. Ellen King, Case 245, San Mateo County, 1881 (affidavit of T. C. Coxhead).

68. Ibid., affidavits of John Swenarton, Mary Swenarton, and W. M. Searby. Many mothers' custody requests maintained that the children were "well cared for and happy"; see, for example, Sarah v. Euclid Isbill, Case 402, San Mateo County, 1882 (formal complaint); Celeste v. Elcano Britton, Case 446, San Mateo County,, 1883 (formal complaint); Nancy v. Harrison Moore, Case 576, San Mateo County, 1884 (formal complaint); and Katherine v. Alfred Cole, Case 644, San Mateo County, 1885 (formal complaint).

69. These examples are from the *Weekly Argus,* 11 Apr. 1874 and 27 June 1874, and *San Jose Daily Mercury,* 25 Dec. 1886.

70. All of the above appeared in the cross-complaint of Fred v. Mary Rohrer, Case 970, San Mateo County, 1874.

71. Ibid., (affidavit of George Webb).

72. Ibid., (affidavit of Annie Wood).

73. Ibid., (affidavit of Minnie Hogan).

74. Fred v. Mary Rohrer, *District Court Minutes,* II, pp. 143, 151, 156.

75. William v. Annie Zander, Case 998,. San Mateo County, 1889 (affidavit by Annie Zander, 15 Mar. 1893.

76. Ibid., (affidavit by Annie Zander, 23 Mar. 1893). This concern with religion is exceptional. One striking aspect of the divorce evidence is how rarely religion is mentioned, not just regarding children's education but regarding all other facets of family life as well.

77. Ibid., (affidavit by Annie Zander, 15 Mar. 1893).

78. Ibid., (affidavit by Mrs. Theodore Grady, 15 Mar. 1893).

79. Ibid., (affidavit by Warring Wilkinson, 15 Mar. 1893). The Zander and Rohrer cases reflect Michael Grossberg's more general finding that nineteenth-century law institutionalized sex role beliefs, especially the belief that women's more natural child-rearing abilities were especially suited for rearing young daughters: Grossberg, "Law and the Family," pp. 601–2.

80. Ibid., (affidavit by Mattie Zander, 28 Mar. 1893).

81. Cott, "Eighteenth-Century Family and Social Life," p. 29.

82. Louisa v. J. C. Koppell, Case 8332, Santa Clara County, 1889 (formal complaint).

83. Antoinette v. Joseph Johnson, Case 3993, Santa Clara County, 1874 (testimony of R. B. Donovan); Mary Ann v. Edward Evans, Case 1360, San Mateo County, 1878 (formal complaint).

84. Caroline v. John Planer, Case 1002, San Mateo County, 1874 (formal complaint).

85. Sarah v. James White, Case 276, San Mateo County, 1881 (formal complaint); Mary Ann v. Thomas O'Connell, Case 1083, San Mateo County, 1876 (testimony of Mary Ann O'Connell).

86. Esther v. George Philbrick, Case 6742, Santa Clara County, 1883 (formal complaint and testimony of Esther Newton).

87. Polly v. James Haun, Case 2417, Santa Clara County, 1866 (testimony of Jacob and Susannah Haun). Jacob was seventeen at the time he testified, but he was testifying about events over the previous five years, that is, since he was twelve. Other women also complained about being verbally abused in the presence of their children, evidence suggesting that women expected marriage to be founded on mutual respect among all members of the family; see Joanna v. Henry Vandervorst, Case 4980, Santa Clara County, 1877 (formal complaint); Eliza v. J. P. Noyes, Case 1304, San Mateo County, 1878 (formal complaint); Ellen v. Daniel Ryan, Case 827, San Mateo County, 1887 (formal complaint); Abbie v. William Steele, Case 6260, Santa Clara County, 1881 (formal complaint); and Mary v. Peter Flynn, Case 6211, Santa Clara County, 1880 (formal complaint).

88. Cott, "Eighteenth-Century Family and Social Life," pp. 28–29.

89. William v. Addie Gray, Case 480, San Mateo County, 1883 (testimony of Carrie Gray). Degler suggests that the low level of child labor in the nineteenth century attests to the high regard for children's special status. In 1870, only 13 percent of youths (from all social classes) ages 10–15 were gainfully employed; that figure rose to 17 percent in 1880, then fell to 12 percent in 1890. By 1901, less than 10 percent of working-class children 10–16 were in the paid work force (Delger, *At Odds,* pp. 69–71).

90. Frank v. Susan Gilbert, Case 1134, San Mateo County, 1875 (formal complaint and affidavit of Caroline Perry).

91. Emma v. Joseph Tuers, Case 2161, Santa Clara County, 1865 (testimony of Eleanor Miles and William Tuers).

92. Will v. Angelina Frisbie, Case 213, San Mateo County, 1880 (formal complaint).

93. Thomas v. Mary Howard, Case 5898, Santa Clara County, 1880

(formal complaint); Wesley v. Ellen Schuyler, Case 1341, San Mateo County, 1878 (formal complaint).

94. John v. Mary Ann Henning, Case 2463, Santa Clara County, 1867 (formal complaint); Catharine v. John Kennedy, Case 5922, Santa Clara County, 1880 (cross-complaint).

95. Cott, *Bonds of Womanhood,* p. 74.

96. Barbara Berg ties urban fathers' absence from home to their declining authority in *Remembered Gate,* pp. 49–50.

97. Norton, *Liberty's Daughters,* p. 95.

98. Ibid, p. 92.

99. Degler, *At Odds,* pp. 75–78.

100. Jeffrey, "Family History," pp. 202, 207, 269.

101. Nancy v. Harrison Moore, Case 576, San Mateo County, 1884 (letter from Harrison to Nancy Moore).

102. Abigail v. William Bennett, Case 3351, Santa Clara County, 1870 (testimony of Mrs. Mary Williams).

103. Joseph v. Arena Gardner, Case 794, San Mateo County, 1887 (testimony of Joseph Gardner). Abbie Steele expressed similar sentiments in 1881. She maintained that she told her husband that if he did not love her "at least respect her and he replied, 'damn you, I have no respect of such a woman as you.' " She then begged him to respect her for the sake of the children. See Abbie v. William Steele, Case 6260, Santa Clara County, 1881 (formal complaint).

104. John v. Mary Ann Henning, Case 2463, Santa Clara County, 1867 (testimony of Samuel Gummer, John Williams, and George Elliott).

105. Martha v. Samuel Brisbine, Case 3623, Santa Clara County, 1872 (defendant's answer). On other fathers who pledged to provide an appropriate environment for their children, see Nancy v. Alexander Little, Case 554, San Mateo County, 1868 (defendant's answer); Eliza v. J. P. Noyes, Case 1304, San Mateo County, 1878 (defendant's cross-complaint). On fathers who pledged to educate their children, see Adelle v. Harvey Kincaid, Case 281, San Mateo County, 1881 (defendant's answer); Catharine v. H. F. Thurston, Case 806, San Mateo County, 1887 (defendant's answer).

106. Camille v. Julia Grosjean, Case 345, San Mateo County, 1882 (testimony of Camille Grosjean).

107. Thus, we find articles like this one from the *Weekly Argus* (18 Apr. 1874) urging fathers to play with their children: "A nap on the lounge is all very well, but after a half-hour of it, if the most tired man will shake off dull sleep, and have a romp with the children, or a game of bo-peep with the baby, he will be rested much more thoroughly than if he drowsed away the whole evening, as too many businessmen do."

108. Marguerita v. Jean Portier, Case 595, Santa Clara County, 1854 (formal complaint).

109. Ibid., (testimony of John O'Neil).

110. Eliza v. J. P. Noyes, Case 1304, San Mateo County, 1878 (formal complaint).

111. Cott, "Eighteenth-Century Family and Social Life," pp. 28–29.

112. Samuel v. Louisa Cook, Case 732, San Mateo County, 1871. This case is a habeas corpus suit involving one of their children, but a year later the couple appeared in divorce court.

113. Susan v. Nicholas Dodge, Case 2829, Santa Clara County, 1869 (testimony of William Hughes).

114. Mary v. William Allen, Case 823, San Mateo County, 1872 (testimony of Mrs. Mary Hull).

115. Adelle v. Harvey Kincaid, Case 281, San Mateo County, 1881 (formal complaint).

116. Kate v. Edward Bliven, Case 4574, Santa Clara County, 1876 (testimony of Ida Turner).

117. Cott, "Eighteenth-Century Family and Social Life," pp. 28–29.

118. Elizabeth v. Jerome Hill, Case 4295, Santa Clara County, 1875 (testimony of Elizabeth Hill; also see testimony of J. M. Spencer and Julia Henderson).

119. Margaret v. Michael Maloney, Case 597, San Mateo County, 1868 (formal complaint).

120. Mary v. David Savage, Case 6065, Santa Clara County, 1880 (formal complaint); Mary Ann v. Edward Evans, Case 1360, San Mateo County, 1878 (formal complaint); Mary v. Christian Schumann, Case 1279, San Mateo County, 1878 (formal complaint); Armenia v. Oliver Boyer, Case 1170, San Mateo County, 1876 (settlement).

121. Eliza v. J. P. Noyes, Case 1304, San Mateo County, 1878 (defendant's cross-complaint).

## *Afterword: The Family, Victorian Culture, and Twentieth-Century Developments*

1. The fine collection of essays in Daniel Walker Howe's *Victorian America* (Philadelphia: University of Pennsylvania Press, 1976) provides a good starting point for exploring Victorian culture in America.

2. On the character-shaping abilities of institutions, see, for example, Rothman, *Discovery of the Asylum,* and Michael Katz, *The Irony of Early School Reform: Educational Innovation in Mid-Nineteenth Century Massachusetts* (Boston: Beacon Press, 1968).

3. This assertion is admittedly impressionistic, but almost any collection of mid-nineteenth-century newspapers confirms the view that the family was the key institution in molding charcter. In the San Mateo and Santa Clara County newspapers, scarcely an issue went by without some word of advice on the building of proper charcter within the family.

4. Daniel Walker Howe, "Victorian Culture in America," in Howe, ed., *Victorian America,* p. 10.

5. On the Benevolent Empire, see Clifford S. Griffin, *Their Brothers' Keepers: Moral Stewardship in the United States, 1800–1865* (New Brunswick, N.J.: Rutgers University Press, 1960); Ronald G. Walters, *American Reformers, 1815–1860* (New York: Hill & Wang, 1978), pp. 21–37; Timothy L. Smith,

*Revivalism and Social Reform: American Protestantism on the Eve of the Civil War* (Nashville: Abingdon Press, 1957); Clifford S. Griffin, "Religious Benevolence as Social Control, 1815–1860," *Mississippi Valley Historical Review,* 44 (1957): 423–44. Lois Banner criticizes the social control theorists (and provides a useful review of the literature) in her essay, "Religious Benevolence as Social Control: A Critique of an Interpretation," *Journal of American History,* 60 (June 1973): 23–41.

6. Johnson, *Shopkeeper's Millennium,* pp. 95–141.

7. Rothman, *Discovery of the Asylum,* p. xviii.

8. Sklar, *Catharine Beecher,* pp. 122–37, 151–67.

9. The issue of deference receives thoughtful treatment in J. R. Pole, "Historians and the Problem of Early American Democracy," *American Historical Review,* 67 (1961–1962): 626–46, and Ronald P. Formisano, "Deferential-Participant Politics: The Early Republic's Political Culture, 1789–1840," *American Political Science Review,* 68 (1974): 473–87.

10. The term "power relations" here refers to the formal democratization of politics—the expansion of the franchise, the increasing influence of party politics, the adoption of open caucuses and conventions, the rising number of elected rather than appointed officials—and not to the power that men of influence exerted as wealth became more unequally distributed and as corporate capitalism emerged later in the century.

11. O'Neill, *Divorce in the Progressive Era,* pp. 6–7; Degler, *At Odds,* pp. 165–77.

12. Clearly, other factors were at work as well. If the sense of self-worth provided by domesticity ultimately led many women to question the confining aspects of the separation of the spheres, so, too, did women's experience outside the home. In fact, William Chafe argues that the experience of working wives during and after World War II established the preconditions for the feminist revival of the 1960s: women were receptive to feminist arguments precisely because their own roles and self-conceptions changed as they entered the work force. Both private and public developments, then, undermined the attraction of domesticity. The high status of women in the home and wives' involvement in the job market led increasing numbers of women to question the assumption that women, by nature, were incapable of performing certain tasks and holding certain positions. See Chafe, *The American Woman: Her Changing Social, Economic, and Political Role, 1920–1970* (New York: Oxford University Press, 1972), parts 2 and 3.

13. To this day, the assumptions of domesticity maintain a strong hold in American society: witness the opposition to the Equal Rights Amendment and the fear that its passage threatens the family. Andrew Hacker explores the opposition to the ERA in his article, "ERA—RIP" in *Harper's Magazine,* 261 (September 1980): 10–14.

14. Barbara Easton, "Feminism and the Contemporary Family," in Cott and Pleck, eds., *Heritage of Her Own,* p. 571. Easton notes that male reluctance to express emotions toward women is a central theme of contemporary feminist literature.

15. Rodgers, *Work Ethic,* chapters 1–3.

16. On work and alienation, see, for example, the Report of a Special Health, Education, and Welfare Task Force, *Work in America* (Cambridge, Mass.: Massachusetts Institute of Technology Press, 1973), and Harry Braverman, *Labor and Monopoly Capital: The Degradation of Work in the Twentieth Century* (New York: Monthly Review Press, 1974).

17. Delger, *At Odds,* pp. 66–110.

18. Grossberg, "Law and the Family," pp. 601. 610.

19. The theme of declining parental autonomy and self-confidence is emphasized in several of Christopher Lasch's recent essays; see *Haven in a Heartless World: The Family Besieged* (New York: Basic Books, 1977) and *The Culture of Narcissism: American Life in an Age of Diminishing Expectations* (New York: Warner Books, 1979), pp. 267–317, 369–97. Two quite different interpretations of Dr. Benjamin Spock have recently appeared: Michael Zuckerman, "Dr. Spock: The Confidence Man," in Charles Rosenberg, ed., *The Family in History* (Philadelphia: University of Philadelphia Press, 1975), pp. 179–207; and William Graebner, "The Unstable World of Benjamin Spock: Social Engineering in a Democratic Culture, 1917–1950," *Journal of American History,* 67 (1980): 612–29. Zuckerman's Spock emphasizes values appropriate to a bureaucratic society (fellowship and amiability), whereas Graebner's Spock is a social engineer concerned with controlling—in a non-autocratic way—the basic instability and aggressiveness of children.

20. The middle and upper classes are surely over-represented among those who turn to such experts for help, but the lower classes encounter psychologists, social workers, and the like in their contacts with schools, welfare agencies, hospitals, etc.

21. Grossberg, "Law and the Family," pp. 587–88, 612.

22. Ibid., pp. 616, 619 ff., 626–28, 633–34. Also see Anthony M. Platt, *The Child Savers: The Invention of Delinquency,* 2d ed. (Chicago: University of Chicago Press, 1977; first published 1969), p. 139.

23. Ibid., pp. 138, 142.

24. Ibid, p. xxii.

25. Elaine May sees early twentieth-century marriages decisively breaking from the Victorian past as urban society, working wives, consumerism, and increased leisure time became more important in American society: see her book *Great Expectations.*

26. Christopher Lasch, "Divorce and the 'Decline of the Family,'" in Lasch's, *The World of Nations: Reflections on American History, Politics and Culture* (New York: Vintage Books, 1974), p. 35.

# *Bibliography*

## I. *Primary Sources*

### A. Manuscripts: Divorce Documents

Finding divorce cases involves a simple two-step process. The *General Index to Civil Cases* is used to find those cases involving a plaintiff and a defendant of the opposite sex with the same surname; almost always such cases involve a divorce suit. The number of the case found in the *Index* is then used to locate the actual proceedings of that case on file; moreover, the *Index* usually gives the volume and page number of entries for a given case in the Judgment and Minute Books.

Divorce Records of District and Superior Courts, 1864–1890. Depository: San Mateo County Hall of Justice and Records, Redwood City, Cal.

Divorce Records of District and Superior Courts, 1850–1890. Depository: Santa Clara County Superior Court House, San Jose, Cal.

Record of Judgments of District and Superior Courts, 1864–1890. Depository: San Mateo County Hall of Justice and Records, Redwood City, Cal.

Record of Judgments of District and Superior Courts, 1850–1890. Depository: Santa Clara County Superior Court House, San Jose, Cal.

Record of Minutes of District and Superior Courts, 1864–1890. Depository: San Mateo County Hall of Justice and Records, Redwood City, Cal.

Record of Minutes of Superior Court, 1880–1890. Depository: Santa Clara County Superior Court House, San Jose, Cal.

### B. Manuscripts: Census Schedules

The census schedules of 1860, 1870, and 1880 were used to find the occupations of men who appeared in divorce court but whose type of employment was not listed in the divorce documents; unfortunately, very few of the litigants could be found in the schedules.

United States Census Office. *Population Schedules of the Eighth Census of the United States, 1860: California.* Washington, D.C.: National Archives and Records Service. General Services Administration, 1967. Microfilm.

———. *Population Schedules of the Ninth Census of the United States, 1870: California.* Washington, D.C.: National Archives and Records Service. General Services Administration, 1965. Microfilm.

———. *Population Schedules of the Tenth Census of the United States, 1880: California.* Washington, D.C.: National Archives and Records Service. General Services Administration, 1971. Microfilm.

C. Newspapers

*San Jose Daily Mercury,* 1886 (San Jose, Cal.).
*San Mateo County Gazette,* January 1859–March 1860) (Redwood City, Cal.).
*Santa Clara Argus,* 1866 (San Jose, Cal.).
*Weekly Argus,* 1874 (San Jose, Cal.).

D. Special Reports on Divorce

United States Bureau of the Census. *Special Reports: Marriage and Divorce, 1867–1906.* 2 vols. Washington, D.C.: Government Printing Office, 1908–1909.
Wright, Carroll. *A Report on Marriage and Divorce in the United States, 1867–1886.* Washington, D.C.: Government Printing Office, 1889.

E. Federal Census Reports

United States Bureau of the Census. *Agriculture of the United States in 1860: The Eighth Census.* Washington, D.C.: Government Printing Office, 1864.
———. *Census Reports: Manufactures: States and Territories.* Vol. VIII, Part 2. Washington , D.C.: Government Printing Office, 1902.
———. *Compendium of the Eleventh Census, 1890, Part 1: Population.* Washington, D.C.: Government Printing Office, 1892.
———. *Compendium of the Eleventh Census, 1890. Part 2.* Washington, D.C.: Government Printing Office, 1894.
———. *Industry and Wealth at the Ninth Census.* Vol. III Washington, D.C.: Government Printing Office, 1872.
——— *Manufactures of the United States in 1860: The Eighth Census.* Washington, D.C.: Government Printing Office, 1865.
——— *Report on the Manufactures of the United States at the Tenth Census.* Washington, D.C.: Government Printing Office, 1883.
——— *Report on Manufacturing Industries at the Eleventh Census, 1890: Part 1, Totals for States and Industries.* Washington, D.C.: Government Printing Office, 1895.
——— *Report on the Production of Agriculture: Tenth Census.* Washington, D.C.: Government Printing Office, 1883.
——— *The Statistics of the Population of the United States Census: The Ninth Census.* Washington, D.C.: Government Printing Office, 1872.
———. *Statistics of the Population of the United States at the Tenth Census.* Washington, D.C.: Government Printing Office, 1883.

F. Legal Documents

Labatt, Henry J. *Reports of Cases Determined in the District Courts of the State of California.* 2 vols. San Francisco: Whitton, Towne, & Co., Printers, 1858.
*The Pacific Reporter,* Vol. XXIV. St. Paul: West Publishing Co., 1891.
———, Vol. XXX. St. Paul: West Publishing Co., 1892.
*Reports of Cases Determined in the Supreme Court of the State of California, 1860.* Vol. XIV, 2d ed. San Francisco: Bancroft & Whitney, 1887.
*Reports of Cases Determined in the Supreme Court of the State of California,* 1862. Vol. XIX, 2d ed. San Francisco: Bancroft & Whitney, 1886.
*Reports of Cases Determined in the Supreme Court of the State of California.* Vol. XXII. San Francisco: H. H. Bancroft Co., 1864.
*Statutes of California. Second Session, 1851.* Eugene Casserly: State Printer, 1851.
*Statutes of California. Eighteenth Session, 1869–1870.* D. W. Gelwicks: State Printer, 1870.
*West's Annotated California Codes: Civil Code, Sections 1 to 192.* St. Paul: West Publishing Co., 1954.

G. City and County Directories

*Bishop's Directory of the City of San Jose for 1876: Also a Directory of Santa Clara.* San Francisco: B. C. Vandall, 1876.
*Directory of the City of San Jose and Santa Clara County, 1881–1882.* San Francisco: L. M. McKenney & Co., 1880.
Paulson, K. L. *Hand-Book and Directory of Santa Clara, San Benito, Santa Cruz, Monterey, and San Mateo Counties.* San Francisco: L. L. Paulson, 1875.
*San Jose City Directory Including Santa Clara, San Mateo, Santa Cruz, San Benito, and Monterey Counties, 1889.* San Francisco: McKenney Directory Co., Publishers, 1889.

II. *Secondary Sources*

A. Dissertations and Theses

Grossberg, Michael Craig. "Law and the Family in Nineteenth Century America," Ph.D. dissertation, Brandeis University, 1979.
Jeffrey, Kirk, Jr. "Family History: The Middle-Class American Family in the Urban Context, 1830–1870." Ph.D. dissertation, Stanford University, 1972.
McGlone, Robert. "Suffer the Children: The Emergence of Modern Middle-Class Family Life, 1820–1870," Ph.D. dissertation, University of California, Los Angeles, 1971.
May, Elaine T. "The Pursuit of Domestic Perfection: Marriage and Divorce in Los Angeles, 1890–1920." Ph.D. dissertation, University of California, Los Angeles, 1975.

Nissenbaum, Stephen. "Careful Love: Sylvester Graham and the Emergence of Victorian Sexual Theory in America, 1830–1840." Ph.D. dissertation, University of Wisconsin, 1968.

B. Reference Works

Floud, Roderick. *An Introduction to Quantitative Methods for Historians.* Princeton: Princeton University Press, 1973.

Israel, Stan. *A Bibliography on Divorce.* New York: Bloch Publishing Co., 1974.

Loether, Herman J., and Donald G. McTavish. *Descriptive Statistics for Sociologists: An Introduction.* Boston: Allyn & Bacon, Inc., 1974.

Nie, Norman H., et al. *Statistical Package for the Social Sciences.* 2d ed. New York: McGraw–Hill, 1975.

Shorter, Edward. *The Historian and the Computer: A Practical Guide.* Englewood Cliffs, N.J.: Prentice–Hall, 1971.

C. Local Histories: Nineteenth and Early Twentieth Centuries

Alexander, Philip W., and Charles P. Hamm. *History of San Mateo County from the Earliest Times with a Description of Its Resources and Advantages and the Biographies of Its Representative Men.* Burlingame, Cal.: Press of Burlingame Publishing, 1916.

Barrows, Henry D., and Luther A. Ingersoll, eds. *A Memorial and Biographical History of the Coast Counties of Central California.* Chicago: Lewis Publishing Co., 1893.

Foote, Horace Stuart, ed. *Pen Pictures from the Garden of the World of Santa Clara County, California: Containing a History of the County of Santa Clara from the Earliest Period of Its Occupancy to the Present Time.* Chicago: Lewis Publishing Co., 1888.

Hall, Frederic. *The History of San Jose and Surroundings with Biographical Sketches of Early Settlers.* San Francisco: Bancroft, 1871.

*History of Santa Clara County, California Including its Geography, Geology . . . and Biographical Sketches of Early and Prominent Settlers and Representative Men.* San Francisco: Alley, Bowen, & Co., 1881.

Moore and DePue. *The Illustrated History of San Mateo County: The Reduced Facsimile of a Volume Entitled "The Illustrated History of San Mateo County,"* first published 1878. Woodside, Cal.: Gilbert Richards Publications, 1974.

Munro–Fraser, J. P. *History of Santa Clara County, California Including Its Geography, Geology, Topography, Climatography, . . . and Biographical Sketches of Early and Prominent Settlers . . .* San Francisco: Alley, Bowen, & Co., 1881.

Owen, J. J. *Santa Clara Valley, Its Resources . . . with Sketches of Prominent Citizens.* San Jose: Mercury Steam Print, 1873.

*The San Jose Mercury. Santa Clara County and Its Resources: Historical, Descriptive, Statistical: A Souvenir of the San Jose Mercury.* San Jose: *San Jose Mercury,* 1895.

Sawyer, Eugene T. *History of Santa Clara County, California with Biographical Sketches of the Leading Men and Women of the County . . . from Early Days to the Present.* Los Angeles: Historic Record Co., 1922.

D. Local Histories: Recent

DeMers, Donald O., and Ann M. Whitesell. *Santa Clara Valley: Images of the Past.* San Jose: San Jose Historical Museum Assn., 1977.

Goodman, Marian. *San Mateo County: Its Story.* Redwood City, Cal.: Goodman Publishing Co., 1967.

Richard, Gilbert. *Crossroads: People and Events of the Redwoods of San Mateo County: A History.* Woodside, Cal.: G. Richard Publications, 1973.

Stanger, Frank M. *Sawmills in the Redwoods: Logging on the San Francisco Peninsula, 1849–1967.* San Mateo, Cal.: San Mateo Historical Assn., 1967.

———. *South from San Francisco; San Mateo County, California: Its History and Heritage.* San Mateo, Cal.: San Mateo County Historical Assn., 1963.

E. Books

Anderson, Michael. *Family Structure in Nineteenth-Century Lancashire.* Cambridge, England: Cambridge University Press, 1971.

Ariès, Philippe. *Centuries of Childhood: A Social History of Family Life.* Trans. Robert Baldick. New York: Vintage Books, 1962.

Banks, J. A. *Prosperity and Parenthood: A Study of Family Planning among the Victorian Middle Classes.* London: Routledge & Kegan Paul, 1954.

———. and Olive Banks. *Feminism and Family Planning in Victorian England.* Liverpool: Liverpool University Press, 1964.

Barker–Benfield, G. J. *The Horrors of the Half-Known Life: Male Attitudes toward Women and Sexuality in Nineteenth-Century America.* New York: Harper & Row, 1976.

Barnett, James H. *Divorce and the American Divorce Novel: A Study in Literary Reflections of Social Influences, 1858–1937.* New York: Russell & Russell, 1968 (first published 1937).

Benson, Mary Sumner. *Women in Eighteenth-Century America: A Study of Opinion and Social Usage.* Columbia Studies in History, Economics, and Public Law, no. 405. New York: Columbia University Press, 1935.

Berg, Barbara J. *The Remembered Gate: Origins of American Feminism: The Woman and the City, 1800–1860.* New York: Oxford University Press, 1978.

Berkin, Carol Ruth, and Mary Beth Norton, eds. *Women of America: A History.* Boston: Houghton Mifflin, Co., 1979.

Blake, Nelson. *The Road to Reno: A History of Divorce in the United States.* New York: Macmillan Co., 1962.

Branca, Patricia. *Silent Sisterhood: Middle Class Women in the Victorian Home.* London: Croom Helm, 1975.

Braverman, Harry. *Labor and Monopoly Capital. The Degradation of Work in the Twentieth Century.* New York: Monthly Review Press, 1974.

Breen, T. H. *The Character of the Good Ruler: Puritan Political Ideas in New England, 1630–1730.* New York: Norton, 1970.

Bremner, Robert H., ed. *Children and Youth in America: A Documentary History.* 3 vols. Cambridge, Mass.: Harvard University Press, 1970–1974.

Bridenthal, Renate, and Claudia Koonz, eds. *Becoming Visible: Women in European History.* Boston: Houghton Mifflin Co., 1977.

Brown, Richard D. *Modernization: The Transformation of American Life, 1600–1865.* New York: Hill & Wang, 1976.

Bushman, Richard L. *From Puritan to Yankee: Character and Social Order in Connecticut, 1690–1765.* New York: Norton, 1970.

Cahen, Alfred. *Statistical Analysis of American Divorce.* Columbia Studies in History, Economics, and Public Law, no. 360. New York: Columbia University Press, 1932.

Calhoun, Arthur. *A Social History of the American Family: Since the Civil War.* New York: Barnes & Noble, 1945.

Cantor, Milton, ed. *American Workingclass Culture: Explorations in American Labor and Social History.* Westport, Conn.: Greenwood Press, 1979.

Cawelti, John G. *Apostles of the Self-Made Man: Changing Concepts of Success in America.* Chicago: University of Chicago Press, 1965.

Chafe, William H. *The American Woman: Her Changing Social, Economic, and Political Role, 1920–1970.* London: Oxford University Press, 1972.

———. *Women and Equality: Changing Patterns in American Culture.* New York: Oxford University Press, 1977.

Cott, Nancy. *The Bonds of Womanhood: "Woman's Sphere" in New England, 1780–1835.* New Haven: Yale University Press, 1977.

Cott, Nancy, and Elizabeth Pleck, eds. *A Heritage of Her Own: Toward A New Social History of American Women.* New York: Simon & Schuster, 1979.

Crow, Duncan. *The Victorian Woman.* London: George Allen & Unwin, 1971.

Curti, Merle. *The Making of an American Community: A Case Study of Democracy in a Frontier County.* Stanford: Stanford University Press, 1959.

Davidoff, Lenore. *The Best Circles: Women and Society in Victorian England.* Totowa, N.J.: Rowman & Littlefield, 1973.

Davis, Natalie. *Society and Culture in Early Modern France: Eight Essays.* Stanford: Stanford University Press, 1975.

Dawley, Alan. *Class and Community: The Industrial Revolution in Lynn.* Cambridge, Mass.: Harvard University Press, 1976.

Degler, Carl. *At Odds: Women and the Family in America from the Revolution to the Present.* New York: Oxford University Press, 1980.

DeMause, Lloyd, ed. *The History of Childhood.* New York: Harper & Row, 1975.

Demos, John. *A Little Commonwealth: Family Life in Plymouth Colony.* London: Oxford University Press, 1970.

Ditzion, Sidney. *Marriage, Morals, and Sex in America: A History of Ideas.* New York: Nelson, 1961.

Douglas, Ann. *The Feminization of American Culture.* New York: Alfred Knopf, 1977.

Doyle, Don H. *The Social Order of a Frontier Community: Jacksonville, Illinois, 1825–1870.* Urbana: University of Illinois Press, 1978.

Ehrenreich, Barbara, and Deirdre English. *Complaints and Disorders: The Sexual Politics of Sickness.* Old Westbury, NY.: Feminist Press, 1973.

Faragher, John Mack. *Women and Men on the Overland Trail.* New Haven: Yale University Press, 1979.

Farber, Bernard. *Guardians of Virtue: Salem Families in 1800.* New York: Basic Books, 1972.

Filene, Peter G. *Him, Her, Self: Sex Roles in Modern America.* New York: Harcourt, Brace, Jovanovich, 1974.

Fine, Sidney. *Laissez Faire and the General Welfare State: A Study of Conflict in American Thought, 1865–1901.* Ann Arbor: University of Michigan Press, 1967.

Flaherty, David H. *Privacy in Colonial New England.* Charlottesville: University Press of Virginia, 1972.

Flexner, Eleanor. *Century of Struggle: The Women's Rights Movement in the United States.* New York: Atheneum, 1970.

Foner, Eric. *Free Soil, Free Labor, Free Men: The Ideology of the Republican Party before the Civil War.* New York: Oxford University Press, 1970.

Foster, Stephen, *Their Solitary Way: The Puritan Social Ethic in the First Century of Settlement in New England.* New Haven: Yale University Press, 1971.

Friedman, Lawrence M. *A History of American Law.* New York: Simon & Schuster, 1973.

Frost, J. William. *The Quaker Family in Colonial America: A Portrait of the Society of Friends.* New York: St. Martin's Press, 1973.

Gillis, John R. *Youth and History: Tradition and Change in European Age Relations, 1770–Present.* New York: Academic Press, 1974.

Goode, William J. *World Revolution and Family Patterns.* New York: Free Press, 1963.

Gordon, Linda. *Woman's Body, Woman's Right: A Social History of Birth Control in America.* New York: Grossman Publishers, 1976.

Gordon, Michael. *The American Family: Past, Present, and Future.* New York: Random House, 1978.

———, ed. *The American Family in Social Historical Perspective.* New York: St. Martin's Press, 1973; 2d ed, St. Martin's Press, 1978.

Grabill, Wilson, et al. *The Fertility of American Women.* New York: John Wiley & Sons, Inc., 1958.

Greven, Philip. *Four Generations: Population, Land, and Family in Colonial Andover, Massachusetts.* Ithaca: Cornell University Press, 1970.

———. *The Protestant Temperament: Patterns of Child-Rearing, Religious Experience, and the Self in Early America.* New York: Alfred Knopf, 1977.

Griffin, Clifford S. *Their Brothers' Keepers: Moral Stewardship in the United States, 1800–1865.* New Brunswick, N.J.: Rutgers University Press, 1960.

Gutman, Herbert G. *The Black Family in Slavery and Freedom, 1750–1925*. New York: Pantheon, 1976.

Hale, Nathan G. *Freud and the Americans: The Beginnings of Psychoanalysis in the United States, 1876–1917*. New York: Oxford University Press, 1971.

Haller, John, and Robin Haller. *The Physician and Sexuality in Victorian America.* Urbana: University of Illinois Press, 1974.

Hareven, Tamara K. *Anonymous Americans: Explorations in Nineteenth-Century Social History.* Englewood Cliffs, N.J.: Prentice-Hall, 1971.

———, ed. *Family and Kin in Urban Communities, 1700–1930*. New York: New Viewpoints, 1977.

———, ed. *Transitions: The Family and the Life Course in Historical Perspective.* New York: Academic Press, 1978.

———, and Maris Vinovskis, eds. *Family and Population in Nineteenth-Century America.* Princeton: Princeton University Press, 1978.

Harris, Barbara. *Beyond Her Sphere: Women and the Professions in American History.* Westport, Conn.: Greenwood Press, 1978.

Hartman, Mary, and Lois Banner, eds. *Clio's Consciousness Raised: New Perspectives on the History of Women.* New York: Harper & Row, 1974.

Hawes, Joseph. *Children in Urban Society.* New York: Oxford University Press, 1971.

Hill, Christopher. *Society and Puritanism in Pre-Revolutionary England.* 2d ed. New York: Schocken Books, 1967.

Hollingsworth, T. H. *Historical Demography.* London: Hodder & Stoughton, 1969.

Houghton, Walter. *The Victorian Frame of Mind, 1830–1870*. New Haven: Yale University Press, 1957.

Howard, George E. *A History of Matrimonial Institutions.* 3 vols. Chicago: University of Chicago Press, 1904.

Howe, Daniel Walker, ed. *Victorian America.* Philadelphia: University of Pennsylvania Press, 1976.

Hunt, David. *Parents and Children in History: The Psychology of Family Life in Early Modern France.* New York: Harper & Row, 1970.

Jacobson, Paul. *American Marriage and Divorce.* New York: Rinehart & Co., 1959.

Jeffrey, Julie Roy. *Frontier Women: The Trans-Mississippi West, 1840–1880*. New York: Hill & Wang, 1979.

Johnson, Paul E. *A Shopkeeper's Millennium: Society and Revivals in Rochester, New York, 1815–1837*. New York: Hill & Wang, 1978.

Katz, Michael. *The Irony of Early School Reform: Educational Innovation in Mid-Nineteenth Century Massachusetts.* Boston: Beacon Press, 1968.

———. *The People of Hamilton, Canada West: Family and Class in a Mid-Nineteenth Century City.* Cambridge, Mass.: Harvard University Press, 1975.

Keller, Morton. *Affairs of State: Public Life in Late Nineteenth-Century America.* Cambridge, Mass.: Harvard University Press, 1977.

Kennedy, David. *Birth Control in America: The Career of Margaret Sanger.* New Haven: Yale University Press, 1970.

Kerber, Linda. *Women of the Republic: Intellect and Ideology in Revolutionary America.* Chapel Hill: University of North Carolina Press, 1980.

Kett, Joseph. *The Rites of Passage: Adolescence in America, 1790 to the Present.* New York: Basic Books, 1977.

Koehler, Lyle. *A Search for Power: The "Weaker Sex" in Seventeenth-Century New England.* Urbana: University of Illinois Press, 1980.

Komarovsky, Mirra. *Blue Collar Marriage.* New York: Random House, 1962.

Kraditor, Aileen. *The Ideas of the Woman Suffrage Movement, 1890–1920.* New York: Columbia University Press, 1965.

Kroninger, Robert H. *Sarah and the Senator.* Berkeley, Calif.: Howell–North, 1964.

Lasch, Christopher. *The Culture of Narcissism: American Life in an Age of Diminishing Expectations.* New York: Warner Books, 1979.

———. *Haven in a Heartless World: The Family Beseiged.* New York: Basic Books, 1977.

———. *The World of Nations: Reflections on American History, Politics and Culture.* New York: Vintage Books, 1974.

Laslett, Peter, ed. *Household and Family in Past Time.* Cambridge, England: Cambridge University Press, 1972.

———. *The World We Have Lost: England before the Industrial Age.* 2d ed. New York: Charles Scribner's Sons, 1971.

Levine, David. *Family Formation in an Age of Nascent Capitalism.* New York: Academic Press, 1977.

Lockridge, Kenneth. *Literacy in Colonial New England: An Enquiry into the Social Context of Literacy in the Early Modern West.* New York: Norton, 1974.

———. *A New England Town: The First Hundred Years: Dedham, Massachusetts, 1636–1736.* New York: W. W. Norton & Co. 1970.

Macfarlane, Alan. *The Family Life of Ralph Josselin: A Seventeenth-Century Clergyman: An Essay in Historical Anthropology.* New York: W. W. Norton & Co., 1970.

McGregor, Oliver R. *Divorce in England: A Centenary Study.* London: Heinemann, 1957.

Marcus, Steven. *The Other Victorians: A Study of Sexuality and Pornography in Mid-Nineteenth Century England.* New York: Basic Books, 1966.

May, Elaine Tyler. *Great Expectations: Marriage and Divorce in Post-Victorian America.* Chicago: University of Chicago Press, 1980.

Mohl, Raymond A. *Poverty in New York, 1783–1825.* New York: Oxford University Press, 1971.

Mohr, James C. *Abortion in America: The Origins and Evolution of National Policy.* New York: Oxford University Press, 1978.

Moore, R. Laurence. *In Search of White Crows: Spiritualism, Parapsychology, and American Culture.* New York: Oxford University Press, 1977.

Morgan, Edmund S. *The Puritan Family: Religion and Domestic Relations in Seventeenth-Century New England.* 2d ed. New York: Harper & Row, 1966 (first published 1944).

Morris, Richard B. *Studies in the History of American Law.* New York: Columbia University Press, 1930.

Norton, Mary Beth. *Liberty's Daughters: The Revolutionary Experience of American Women, 1750–1800*. Boston:Little, Brown & Co., 1980.

Oakley, Ann. *Woman's Work: The Housewife, Past and Present.* New York:Pantheon Books, 1974.

O'Neill, William. *Divorce in the Progressive Era.* New Haven: Yale University Press, 1969.

———. *Everyone Was Brave: The Rise and Fall of Feminism in America.* Chicago: Quadrangle Books, 1969.

Pearsall, Ronald. *Public Purity, Private Shame: Victorian Sexual Hypocrisy Exposed.* London: Weidenfeld and Nicolson, 1976.

———. *The Worm in the Bud: The World of Victorian Sexuality.* Toronto: Macmillan Co., 1969.

Pivar, David J. *Purity Crusade: Sexual Morality and Social Control, 1868–1900.* Westport, Conn.: Greenwood Press, 1973.

Platt, Anthony M. *The Child Savers: The Invention of Delinquency.* 2d ed. Chicago: The University of Chicago Press, 1977 (first published 1969).

Pleck, Elizabeth and Joseph Pleck, eds. *The American Man.* Englewood Cliffs, N.J.: Prentice–Hall, 1980.

Rabb, Theodore, and Robert Rotberg, eds. *The Family in History: Interdisciplinary Essays.* New York: Harper & Row, 1971.

Rapson, Richard L. *Britons View America: Travel Commentary, 1860–1935.* Seattle: University of Washington Press, 1971.

Report of a Special Health, Education, and Welfare Task Force. *Work in America.* Cambridge, Mass.: Massachusetts Institute of Technology Press, 1973.

Rodgers, Daniel T. *The Work Ethic in Industrial America, 1850–1920.* Chicago: University of Chicago Press, 1974.

Rorabaugh, W.J. *The Alcoholic Republic: An American Tradition.* New York: Oxford University Press, 1979.

Rosaldo, Michelle Zimbalist, and Louise Lamphere, eds. *Woman, Culture, and Society.* Stanford: Stanford University Press, 1974.

Rothman, David, *The Discovery of the Asylum: Social Order and Disorder in the New Republic.* Boston: Little, Brown, & Co., 1971.

Rugoff, Milton. *Prudery and Passion.* New York: Putnam, 1971.

Ryan, Mary. *Cradle of the Middle Class: The Family in Oneida County, New York, 1790–1865.* Cambridge: Cambridge University Press, 1981.

———. *Womanhood in America: From Colonial Times to the Present.* New York: New Viewpoints, 1975.

Saxton, Alexander. *The Indispensable Enemy: Labor and the Anti-Chinese Movement in California.* Berkeley: University of California Press, 1971.

Schucking, Levin L. *The Puritan Family.* New York: Schocken Books, 1970 (first published 1929).

Scott, Anne. *The Southern Lady: From Pedestal to Politics, 1830–1930.* Chicago: University of Chicago Press, 1970.

Sennett, Richard. *Families against the City: Middle Class Homes of Industrial Chicago, 1872–1890.* Cambridge, Mass.: Harvard University Press, 1970.

Shorter, Edward. *The Making of the Modern Family.* New York: Basic Books, Inc., 1975.

Sklar, Kathryn Kish. *Catharine Beecher: A Study in American Domesticity.* New Haven: Yale University Press, 1973.

Smith, Daniel Blake. *Inside the Great House: Planter Family Life in Eighteenth-Century Chesapeake Society.* Ithaca: Cornell University Press, 1980.

Smith, Timothy L. *Revivalism and Social Reform: American Protestantism on the Eve of the Civil War.* Nashville: Abingdon Press, 1957.

Spruill, Julia Cherry. *Women's Life and Work in the Southern Colonies.* New York: W. W. Norton & Co., 1972 (first published 1938).

Stone, Lawrence. *The Family, Sex, and Marriage in England, 1500–1800.* New York: Harper & Row, 1977.

Thernstrom, Stephan. *The Other Bostonians: Poverty and Progress in the American Metropolis, 1880–1970.* Cambridge, Mass.: Harvard University Press, 1973.

———. *Poverty and Progress: Social Mobility in a Nineteenth-Century City.* New York: Antheneum, 1971.

Thompson, Roger. *Women in Stuart England and America: A Comparative Study.* London: Routledge & Kegan Paul, 1974.

Tilly, Louise, and Joan Scott. *Women, Work and Family.* New York: Holt, Rinehart, & Winston, 1978.

Tocqueville, Alexis de. *Democracy in America.* Vol. 2. New York: Vintage Books, 1945.

Trudgill, Eric. *Madonnas and Magdalens: The Origins and Development of Victorian Sexual Attitudes.* New York: Holmes & Meier, 1976.

Trumbach, Randolph. *The Rise of the Egalitarian Family: Aristocratic Kinship and Domestic Relations in Eighteenth-Century England.* New York: Academic Press, 1978.

Walters, Ronald G. *American Reformers, 1815–1860.* New York: Hill & Wang, 1978.

———. ed. *Primers for Prudery: Sexual Advice to Victorian America.* Englewood Cliffs, N.J.: Prentice–Hall, 1974.

Warner, Sam Bass. *Streetcar Suburbs: The Process of Growth in Boston, 1870–1900.* New York: Antheneum, 1971.

Wells, Robert V. *The Population of the British Colonies in America before 1776: A Survey of Census Data.* Princeton: Princeton University Press, 1975.

Welter, Barbara. *Dimity Convictions: The American Woman in the Nineteenth Century.* Athens: Ohio University Press, 1976.

Wertheimer, Barbara M. *We Were There: The Story of Working Women in America.* New York: Pantheon, 1977.

Willcox, Walter. *The Divorce Problem: A Study in Statistics.* Columbia Studies in History, Economics and Public Law, no. l. New York: Columbia University Press, 1891.

Wishy, Bernard. *The Child and the Republic: The Dawn of Modern American Child Nurture.* Philadelphia: University of Pennsylvania Press, 1968.

Wolf, Stephanie Grauman. *Urban Village: Population, Community, and Family*

*Structure in Germantown, Pennsylvania, 1683–1800*. Princeton: Princeton University Press, 1976.

Wrigley, E. A., ed. *An Introduction to English Historical Demography.* London: Weidenfeld & Nicholson, 1966.

———. *Population and History.* New York: McGraw Hill, 1969.

Wylie, Irvin G. *The Self-Made Man in America: The Myth of Rags to Riches.* New Brunswick, N.J.: Rutgers University Press, 1954.

Yans–McLaughlin, Virginia. *Family and Community: Italian Immigrants in Buffalo, 1880–1930.* Ithaca: Cornell University Press, 1971.

Yasuba, Yasukichi. *Birth Rates of the White Population in the United States, 1800-1860.* Baltimore, Johns Hopkins University Press, 1962.

Young, Michael, and Peter Willmott. *Family and Kinship in East London.* Glencoe, Ill.: Free Press, 1957.

———. *The Symmetrical Family.* London: Routledge & Kegan Paul, 1973.

Zaretsky, Eli. *Capitalism, the Family, and Personal Life.* New York: Harper & Row, 1976.

F. Articles

Achenbaum, W. Andrew. "The Obsolescence of Old Age in America, 1865-1914." *Journal of Social History,* 8(Fall 1974): 48–62.

Anderson, Michael. "Family, Household, and the Industrial Revolution." In *The American Family in Social-Historical Perspective,* ed. Michael Gordon. New York: St. Martin's Press, 1973, pp. 59–75.

Banner, Lois. "On Writing Women's History." *Journal of Interdisciplinary History,* 2 (Autumn 1971): 347–58.

———. "Religious Benevolence as Social Control: A Critique of an Interpretation." *Journal of American History,* 60 (June 1973): 23–41.

Barker–Benfield, Ben. "The Spermatic Economy: A Nineteenth-Century View of Sexuality." *Feminist Studies,* 1 (Summer 1972): 45–74.

Basch, Norma. "Invisible Women: The Legal Fiction of Marital Unity in Nineteenth-Century America." *Feminist Studies,* 5 (Summer 1979): 346–66.

Beales, Ross W., Jr. "In Search of the Historical Child: Miniature Adulthood and Youth in Colonial New England." *American Quarterly,* 27 (October 1975): 379–98.

Benson, Susan Porter. "Business Heads and Sympathizing Hearts: The Women of the Providence Employment Society, 1837-1858." *Journal of Social History,* 12 (Winter 1978): 302–12.

Berkner, Lutz. "Recent Research on the History of the Family in Western Europe." *Journal of Marriage and the Family,* 35 (August 1973): 395–405.

———. "The Use and Misuse of Census Data for the Historical Analysis of Family Structure." *Journal of Interdisciplinary History,* 5 (Spring 1975): 721–38.

Bloch, Ruth. "American Feminine Ideals in Transition: The Rise of the Moral Mother, 1785–1815." *Feminist Studies,* 4 (June 1978): 101–26.

Blumin, Stuart. "The Historical Study of Vertical Mobility." *Historical Methods Newsletter,* 1 (September 1968): 1–13.

Branca, Patricia. "A New Perspective on Women's Work: A Comparative Typology." *Journal of Social History,* 9 (Winter 1975): 129–53.

Bridges, William. "Family Patterns and Social Values in America, 1825–1875." *American Quarterly,* 17 (Spring 1965): 3–11.

Brown, Richard D. "The Emergence of Urban Society in Rural Massachusetts, 1760–1830." *Journal of American History,* 61 (June 1974): 29–51.

———. "Modernization and Modern Personality in America, 1680–1865: A Sketch of a Synthesis." *Journal of Interdisciplinary History,* 2 (Winter 1972): 201–28.

Burnham, John C., and Robert E. Riegel. "Changing American Attitudes toward Prostitution, 1800–1920." *Journal of the History of Ideas,* 29 (July 1968): 437–52.

Burstyn, Joan N. "Catharine Beecher and the Education of American Women." *New England Quarterly,* 47 (September 1974): 386–403.

Calvert, Karin. "Children in American Family Portraiture, 1670 to 1810." *William and Mary Quarterly,* 39 (January 1982): 87–113.

Carr, Lois Green, and Lorena S. Walsh. "The Planter's Wife: The Experience of White Women in Seventeenth-Century Maryland." *William and Mary Quarterly,* 34 (October 1977): 542–71.

Clark, Christopher. "The Household Economy, Market Exchange, and the Rise of Capitalism in the Connecticut Valley, 1800–1860." *Journal of Social History,* 13 (Winter 1979): 169–90.

Clark, Clifford E. "Domestic Architecture as an Index to Social History: The Romantic Revival and the Cult of Domesticity in America, 1840–1870." *Journal of Interdisciplinary History,* 7 (Summer 1976): 33–56.

Clinton, Katherine. "Pioneer Women in Chicago, 1833–1837." *Journal of the West,* 12 (April 1973): 317–24.

Cominos, Peter. "Late Victorian Sexual Respectability and the Social System." *International Review of Social History,* 8 (1963): 18–48, 216–50.

Cott, Nancy. "Divorce and the Changing Status of Women in Eighteenth-Century Massachusetts." *William and Mary Quarterly,* 33 (October 1976): 586–614.

———. "Eighteenth-Century Family and Social Life Revealed in Massachusetts Divorce Records." *Journal of Social History,* 10 (Fall 1976): 20–43.

———. "Passionlessness: An Interpretation of Victorian Sexual Ideology, 1790–1850." *Signs,* 4 (Winter 1978): 219–36.

———. "Young Women in the Second Great Awakening in New England." *Feminist Studies,* 3 (Fall 1975): 15–29.

Cumbler, John T. "The Politics of Charity: Gender and Class in Late Nineteenth-Century Charity Policy," *Journal of Social History,* 14 (Fall 1980): 99–112.

Davidoff, Lenore. "Mastered for Life: Servant and Wife in Victorian and Edwardian England." *Journal of Social History,* 7 (Summer 1974): 406–28.

Davis, Natalie. "Ghosts, Kin, and Progeny: Some Features of Family Life in Early Modern France." *Daedalus,* 106 (Spring 1977): 87–114.

Degler, Carl. "What Out to Be and What Was: Women's Sexuality in the Nineteenth Century." *American Historical Review,* 79 (December 1974): 1467–90.

Demos, John. "Developmental Perspectives on the History of Childhood." *Journal of Interdisciplinary History,* 2 (Autumn 1971): 315–28.

———, and Virginia Demos. "Adolescence in Historical Perspective." *Journal of Marriage and the Family,* 21 (November 1969): 632–38.

Duberman, Martin. "Male Impotence in Colonial Pennsylvania." *Signs,* 4 (Winter 1978): 395–401.

Dublin, Thomas. "Women, Work and the Family: Female Operatives in the Lowell Mills, 1830–1860." *Feminist Studies,* 3 (Fall 1975): 30–39.

———. "Women, Work, and Protest in the Early Lowell Mills." *Labor History,* 16 (Winter 1975): 99–116.

DuBois, Ellen. "The Radicalism of the Woman Suffrage Movement: Notes toward the Reconstruction of Nineteenth-Century Feminism." *Feminist Studies,* 3 (Fall 1975): 63–71.

Easterlin, Richard A. "Factors in the Decline of Farm Family Fertility in the United States: Some Preliminary Research Results." *Journal of American History,* 63 (December 1976): 600–614.

Easton, Barbara. "Feminism and the Contemporary Family." In *A Heritage of Her Own: Toward a New Social History of American Women,* ed. Nancy Cott and Elizabeth H. Pleck. New York: Simon & Schuster, 1979.

Fairchilds, Cissie. "Female Sexual Attitudes and the Rise of Illegitimacy: A Case Study." *Journal of Interdisciplinary History,* 8 (Spring 1978): 627–68.

Faler, Paul. "Cultural Aspects of the Industrial Revolution: Lynn, Massachusetts, Shoemakers and Industrial Morality, 1826–1860." *Labor History,* 15 (Summer 1974): 367–94.

———, and Alan Dawley. "Workingclass Culture and Politics in the Industrial Revolution: Sources of Loyalism and Rebellion." *Journal of Social History,* 9 (June 1976): 466–80.

Feldman, Egal. "Prostitution, the Alien Woman, and the Progressive Imagination." *American Quarterly,* 19 (Summer 1967): 192–206.

Finkelstein, Barbara. "Pedagogy as Intrusion: Teaching Values in Popular Primary Schools in Nineteenth-Century America.," *History of Childhood Quarterly,* 2 (Winter 1975): 349–78.

Formisano, Ronald P. "Deferential-Participant Politics: The Early Republic's Political Culture, 1789–1840." *American Political Science Review,* 68 (1974): 473–87.

Furstenberg, Frank, Jr. "Industrialization and the American Family: A Look Backward." *American Sociological Review,* 31 (June 1966): 326–37.

———, Theodore Hershberg, and John Modell. "The Origins of the Female-Headed Black Family: The Impact of the Urban Experience." *Journal of Interdisciplinary History,* 6 (Autumn 1975): 211–33.

Gadlin, Howard. "Scars and Emblems: Paradoxes of American Family Life." *Journal of Social History,* 11 (September 1978): 305–27.

Gillis, John. "Youth in History: Progress and Prospects." *Journal of Social History,* 7 (Winter 1974): 201–7.

Gladwin, Lee. "Tobacco and Sex: Some Factors Affecting Non-Marital Sexual Behavior in Colonial Virginia." *Journal of Social History,* 12 (Fall 1978): 57–75.

Glasco, Lawrence A. "Life Cycles and Household Structure of American Ethnic Groups: Irish, Germans, and Native-Born Whites in Buffalo, New York, 1855." *Journal of Urban History,* 1 (May 1975): 339–64.

Gordon, Linda. "Voluntary Motherhood: The Beginnings of Feminist Birth Control Ideas in the United States." *Feminist Studies,* 1 (Winter–Spring 1973): 5–22.

Gordon, Michael. "From an Unfortunate Necessity to a Cult of Mutual Orgasm: Sex in American Marital Educational Literature, 1830–1940." In *Studies in the Sociology of Sex,* ed. James Henslin. New York: Appleton–Century Crofts, 1971, pp. 53–80.

———. "The Ideal Husband as Depicted in the Nineteenth-Century Marriage Manual." *Family Coordinator,* 18 (July 1969): 226–31.

———, and M. Charles Bernstein. "Mate Choice and Domestic Life in the Nineteenth-Century Marriage Manual." *Journal of Marriage and the Family,* 32 (November 1970): 665–74.

Graebner, William. "The Unstable World of Benjamin Spock: Social Engineering in a Democratic Culture, 1917–1950." *Journal of American History,* 67 (December 1980): 612–29.

Greenfield, Sidney. "Industrialization and the Family in Sociological Theory." *American Journal of Sociology,* 67 (November 1961): 312–22.

Greven, Philip J. "Family Structure in Seventeenth-Century Andover, Massachusetts." *William and Mary Quarterly,* 23 (1966): 234–56.

Griffen, Clyde. "Occupational Mobility in Nineteenth-Century America: Problems and Possibilities." *Journal of Social History,* 5 (Spring 1972): 310–30.

Griffin, Clifford S. "Religious Benevolence as Social Control, 1815–1860." *Mississippi Valley Historical Review,* 44 (December 1957): 423–44.

Griswold, Robert L. "Apart But Not Adrift: Wives, Divorce, and Independence in California, 1850–1890." *Pacific Historical Review,* 49 (May 1980), 265–83.

Gundersen, Joan R., and Gwen Victor Gampel. "Married Women's Legal Status in Eighteenth-Century New York and Virginia." *William and Mary Quarterly,* 39 (January 1982): 114–134.

Gutman, Herbert G. "Persistent Myths about the Afro-American Family." *Journal of Interdisciplinary History,* 6 (Autumn 1975): 181-210.

———. "Work, Culture, and Society in Industrializing America, 1815–1919." *American Historical Review,* 78 (June 1973): 531–88.

Hacker, Andrew. "ERA—RIP." *Harper's Magazine,* 261 (September 1980): 10–14.

Hareven, Tamara. "Cycles, Courses and Cohorts: Reflections on Theoretical and Methodological Approaches to the Historical Study of Family Development." *Journal of Social History,* 12 (Fall 1978): 97–109.

———. "The Family as Process: The Historical Study of the Family Cycle." *Journal of Social History,* 7 (Spring 1974): 322–29.

———. "Family Time and Industrial Time: Family and Work in a Planned Corporation Town, 1900–1924." *Journal of Urban History,* 1 (May 1975): 365–89.

———. "The Historical Study of the Family in Urban Society." *Journal of Urban History,* 1 (May 1975): 259–67.

———. "The History of the Family as an Interdisciplinary Field." *Journal of Interdisciplinary History,* 2 (Autumn 1971): 399–414.

———. "The Laborers of Manchester, New Hampshire, 1912–1922: The Role of the Family and Ethnicity in Adjustment to Industrial Life." *Labor History,* 16 (1975): 249–65.

———. "Modernization and Family History: Perspectives on Social Change." *Signs,* 2 (Autumn 1976), 190–206.

Henretta, James A. "Families and Farms: *Mentalité* in Pre-Industrial America." *William and Mary Quarterly,* 3d ser., 35 (January 1978):3–32.

Hersh, Blanche. "A Partnership of Equals: Feminist Marriages in Nineteenth-Century America." In *The American Man,* ed. Elizabeth Pleck and Joseph Pleck. Englewood Cliffs, N.J.: Prentice–Hall, 1980, pp. 183–215.

Illick, Joseph. "Child-Rearing in Seventeenth-Century England and America." In *The History of Childhood,* ed. Lloyd DeMause. New York: Harper & Row, 1975, pp. 303–50.

Jameson, Elizabeth. "Imperfect Unions: Class and Gender in Cripple Creek, 1894–1904." In *Class, Sex, and the Woman Worker,* ed. Milton Cantor and Bruce Laurie. Westport, Conn.: Greenwood Press, 1977.

Jeffrey, Kirk, Jr. "The Family as Utopian Retreat from the City." In *The Family, Communes, and Utopian Societies,* ed. Sallie Teselle. New York: Harper & Row, 1972, pp. 21–41.

———. "Marriage, Career, and Feminine Ideology in Nineteenth-Century America: Reconstructing the Marital Experience of Lydia Maria Child, 1828–1874." *Feminist Studies,* 2 (1975): 113–30.

Jensen, Joan M., and Darlis A. Miller. "The Gentle Tamers Revisited: New Approaches to the History of Women in the American West." *Pacific Historical Review,* 49 (May 1980): 173–213.

Johnson, James. "The Covenant Idea and the Puritan View of Marriage." *Journal of the History of Ideas,* 32 (January–March 1971): 107–18.

Katz, Michael. "Occupational Classification in History." *Journal of Interdisciplinary History,* 3 (Summer 1973): 63–88.

Kerber, Linda. "Daughters of Columbia: Educating Women for the Republic, 1787–1805." In *The Hofstadter Aegis: A Memorial,* ed. Stanley Elkins and Eric McKitrick. New York: Alfred Knopf, 1974, pp. 36–59.

———. "The Republican Mother: Women and the Enlightenment: An American Perspective." *American Quarterly,* 28 (Summer 1976): 187–205.

Kett, Joseph. "Adolescence and Youth in Nineteenth-Century America." *Journal of Interdisciplinary History,* 2 (Autumn 1971): 283–98.

———. "Growing Up in Rural New England, 1800–1840." In *Anonymous*

*Americans,* ed. Tamara Hareven. Englewood Cliffs, N.J.: Prentice–Hall, 1971, pp. 1–16.

Keyssar, Alexander. "Widowhood in Eighteenth-Century Massachusetts: A Problem in the History of the Family." *Perspectives in American History,* 8 (1974): 83–119.

Kingsdale, Jon M. "The 'Poor Man's Club': Social Functions of the Urban Working-class Saloon." In *The American Man,* ed. Elizabeth Pleck and Joseph Pleck. Englewood Cliffs, N.J.: Prentice–Hall, 1980, pp. 257–83.

Klebaner, Benjamin. "Poverty and Its Relief in American Thought, 1815–1861." *Social Science Review,* 38 (1964): 382–89.

Krom, Howard. "California's Divorce Law Reform: An Historical Analysis." *Pacific Law Journal,* 1 (January 1970): 156–81.

Kunzle, David. "Dress Reform as Antifeminism: A Response to Helene Roberts' 'The Exquisite Slave.' " *Signs,* 2 (Spring 1977): 570–79.

Lantz, Herman, et al. "The Changing American Family from the Preindustrial to the Industrial Period: A Final Report." *American Sociological Review,* 42 (June 1977): 406–21.

———. "Pre-Industrial Patterns in the Colonial Family in America: A Content Analysis of Colonial Magazines." *American Sociological Review,* 33 (June 1968): 413–26.

Lasch, Christopher. "Divorce and Family in America." *Atlantic Monthly,* 218 (November 1966): pp. 57–61.

———. "The Family and History." *New York Review of Books,* 22 (13 Nov. 1975), 33–38.

———, and William R. Taylor. "Two 'Kindred Spirits': Sorority and Family in New England, 1839–1846." *New England Quarterly,* 36 (1963): 25–41.

Laslett, Barbara. "Household Structure on an American Frontier, Los Angeles in 1850." *American Journal of Sociology,* 81 (July 1975): 109–28.

Laslett, Peter. "The Comparative History of Household and Family." In *The American Family in Social-Historical Perspective,* ed. Michael Gordon. New York: St. Martin's Press, 1973, pp. 19–33.

LeMasters, Ersel. "The Passing of the Dominant Husband Father." In *Recent Sociology: Family, Marriage, and the Struggle of the Sexes,* ed. Hans Peter Dreitzel. New York: Macmillan Co., 1972, pp. 107–20.

Lerner, Gerda. "The Lady and the Mill Girl: Changes in the Status of Women in the Age of Jackson." *American Studies,* 10 (Spring 1969): 5–15.

Levy, Barry. " 'Tender Plants': Quaker Farmers and Children in the Delaware Valley, 1681–1735." *Journal of Family History,* 3 (Summer 1978): 116–35.

Lewis, Jan. "Domestic Tranquillity and the Management of Emotion among the Gentry of Pre-Revolutionary Virginia." *William and Mary Quarterly,* 39 (January 1982): 135–49.

McLaughlin, Virginia Yans. "Patterns of Work and Family Organization: Buffalo's Italians." *Journal of Interdisciplinary History,* 2 (Autumn 1971): 299–314.

McLaughlin, William G. "Evangelical Childrearing in the Age of Jackson:

Francis Wayland's Views on When and How to Subdue the Willfulness of Children." *Journal of Social History,* 9 (Fall 1975): 20–43.

Mechling, Jay. "Advice to Historians on Advice to Mothers." *Journal of Social History,* 9 (Fall 1975): 45–63.

Mergen, Benard. "The Discovery of Children's Play." *American Quarterly,* 27 (October, 1975): 399–420.

Mills, C. Wright. "Situated Actions and Vocabularies of Motive." *American Sociological Review,* 5 (1940): 904–13.

Modell, John. "Suburbanization and Change in the American Family." *Journal of Interdisciplinary History,* 9 (Spring 1979): 621–46.

———, and Tamara Hareven. "Urbanization and the Malleable Household: An Examination of Boarding and Lodging in American Families." *Journal of Marriage and the Family,* 35 (August 1973): 467–79.

Moran, Gerald F. "Religious Renewal, Puritan Tribalism, and the Family in Seventeenth-Century Milford, Connecticut." *William and Mary Quarterly,* 3d ser., 36 (April 1979): 236–54.

———, and Maris Vinovskis. "The Puritan Family and Religion: A Critical Reappraisal." *William and Mary Quarterly,* 39 (January 1982):29–63.

Morantz, Regina. "The Lady and Her Physician." In *Clio's Consciousness Raised: New Perspectives on the History of Women,* ed. Mary Hartman and Lois W. Banner. New York: Harper & Row, 1974, pp. 38–53.

Morgan, Edmund S. "The Puritans and Sex." *New England Quarterly,* 15 (December 1942): 591–607.

Neuman, R. P. "Masturbation, Madness, and the Modern Concepts of Childhood and Adolescence." *Journal of Social History,* 8 (Spring 1975): 1–28.

Norton, Mary Beth. "Eighteenth-Century American Women in Peace and War: The Case of the Loyalists." *William and Mary Quarterly,* 33 (July 1976): 386–409.

O'Neill, William. "Divorce in the Progressive Era." *American Quarterly,* 17 (Summer 1965): 205–17.

Pleck, Elizabeth. "The Two-Parent Household: Black Family Structure in Late Nineteenth-Century Boston." *Journal of Social History,* 6 (Fall 1972): 1–31.

———. "Two Worlds in One: Work and Family." *Journal of Social History,* 10 (Winter 1976): 178–95.

Pole, J. R. "Historians and the Problem of Early American Democracy." *American Historical Review,* 67 (1961–62): 626–46.

Rapson, Richard. "The American Child as Seen by British Travelers, 1845–1935." *American Quarterly,* 18 (Fall 1965): 520–34.

Reinier, Jacqueline. "Rearing the Republican Child: Attitudes and Practices in Post-Revolutionary Philadelphia." *William and Mary Quarterly,* 39 (January 1982): 150–63.

Riley, Glenda. "'Not Gainfully Employed': Women on the Iowa Frontier, 1833–1870." *Pacific Historical Review,* 49 (May 1980): 237–64.

Roberts, Helene. "The Exquisite Slave: The Role of Clothes in the Making of the Victorian Woman." *Signs,* 2 (Spring 1977): 554–69.

Rodgers, Daniel T. "Socializing Middle-Class Children: Institutions, Fables, and Work Values in Nineteenth-Century America." *Journal of Social History,* 13 (Spring 1980): 354–67.

———. "Tradition, Modernity, and the American Industrial Worker: Reflections and Critique." *Journal of Interdisciplinary History,* 7 (Spring 1977): 655–82.

Rosenberg, Charles. "Sexuality, Class, and Role in Nineteenth-Century America." *American Quarterly,* 25 (May 1973): 131–53.

Rothman, David. "Documents in Search of a Historian: Toward a History of Childhood and Youth in America." *Journal of Interdisciplinary History,* 2 (Autumn 1971): 367–78.

Sanderson, Warren D. "Quantitative Aspects of Marriage Fertility and Family Limitation in Nineteenth-Century America: Another Application of the Coale Specification." *Demography,* 16 (August 1979): 339–58.

Saveth, Edward. "The Problem of American Family History." *American Quarterly,* 21 (Summer 1969): 311–30.

Scholten, Catherine M. " 'On the Importance of the Obstetrick Art': Changing Customs of Childbirth in America, 1760 to 1825." *William and Mary Quarterly,* 34 (July 1977): 426–45.

Scott, Joan, and Louise Tilly. "Women's Work and the Family in Nineteenth-Century Europe." *Comparative Studies in Society and History,* 17 (January 1975): 36–64.

Sennett, Richard. "Middle-Class Families and Urban Violence: The Experience of a Chicago Community in the Nineteenth Century." In *Nineteenth-Century Cities: Essays in the New Urban History,* ed. Stephan Ternstrom and Richard Sennett. New Haven: Yale University Press, 1969, pp. 386–420.

Shammas, Carole. "The Domestic Environment in Early Modern England and America." *Journal of Social History,* 14 (Fall 1980): 3–24.

Shifflett, Crandall A. "The Household Composition of Rural Black Families: Louisa County, Virginia, 1880." *Journal of Interdisciplinary History,* 6 (Autumn 1975): 235–60.

Shorter, Edward. "Female Emancipation, Birth Control, and Fertility in European History." *American Historical Review,* 78 (June 1973): 605–35.

———. "Illegitimacy, Sexual Revolution, and Social Change in Modern Europe, 1750–1900." *Journal of Interdisciplinary History,* 2 (Autumn 1971): 237–72.

Smelser, Neil J. "Sociological History: The Industrial Revolution and the British Working-Class Family." *Journal of Social History,* 1 (Fall 1967): 17–35.

Smith, Daniel Blake. "The Study of the Family in Early America: Trends, Problems, and Prospects." *William and Mary Quarterly,* 39 (January 1982): 3–28.

Smith, Daniel Scott. "The Dating of the American Sexual Revolution: Evidence and Interpretation." In *The American Family in Social-Historical Perspective,* ed. Michael Gordon. New York: St. Martin's Press, 1973, pp. 321–35.

———. "The Demographic History of Colonial New-England." In *The American Family in Social-Historical Perspective,* ed. Michael Gordon. New York: St. Martin's Press, 1973, pp. 397–415.

———. "Family Limitation, Sexual Control, and Domestic Feminism in Victorian America." *Feminist Studies,* 1 (Winter–Spring 1973): 40–58.

———. "Parental Power and Marriage Patterns: An Analysis of Historical Trends in Hingham, Massachusetts." *Journal of Marriage and the Family,* 35 (August 1973): 419–39.

———, and Michael Hindus. "Premarital Pregnancy in America, 1640–1971: An Overview and Interpretation." *Journal of Interdisciplinary History,* 5 (Spring 1975): 537–70.

Smith–Rosenberg, Carroll. "Beauty, the Beast, and the Militant Woman." *American Quarterly,* 23 (October 1971): 562–84.

———. "The Female World of Love and Ritual: Relationships between Women in Nineteenth-Century America." *Signs,* 1 (1975): 1–30.

———. "The Hysterical Woman: Sex Roles and Role Conflict in Nineteenth-Century America." *Social Research,* 39 (Winter 1972): 652–78.

———. "Puberty to Menopause: The Cycle of Femininity in Nineteenth-Century America." In *Clio's Consciousness Raised: New Perspectives on the History of Women,* ed. Mary Hartman and Lois W. Banner. New York: Harper & Row, 1974, pp. 23–37.

———, and Charles Rosenberg. "The Female Animal: Medical and Biological Views of Woman and Her Role in Nineteenth-Century America." *Journal of American History,* 60 (September 1973): 332–56.

Stannard, David E. "Death and the Puritan Child." *American Quarterly,* 26 (December 1974): 456–76.

Stewart, Abigail, David Winter, and A. David Jones. "Coding Categories for the Study of Child-Rearing from Historical Sources." *Journal of Interdisciplinary History,* 5 (Spring 1975): 687–701.

Strong, Bryan. "Toward the History of the Experiential Family: Sex and Incest in the Nineteenth-Century Family." *Journal of Marriage and the Family,* 35 (1975): 457–66.

Thernstrom, Stephan, and Peter Knights. "Men in Motion: Some Data and Speculations about Urban Population Mobility in Nineteenth-Century America." *Journal of Interdisciplinary History,* 1 (Autumn 1970): 7–36.

Thompson, E. P. "Time, Work-Discipline, and Industrial Capitalism." *Past and Present,* 38 (1967): 56–97.

Tilly, Louise A., Joan W. Scott, and Miriam Cohen. "Women's Work and European Fertility Patterns." In *The American Family in Social–Historical Perspective,* ed. Michael Gordon. 2d ed. New York: St. Martin's Press, 1978, pp. 289–312.

Tomes, Nancy. "A 'Torrent of Abuse': Crimes of Violence between Working Class Men and Women in London, 1840–1875." *Journal of Social History,* 11 (Spring 1978): 328–45.

Ulrich, Laurel T. "Vertuous Women Found: New England Ministerial Literature, 1668–1735." *American Quarterly,* 28 (Spring 1976): 20–40.

Verbrugge, Martha. "Women and Medicine in Nineteenth-Century America." *Signs,* 1 (Summer 1976): 957–72.

Vicinus, Martha. "Introduction: The Perfect Victorian Lady." In *Suffer and Be Still: Women in the Victorian Age,* ed. Martha Vicinus. Bloomington: Indiana University Press, 1972, vii–xv.

Walkowitz, Daniel J. "Working Class Women in the Gilded Age: Factory, Community and Family Life Among Cohoes, New York Cotton Workers." *Journal of Social History,* 5 (Summer 1972): 464–90.

Walsh, Lorena. " 'Till Death Us Do Part': Marriage and Family in Seventeenth-Century Maryland." In *The Chesapeake in the Seventeenth Century: Essays on Anglo-American Society and Politics,* ed. Thad W. Tate and David L. Ammerman. New York: Norton, 1979, pp. 126–52.

Walters, Ronald G. "The Erotic South: Civilization and Sexuality in American Abolitionism." *American Quarterly,* 25 (May 1973): 177–201.

Weisberg, K. Kelly. " 'Under Greet Temptations Heer': Women and Divorce in Puritan Massachusetts." *Feminist Studies,* 2 (1975): 183–93.

Weiss, Nancy Pottishman. "Mother, the Invention of Necessity: Dr. Benjamin Spock's *Baby and Child Care*." *American Quarterly,* 29 (Winter 1977): 519–46.

Wells, Robert V. "Demographic Change and the Life Cycle of American Families." *Journal of Interdisciplinary History,* 2 (Autumn 1971): 273–82.

———. "Family History and Demographic Transition." *Journal of Social History,* 9 (Fall 1975): 1–19.

———. "Family Size and Fertility Control in Eighteenth-Century America: A Study of Quaker Families." *Population Studies,* 25 (March 1971): 73–82.

———. "Household Size and Composition in the British Colonies in America, 1675–1775." *Journal of Interdisciplinary History,* 4 (1974): 543–70.

———. "Quaker Marriage Patterns in A Colonial Perspective." *William and Mary Quarterly,* 29 (July 1972): 415–42.

Welter, Barbara. "The Cult of True Womanhood: 1820–1860." *American Quarterly,* 18 (1966): 151–74.

———. "The Feminization of American Religion: 1800–1860." In *Clio's Consciousness Raised: New Perspectives on the History of Women,* ed. Mary Hartman and Lois W. Banner. New York: Harper & Row, 1974, pp. 137–57.

Wilson, Joan H. "The Illusion of Change: Women and the American Revolution." In *The American Revolution: Explorations in the History of American Radicalism,* ed. Alfred Young. Dekalb: Northern Illinois University Press, 1976, pp. 383–446.

Wood, Ann Douglas. " 'The Fashionable Diseases': Women's Complaints and Their Treatment in Nineteenth-Century America." *Journal of Interdisciplinary History,* 4 (Summer 1973): 25–52.

———. "The 'Scribbling Women' and Fanny Fern: Why Women Wrote." *American Quarterly,* 23 (Spring 1971): 3–24.

Wrigley, E. A. "The Process of Modernization and the Industrial Revolution in England." *Journal of Interdisciplinary History,* 3 (1972): 225–60.

Zuckerman, Michael. "Dr. Spock: The Confidence Man." In *The Family in History,* ed. Charles Rosenberg. Philadelphia: University of Pennsylvania Press, 1975.

# Index